Early Medieval Philosophy

The Author

John Marenbon is a Fellow of Trinity College, Cambridge. Born in London, he was educated at Westeminster School and at Trinity College. He is the author of *From the Circle of Alcuin to the School of Auxerre* (Cambridge University Press, 1981) and *Later Medieval Philosophy (1150-1350)*, (Routledge & Kegan Paul, 1987).

Early Medieval Philosophy (480–1150)

An Introduction

John Marenbon

Revised edition

ROUTLEDGE
London and New York

To Sheila, again

First published in 1983
Second edition 1988 by
Routledge
11 New Fetter Lane, London EC4P 4EE

Published in the USA by
Routledge, Chapman & Hall, Inc.
29 West 35th Street, New York, NY 10001

Printed in Great Britain by
T.J. Press (Padstow) Ltd
Padstow, Cornwall

Library of Congress Cataloging in Publication Data
Marenbon, John,
    Early medieval philosophy (480–1130): an introduction/John
    Marenbon. — 2nd ed.
    p. cm.
    Bibliography: p.
    Includes index.
    ISBN 0-415-0070-X (U.S.)
    1. Philosophy, Medieval. 2. Philosophy, Ancient. I. Title.
    B721.M338 1988
    189—dc19   87–37106

British Library CIP Data also available

ISBN 0-415-00070-X

Contents

Preface to the second edition

I

When I wrote *Early Medieval Philosophy* five years ago, I thought of philosophy as a single, identifiable subject. Although I tried in passing to provide a definition of it ('rational argument based on premises self-evident from observation, experience and thought'), in practice I assumed that any thinker who appeared to share the methods and interests of modern British philosophers was a philosopher, and that all other thinkers were theologians, mystics, poets, scientists or whatever, but not philosophers. I knew that early medieval thinkers themselves did not make any such distinction between philosophy and non-philosophy. Indeed, I prefaced the book by noting that 'philosophical speculation was one – often minor – part of their activity, which they rarely separated from other types of thought, logical, grammatical, scientific or theological'. But it was part of my duty as an historian of philosophy, I thought, to distinguish the texts and passages of the period which were philosophical from those which were not. In this way I would show that 'it is possible to speak of early medieval philosophy, just as it is possible to speak of antique, later medieval or modern philosophy'.

After I had finished *Early Medieval Philosophy* I began work on a sequel, dealing with the period from 1150 to 1350 (*Later Medieval Philosophy*, 1987). When I reflected more about philosophy and its history, I began – gradually but firmly – to consider that my earlier approach was misleading. *Later Medieval Philosophy* rejects the principles which I had previously followed. In it (see especially pp. 1–2, 83–90, 189–91) I suggest that there is no single, identifiable subject – 'philosophy' – which has been studied by thinkers from Plato's time to the present day. Although some of the problems discussed by thinkers in the past are similar to those discussed by philosophers today, each belongs to a context shaped by the disciplines recognized at the time. The historian who isolates 'philosophical' arguments of the past from their contexts, studying them without reference to the presuppositions and aims of their proponents, will not understand them. For instance, the treatment of human knowledge by Aquinas, Duns Scotus and Ockham should be seen in the context of thirteenth- and fourteenth-century theology, where investigation of the human intellect was conducted, not for its own sake, but as a way of exploring the nature and cognitive powers of disembodied souls, angels and God. The historian of philosophy is indeed entitled to select which problems he examines, and he may, if he wishes, explicity choose those which seem closest to modern philosophical concerns; but he must then be able to relate past discussion of them to its context, otherwise he will misunderstand the arguments which he is trying to interpret.

Early Medieval Philosophy and *Later Medieval Philosophy* reflect the different ideas about philosophy and its history which I held at the time of writing each of them. The earlier book offers a history of how thinkers in its period discussed some of the supposedly perennial problems of philosophy. The later book describes the organization, presuppositions and aims of studies in thirteenth- and fourteenth-century universities. It goes on to consider how some thinkers of the time treated one important question, the nature of intellectual knowledge. This question has similarities to some which modern philosophers try to answer, but it is not identical to any of them.

If I were to write *Early Medieval Philosophy* again now, I would adopt the approach of its sequel. The claims of the earlier book to provide a 'history of philosophy' and to show 'how early medieval thinkers first came to engage in philosophy' seem to me now to be partly meaningless and partly unsustainable. However, there are two important ways in which the two books are less unlike each other than their difference in aims and method might suggest. It is in the light of these similarities that I offer this new, but largely unaltered, edition of *Early Medieval Philosophy*.

First, *Early Medieval Philosophy*, like its sequel, does – for a somewhat paradoxical reason – consider the general context of intellectual life in its period. When I wrote the book I knew that other historians had included within early medieval philosophy all sorts of material which, in my view then, was not 'philosophy' but theology, logic, poetry, science or antiquarian scholarship. I wanted to make it clear that such material was not 'philosophy', and so I had to examine it in some detail. *Early Medieval Philosophy*, therefore, contains many sections which a history of 'philosophy', in the sense I gave it, should have omitted. If the reader will ignore the over-confident labelling of material as 'philosophy' or 'not philosophy', he will find in the book a reasonable account of the relations between the framework of early medieval studies and individual discussions of problems similar to those which interest modern philosophers.

Second, both books respect the argumentative nature of their material, and they attempt to make the arguments they discuss comprehensible to the modern reader. The mere repetition of a thinker's views in his own terms would not achieve this result. In both books, therefore, I try to translate arguments into terms which can be grasped by a reader today but which do not betray the original author's intentions. Unfortunately, this act of translation can become a process of transformation, which makes a past thinker's problems and ideas the same as those which concern us now: *Early Medieval Philosophy* provides some instances of this fault (three of which are discussed below). But the historian can avoid the risks of translating material from the past only by abandoning the attempt to understand it.

II

There are three sections of *Early Medieval Philosophy* where I seriously misrepresented my subjects, by failing to recognize the difference between their interests and my own: those concerning John Scottus's *Periphyseon*, Abelard's ethical thought, and Gilbert of Poitiers.

The 'Periphyseon'

John Scottus's *Periphyseon* has usually been presented as a masterpiece of philosophy – the only comprehensive metaphysical account of reality from the early Middle Ages. My view (pp. 60–70) was very different. The philosophy which historians admired in the *Periphyseon* was not philosophy but 'systematizing', an arrangement of Neoplatonic concepts into a system which was internally coherent but lacking in any explanatory power. I justified this assessment by a survey of the Neoplatonic elements in John's thought. Certainly, from this summary account John does appear to use Neoplatonic notions in a nearly meaningless way, and to make wild assertions ('The soul creates its own mortal body. . .') without justification. But the account is a caricature, in the manner of Bertrand Russell's *History of Western Philosophy* but without Russell's wit.

There is indeed reason to suspect some of the more adulatory expositions of the *Periphyseon*'s metaphysics, especially those which reconstruct John's thought by reference to pagan Neoplatonic sources which he knew only indirectly. My discussion of the *Periphyseon* went on to consider the peculiarly Christian aspects of John's thought, but this exercise was flawed by the rigid distinction I made between 'expounding Christian texts and dogma', 'reviving a metaphysical system' and 'tackling genuine problems of philosophy'. It would be more accurate to see John Scottus as a Christian thinker, who drew his metaphysical notions both from Augustine and from the Greek Christian Neoplatonists. Rather than describe his reasoning by its dissimilarity to that of 'modern philosophers', it would be more helpful to ask what John was aiming to do. What, in particular, was John's attitude to his role as commentator of an irrefragable authority, the Bible? *Early Medieval Philosophy* begins to answer this question (pp. 64–5), but the discussion is restricted by the insistence that 'philosophy' and 'expounding Christian texts and dogma' should be rigidly distinguished.

Although, by my account, most of the *Periphyseon* was given over to systematizing and dogmatic exposition, I allowed that those parts of it concerned with logic dealt with 'genuine problems of philosophy'. But, although John Scottus was from time to time a philosopher, he was – I insisted – a bad one: 'though he may be one of the most sophisticated logicians of his age, he is also one of the most confused'. His main confusion, according to *Early Medieval Philosophy* (pp. 66–9) was about *ousia*, the first of Aristotle's categories (normally translated 'substance' or 'essence'). John was guilty, I said, of treating *ousia* at times as a 'type' universal (like Man or Animal) and at times as a 'qualitative' universal (like Goodness or Beauty).

Is this accusation just? Not only did John himself not distinguish between 'type' and 'qualitative' universals; it is most unlikely that he would have thought that such a distinction could be made. Universals were for him an ordered set of immutable Ideas (or 'primordial causes'), created by God and themselves responsible for the creation of the rest of nature. The first of these Ideas is Goodness; then comes *ousia* and then various other Ideas including Animal and Man. John Scottus does not represent *ousia* as a quality: rather, the Ideas of other genera and species are determinations of *ousia*, and individuals are distinguished by accidental differences. This is not to say that John's treatment of universals, individuals and being is entirely clear and coherent. He has difficulties in reconciling his Neoplatonic theory of Ideas with Aristotelian logic, and with his need, as a Christian, to recognize the importance of the individual and the corporeal. Such difficulties, however, are deeper and more interesting than simple confusions. They require patient investigation in the light of the aims – doctrinal, metaphysical and logical – of the *Periphyseon*. Such patience is lacking in *Early Medieval Philosophy*.

Abelard's ethical thought

Whereas the account of the *Periphyseon* in *Early Medieval Philosophy* is unjustly unappreciative, the treatment of Abelard's ethical thought is appreciative, and justly so. It *is* true that in his *Collationes* and *Scito teipsum* 'Abelard succeeds in formulating the beginnings of . . . an ethical theory'; and true, also, that Abelard far surpasses his contemporaries by the subtlety and depth with which he investigates this field. However, my wish (in line with the whole project of the book) to show that Abelard was a 'philosopher' whereas his contemporaries were merely 'speculative theologians' led me to distort the shape of Abelard's thought about ethics, even while explaining his individual arguments correctly. Abelard was not a twelfth-century G.E. Moore, trying to isolate a special, 'moral' sense of the word 'good'. He was a Christian thinker who used his sophisticated logic to discuss goodness and evil in the light of his revealed knowledge of God.

Abelard's *Collationes* consist of two dialogues: between a Jew and a *Philosophus*, and between the *Philosophus* and a Christian. The *Philosophus* is a thinker who uses his reason without the aid of revelation. This led me to suggest in *Early Medieval Philosophy* that the discussion of ethics here became purely 'philosophical'. This view is misleading. A considerable part of the dialogue between the Christian and the *Philosophus* is in fact taken up with specifically Christian subjects, such as beatification and damnation. Moreover, the *Philosophus* shares with the Christian a premise which rarely enters into debates which are nowadays called 'philosophical': that there exists a God who is the supreme good. The philosopher has indeed reached this position by the use of reason, but the *Collationes* insist upon a Christian understanding of human reason. There are three sorts of law, as Abelard's characters explain: the Old Law, given to the Jews in the Old Testament; the New Law, contained in the New Testament; and natural law, which is discovered by the right use of human reason and so has been available to all men at all times.

Abelard's interests and purposes in ethics are made clearer by another of his works, which *Early Medieval Philosophy* mentions only in passing (under the disparaging rubric of 'theology'): the commentary on St Paul's Letter to the Romans. This commentary deals with many topics found in the *Collationes* and *Scito teipsum*, such as divine omnipotence, predestination and natural law. But it places them within the context of its main theme, God's justice and his grace, and Abelard's bold defence of the power of men to accept the grace which God freely offers them. An account of Abelard's 'philosophy' which places such subjects beyond its scope merely illustrates the inadequacy of 'philosophy' to account for Abelard.

Gilbert of Poitiers

Authors – even the authors of sober books about the history of philosophy – never like to leave their stories without a hero; and if no such figure can be discovered by legitimate means they are apt to invent one. Gilbert of Poitiers became the hero of *Early Medieval Philosophy*: an early medieval thinker who not only *was* a philosopher, but who knew he was one. In his commentary on Boethius's *De trinitate*, Gilbert distinguishes three sorts of speculation: theological, mathematical and natural. I claimed that mathematical speculation came 'to mean, for Gilbert, something very like philosophical investigation in the strict sense of the term', and went on to present him as a thinker mainly engaged in such investigation, who did not engage in 'multiplying entities, merely analysing objects'. This presentation was very misleading. Mathematical speculation is in fact for Gilbert a specialized activity, concerned with what later logicians would call 'second intentions': little of Gilbert's work is devoted to it. And Gilbert *does* multiply entities, by positing the real (though not separable) existence of a very important class of entities he calls '*quo est*'s. Neither of these observations implies that Gilbert was uninteresting or unimportant as a thinker: just that he was not the hero of the tale I once tried to tell. I have entirely re-written the section on Gilbert for this edition.

Trinity College,
Cambridge
1987

Preface

No period in the history of philosophy is so neglected as the early Middle Ages. In general accounts, it is represented as a time of intellectual decline between the achievements of antique philosophy and the philosophy which developed, from the late twelfth century onwards, on the basis of Aristotle's newly rediscovered metaphysics and ethics; whilst specialized studies have rarely done more than to argue the philosophical interest of isolated figures, such as Anselm and Abelard.

The main cause of this neglect is the manner in which early medieval thinkers engaged in philosophy. Philosophical speculation was one – often minor – part of their intellectual activity, which they rarely separated from other types of thought, logical, grammatical, scientific or theological. Early medieval philosophy will not, therefore, be found in independent philosophical treatises: it occurs for the most part incidentally, in the course of works on logic, physical science, grammar and theology. Its subject is often suggested by the scientific, logical, grammatical or theological aims of its author, and frequently it cannot be understood without some knowledge of these aims and interests. Yet, for all that, it remains philosophy; and it is possible to speak of early medieval philosophy, just as it is possible to speak of antique, later medieval or modern philosophy.

This book is an attempt, not merely to identify and discuss the material of philosophical importance produced during the early Middle Ages, but also to ask how early medieval thinkers first came to engage in philosophy. It suggests that the relationship between Christianity and philosophy in late antiquity and the following centuries is very different from that which most historians have supposed; that revealed religion, so far from being an obstacle to philosophical speculation, encouraged some of its most profitable developments.

It is impossible to understand how early medieval scholars came to philosophy without a knowledge of the antique heritage on which they drew. The first three chapters of this book examine ancient philosophy, logic and patristic theology. They are not in any sense an attempt to epitomize these vast and difficult subjects, but merely record points of particular importance for the development of early medieval philosophy. The first thinker to be examined in detail is Boethius. In some ways, he belongs to the ancient rather than the medieval tradition, since by his schooling he became familiar with a wide range of Greek Neoplatonic philosophy, most of it unknown in the Middle Ages. Yet his great importance as a direct source for thinkers from the ninth century onwards marks him more clearly as an instigator of early medieval philosophy than any other single figure in the ancient world.

The two and a half centuries which followed the death of Boethius are barren years in the history of philosophy. By the late eighth century, when interest in philosophy began to revive, Latin Europe was culturally separate from the Greek East; and intellectual contacts with the Islamic world began to be of importance for philosophy only in the later twelfth century. This book deals only with the Latin West. The choice of 1150 as the date which marks the end of the early Middle Ages is not an arbitrary one. The following decades saw the rise of a new generation of philosophers, familiar with a wider range of ancient sources than any of their medieval predecessors; both the questions asked, and the way in which they were approached began to change, disrupting a continuity of subject-matter and method which, for all the developments of the intervening centuries, had existed from the time of Boethius to that of Abelard. The year 1150 is not, however, treated rigidly as the end of this survey: certain work of the 1150s and 1160s, linked directly with that of preceding years, is discussed; whilst the writing of, for example, Hermann of Carinthia, heavily influenced by his translations from the Arabic, has been excluded, although some of it dates from the 1140s.

I should like to thank the Master and Fellows of Trinity College, Cambridge, for their generous support; and Oliver Letwin for discussing many of the abstract issues raised by the book. The dedication expresses a different, and deeper, gratitude.

Note on references

References to the pages (and, where applicable, lines) of primary works are given in the text within brackets. The editions to which these references apply are those listed in the Bibliography under Primary Works (below, pp.165–74). Where line numbers are given, they are preceded by a colon: thus '27:41–28:5' means 'from p.27, line 41, to p.28, line 5'. The works of Plato and Aristotle are referred to by means of standard reference numbers and letters, found in all modern editions; and patristic works – not listed in the Bibliography – are referred to by book and chapter. In the case of certain medieval authors, whose works are available in translation and in a number of editions, a reference to book and chapter has been included in addition to a precise reference to the best Latin text, as listed in the Bibliography.

Part One

The antique heritage

1 *Platonism in the ancient world*

Throughout the early Middle Ages, the philosophers of antiquity excited fervent curiosity and, in many cases, deep respect. Yet it was not by reading ancient books of philosophy that early medieval thinkers first came to ask themselves philosophical questions, or arrived at their most profound philosophical reflections. Why did the early Middle Ages benefit so little from the antique philosophical tradition?

The answer to this question seems, at first sight, a most straightforward one. Scholars of the early Middle Ages had no direct contact with the sources which could have transmitted to them the fundamental questions, arguments and theories of ancient philosophy. Their direct reading of Plato was limited to an incomplete translation of one dialogue, the *Timaeus*; Aristotle's philosophical works – as opposed to his logic – began to become known only in the mid-twelfth century. For their knowledge of ancient thought they had to rely principally on later antique material of uncertain quality: the few treatises and textbooks by Latin-speaking Platonists and the more philosophical passages in the writings of the Church Fathers. Is it surprising that early medieval thinkers could not continue the traditions of Plato, Aristotle and Plotinus?

This answer raises another, far deeper question: *why* was the philosophical material transmitted from late antiquity to the early Middle Ages so restricted and so limited in its value to the would-be philosopher? A brief (and highly simplified) sketch of the development of ancient philosophy in some of its aspects will show that the answer is to be found in the nature of the philosophical tradition itself, rather than in the accidents of textual transmission.

Plato

Plato is justly regarded as a philosopher (and the earliest one whose
works survive in quantity) because his method, for the most part,
was to proceed to his conclusions by rational argument based on
premises self-evident from observation, experience and thought.
For him, it was the mark of a philosopher to move from the
particular to the general, from the perceptions of the senses to the
abstract knowledge of the mind. Where the ordinary man would
be content, for instance, to observe instances of virtue, the philosopher asks himself about the nature of virtue-in-itself, by which
all these instances are virtuous. Plato did not develop a single,
coherent theory about universals (for example, Virtue, Man, the
Good, as opposed to an instance of virtue, a particular man, a
particular good thing); but the Ideas, as he called universals, play
a fundamental part in most of his thought and, through all his
different treatments of them, one tendency remains constant. The
Ideas are considered to exist in reality; and the particular things
which can be perceived by the senses are held to depend, in some
way, on the Ideas for being what they are. One of the reasons why
Plato came to this conclusion and attached so much importance to
it lies in a preconception which he inherited from his predecessors.
Whatever really *is*, they argued, must be changeless; otherwise it
is not something, but is always becoming something else. All the
objects which are perceived by the senses can be shown to be
capable of change: what, then, really *is*? Plato could answer con-
fidently that the Ideas were unchanging and unchangeable, and so
really *were*. Consequently, they – and not the world of changing
particulars – were the object of true knowledge. The philosopher,
by his ascent from the particular to the general, discovers not facts
about objects perceptible to the senses, but a new world of true,
changeless being.

As the result of what, quite often, he presented as a purely
rational argument, Plato could thus make promises and revelations
more often associated with religion than philosophy: he could
prove the immortality of the soul, the happiness of the virtuous
man, the danger of the bodily passions. But Plato did not always
expound his thoughts by means of argument; and his use of the
dialogue-form, in which a number of different speakers follow a
sometimes rambling course of discussion, provided many oppor-
tunities for other types of exposition. Through his characters, Plato
would talk in the similes and metaphors of poets, the paradoxes
of myth and the cryptic certainties of the seer. How he intended

such passages to be taken is a matter much disputed by modern scholars; but many of Plato's more immediate followers were untroubled by these doubts.

Of all Plato's dialogues, the *Timaeus* (which alone was available in the early medieval West) relies the least on philosophical reasoning. It is devoted, in the main, to an account of the formation of the Universe, which, although based on some of Plato's most characteristic philosophical preconceptions, is expounded loosely, rather as a religious story, embellished with metaphor and filled out with a mass of physical, cosmological and physiological discussion.

Many thinkers have argued from the order and beauty of the Universe to the existence of a deity which created it. Plato's discussion moves in the opposite direction. The world of becoming, which we perceive with our senses, must have been made by a maker who really *is* and does not become. Since such a maker is good, he must have made the world, not according to the model of that which has come to be, but of that which is unchanging and has true being (27d–29a). Moreover, because the maker is good, and lacks all jealousy, he must have made the world as good as possible. What has intelligence is better than what lacks it; and intelligence can only be present in a soul. The world, therefore, must have been made like a single living creature, with intelligence in its soul; and it must have been copied from an intelligible living creature (29d–30c). The maker is described as making the World-Soul by blending divisible and indivisible kinds of Existence, Sameness and Difference (35a) – the three Ideas which, according to another of Plato's dialogues, the *Sophist*, cannot be identified with or derived from one another. Then, metaphorically, he speaks of the World-Soul as if it were a strip of material, being marked out according to harmonic intervals; the mathematics of which is discussed at some length (35b–36b). Finally, describing the Soul in terms of its body, he imagines this strip being cut and twisted into the shape of an armillary sphere, showing the structure and revolutions of the Universe. In developing this metaphor, Plato expounds his cosmology (35b–36d), a subject on which he continues when he describes the world's body, which is fitted to the soul and woven into it.

The *Timaeus* also includes a parallel description of the process of copying by which the world was made; this provides a physical account of the Universe in the same way as the earlier part of the dialogue provided a cosmological account. The Ideas of the four elements – fire, air, earth and water – are said to have been imposed

on a characterless receptacle, in which the elements, initially confused, are separated (48e–52c). At this point (53c) Calcidius' translation ends, depriving medieval readers of the further discussion
of the elements in geometrical terms which has been promised,
and the elaborate physical and physiological expositions with
which Plato ends his dialogue.

In the context of Plato's work, the *Timaeus* is remarkable for the
space it devotes to presenting the physical constitution of the universe. This is placed within a metaphysical framework, the concepts and principles of which Plato advocates, analyses or, indeed,
contradicts in other dialogues. Argument, logical but loose, is used
in the *Timaeus* to connect together these abstract ideas to form the
outlines of a metaphysical system. It seems probable that Plato
intended some aspects of this system – the World-Soul, perhaps
even the maker – to be taken figuratively, and that the metaphysics
in this dialogue was included rather to place and order the physical
discussion than to represent in any fullness the author's philosophical conclusions. The early medieval reader, ignorant of all but the
most general lines of Plato's other work, might be expected to
take a different view. The *Timaeus* was his Plato.

Why was it the *Timaeus*, of all Plato's dialogues, which was
translated into Latin and preserved for the early Middle Ages? It
was not merely the result of chance. The *Timaeus* was the most
popular of Plato's dialogues in antiquity; it was commented on at
length by many of Plato's later followers; and, as well as that of
Calcidius, there was another Latin translation of it by Cicero,
which survived only in a very incomplete form. The very unargumentative, metaphysically systematic qualities of the *Timaeus*,
which make it so poor a representative of Plato's philosophizing,
recommended it to his followers: it accorded with their Platonism
more than anything more characteristically Plato's. In having the
Timaeus as the main source for their knowledge of Plato's thought,
the early Middle Ages was the beneficiary, or the victim, of the
philosophical attitudes of Plato's ancient followers. But how did
these attitudes come to develop? How, apart from their bequest of
the *Timaeus*, did the philosophers who succeeded Plato influence
the thought of early medieval times?

From Platonism to Neoplatonism

The most intelligent of Plato's followers was Aristotle. His approach to philosophy was quite the opposite of that just described
as widespread in antiquity. He read Plato's mythical and meta-

phorical passages literally only in order to hold them to ridicule. Much of his effort was directed towards showing that Plato's arguments for the existence of immutable Ideas were baseless; and that ethics, psychology, physics and cosmology could be studied fruitfully in the absence of such extensive metaphysical foundations. However, Aristotle had few direct followers among the ancients in his manner of approaching philosophy, and their bearing on the early Middle Ages is negligible. Both Aristotle's philosophy and his logic had their most widespread influence on and through the exponents of Platonism. But, whereas the Platonists followed much of Aristotle's logical teaching faithfully (see below, pp.23–6), the effect of their adaptations of his metaphysics was to strengthen the very aspects of Plato's thought which must have seemed least admirable to a philosopher of Aristotle's temperament.

To one concept, Aristotle grants the transcendence which he denied to Plato's Ideas and to the soul: Intellect (*nous*). In his discussion of psychology, Aristotle treats the Intellect as immortal and not bound to the body; and when his theory of cause and effect requires that he postulate an ultimate, unchanging principle of the universe, he identifies this as Intellect.

The development of philosophy between the death of Aristotle and the third century A.D., when Neoplatonism took on a definite and well-documented form, is complex, disputed and, in part, obscure. There were many different schools: Pythagoreans, Stoics, Aristotelians (of a kind) and various types of Platonists. The doctrines which would characterize Neoplatonism began to be evolved. The Platonists proved to be less interested in the analysis of problems about the world of change and decay than in providing a systematic description of a world of true, immutable being, to which the way had been opened by their favourite Platonic dialogues. Aristotle's concept of the Intellect appealed to these thinkers and was incorporated into some of their systems.

The philosophical ideas of these centuries were contained in a few of the texts available in the early Middle Ages. Cicero (d.43 B.C.) provided a somewhat eclectic assemblage of views in his philosophical works; his *Tusculan Disputations* present a brand of Platonism distinct both from that of its founder and that of the Neoplatonists. Seneca (d.65 A.D.) reflects the thought of various of the schools in his letters – Stoics, Epicureans and Platonists. In one of the letters (65) he speaks of the ideas as existing in God's mind – a theme which would become important in Neoplatonism. Apuleius (second century A.D.) offered in his *De dogmate Platonis* a pre-echo of the threefold division of the intelligible world characteristic in Neoplatonism. Calcidius, translator of the *Timaeus*, attached to Plato's dialogue a lengthy commentary; and, although Calcidius lived most probably in the late fourth to early fifth century, his work shows the influence of other, earlier philosophers, as well as that of the Neoplatonists. An especial source seems to have been Numenius of Apameia, a Pythagorean whose interpretation of Plato helped to prepare the way for Neoplatonism. Calcidius' doctrine on matter (303:9 ff) as without quality, immutable, eternal and neither corporeal nor incorporeal may be particularly close to that of Numenius.

It would be wrong to place much importance on any of these works as a source for early medieval philosophy. It has required the refinements of modern scholarship to gain a coherent picture of the various doctrines which preceded Neoplatonism. The isolated texts available in the early Middle Ages might suggest a phrase, a quotation or even an idea: they could have little effect on the main lines of their readers' thoughts. Even Calcidius' detailed material, which has provided such quarry for recent researchers, received little attention. Moreover, it was natural for medieval scholars to assimilate the Platonic theories in these texts to the Neoplatonic formulations with which they were more familiar.

Plotinus, Porphyry and Latin Neoplatonism

Many aspects of the thought of the preceding centuries went towards forming the philosophy of Plotinus (*c.* 204/5–270), which his pupil Porphyry (*c.* 232–*c.* 304) edited as the *Enneads* and helped to popularize, not without some modification, in his own writings. None of Plotinus' works was available in the early medieval West; but his indirect influence, not slight in terms of specific doctrines, became vast through the character and direction his thought imparted to the whole subsequent tradition of ancient philosophy. A sketch must therefore be made of a set of ideas which are notoriously subtle, intricate and profound.

For Plotinus, the Ideas, which are identified with the Intellect, are only the second highest stage of reality. Even if the Intellect's only object of understanding was itself (as Aristotle had said), this notion, Plotinus believed, carried with it a suggestion of duality. The highest principle of reality must be absolutely simple and unitary: above the Intellect there must be the One. The One has not merely true being like Intellect, but unlimited being; and so

Plotinus can even say – in the sense that its being is not finite – that the One is beyond being.

Intellect proceeds from the One without its production in any way affecting its source. In a similar way, Soul, the lowest level of the intelligible world, is produced by Intellect. Plotinus argued for the existence of this third level of reality, because it provided a necessary intermediary between the changeless world of Ideas (Intellect) and the ever-changing world perceived by the senses. The concept owes something to the World-Soul of the *Timaeus*, which was responsible for vitalizing the sensible world in accordance with the pattern of the Ideas; and something also to the concept of the individual soul which, in Plato, collects and classifies perceptions, engages in reasoning and can ascend to contemplate the Ideas. Soul is not, however, the same as the World-Soul or the individual soul, although the roles of the three concepts sometimes merge in Plotinus' exposition. All that part of reality concerned with life, growth and discursive thought is embraced by Soul; and to this level of reality is attributed the formation of bodies. The material world is not considered to be part of Soul, but whatever is real in it belongs to Soul. The One, Intellect and Soul thus constitute the three levels of reality, or 'hypostases'.

It might be suggested that, by making the material world a merely derivative and unimportant aspect of reality as he describes it, Plotinus shows that he has lost all sense of the task of philosophy as one of explanation, and has occupied himself with forming empty concepts into meaningless patterns. Plotinus could reply Platonically that a philosopher should seek knowledge of what really *is*, not what becomes; or, anticipating Descartes, he could insist that a philosopher can begin his search for certainty only from within his own soul, and then argue that soul is led by its contemplations, not outwards to the sensible world, but to a reality which is found by looking inwards, to the Ideas and, ultimately, to the One. And Plotinus might well add that, for all the metaphorical elusiveness of his style, his arguments have a rigour and a capacity to anticipate and forestall objections to which no summary can do justice.

Yet there are concepts within Plotinus' thought which remain mystical, in the sense that no literal formulation is adequate to express them. Among them are the One itself, and the concept of emanation – the production by a higher hypostasis of its successor without its being itself affected. Both concepts are fundamental to Plotinus' philosophy: the One because it is the source of all reality; emanation, because it allows the One to be represented at once as utterly immutable and yet the cause of all things. Like Plato, Plotinus arrives through speculations which are philosophical at conclusions which come near to being religious. But the comparison must be qualified: first, because Plotinus' starting-point was provided by Plato's thought, along with the theistic and mystical consequences which generations of followers had drawn from it; and second, because the presence of religious elements, perhaps explicable in Plato as ornament or metaphor, is explicit and irrefragable in Plotinus. Another point of comparison with Plato need be less qualified. Both philosophers produced a body of thought which all but the most gifted of its adherents found easy to divest of its explanatory and argumentative aspects, leaving a system of abstract concepts which explained nothing save the devotee's own preconceptions.

Concepts originally developed by Plotinus reached the early Middle Ages in three main ways: through secular handbooks which show the influence of Porphyry but not of any later Neoplatonists; through the Greek Christian writers, and through the Latin writer, Boethius, who followed the Neoplatonism of Porphyry's successors (see below, pp.27–42); and through the Latin Fathers, especially Augustine, who read Plotinus and Porphyry. The first two of these channels of Neoplatonic influence are marked by the tendency to empty systematization particularly common among developments of Plotinus' thought. From the Latin Fathers, however, Plotinus received, not misrepresentation so much as a reasoned reaction; and for them – for Augustine above all – the profoundest legacy of Neoplatonism lay, not in any specific concept, but in the view of philosophy and its relations to religion which it provoked.

Before looking in more detail at Christian attitudes towards Neoplatonism, a few words on the secular handbooks which transmitted early Neoplatonism to the Middle Ages. Two are of some philosophical importance. One is the commentary to the *Timaeus* by Calcidius; the other – probably written at much the same time – is a commentary on Cicero's *Somnium Scipionis* by Macrobius. Calcidius was probably a Christian; Macrobius probably not. But both men's works are secular, containing a view of philosophy not seriously changed by contact with revealed religion. Calcidius' use of pre-Plotinian thought has already been mentioned (see above, p.8); and it is his fondness for philosophers of this more distant period which limits the value of his commentary as a medieval source for Neoplatonism. He had read and made extensive use of Porphyry, though not Plotinus, and his work contains some characteristically Neoplatonic ideas; but these are lost among the welter of earlier philosophical opinions (many probably culled from no other source than Porphyry).

Like Calcidius, Macrobius' commentary is a discursive examination of ideas raised by his text, not a line-by-line exegesis. The *Somnium Scipionis* is the final section of Cicero's *De republica*, an account of a dream in which virtue, patriotism and contempt for the body are exhorted. These ethical concerns make little impression on Macrobius, although a division of the virtues, which Plotinus had propounded, became one of the most influential passages in his book (37:5–39:32). Macrobius' metaphysics is entirely unoriginal, derived from Porphyry and, on occasion, probably from Plotinus. There is a clear, systematic account of the three hypostases: the One, Mind (*mens*) and Soul (19:27–20:9; 55:19–58:13). Macrobius says nothing about why the hypostases should be thought to exist. But he does point to the important conclusion that, since Mind is derived from the One, and Soul from Mind, and since Soul enlivens all things which follow below it, there is a chain binding together all things, from the lowest dreg to God (58:2–11). At another point (99:19 ff) Macrobius offers some explanation of the mathematical and geometrical description of the World-Soul. He remarks that the World-Soul is not intended to be portrayed as corporeal, but does not otherwise doubt the literalness of Plato's description. He also discusses (47:5–51:17) the descent of the individual soul into the body, all but avoiding the difficult question of why it should choose to abandon its blessed, incorporeal state, and concentrating, rather, on the details of its descent through the planetary spheres. Other more purely cosmological passages, discussions of geography and arithmetic make up much of the commentary.

Two further sources of Neoplatonism highly influential in the early Middle Ages are less philosophical in their approach than Calcidius or even Macrobius. Martianus Capella's *De nuptiis Philologiae et Mercurii* (to be dated either between 410 and 439 or in the 470s), a work in prose and verse of unusual difficulty, is devoted mainly to a set of epitomes of the seven liberal arts, grammar, logic, rhetoric, geometry, arithmetic, astronomy and music. The first two books present an allegorical marriage of Philology to Mercury, heavenly wisdom, which includes a number of vaguely Neoplatonic religious motifs, including an ascent through the planetary spheres and a prayer to a Chaldean trinity. Pagan religion is even more evident in the *Asclepius*, which was once (probably wrongly) attributed to Apuleius. The work is a dialogue between Asclepius and Hermes Trismegistus, the god who was worshipped in late antiquity in a cult which mixed Neoplatonism with ideas derived from Egyptian religion. The *Asclepius* reflects the characteristics of the cult; but, although parts of the work are unmistakably pagan, it also contains some general reflections on the unity and incomprehensibility of God phrased in a language sufficiently vague to pass as a pre-echo of Christianity.

Early medieval scholars might be thought unfortunate to have had, as their secular sources for early Neoplatonism, texts so unphilosophical (or, in the case of Calcidius, so bewilderingly eclectic) as these. But, in many ways, they are typical of the vulgarizations of Neoplatonism: systematic in their approach to concepts, reverential towards authority, uninquisitively solemn, lacking in argument. The same characteristics will be found in the more sophisticated adaptations of later Neoplatonism (see below, pp. 18 ff). After Plotinus, Platonic philosophy had all but ceased to be a matter of rational inquiry where first principles are always open to doubt. For Plotinus the claims of philosophy had become those of religion; for his successors, the doctrines of Neoplatonism themselves came to be treated like those of religion: to be studied, arranged, elaborated, even silently transformed, but never to be questioned. Paradoxically, it was through its contact with a revealed religion that Neoplatonism was to regain its power to stimulate more truly philosophical inquiry.

2 Neoplatonism and the Church Fathers

Christianity was one of many religions which flourished in the Roman Empire. Zoroastrians, Mithraists, Jews, Manichees, traditional worshippers of the pagan gods: each sect upheld the truth of its faith and demanded the allegiance of its members. To the Christians, these groups were rivals, and their religious claims deserved only scorn and refutation. But the philosophical religion of Plotinus and Porphyry the Christians found it less easy to dismiss. In the earliest days of the Church, zealots had little need for abstract speculation in order to preach the commands of the Gospels and elaborate their obvious moral consequences. As Christianity became first the leading, and then the official, religion of the Empire, it gained more and more followers who would not so easily sacrifice the rational and humane values of a classical education. Some found it possible to cultivate traditional literary and rhetorical skills, whilst retaining a suspicion or wilful ignorance in the face of 'pagan' philosophy; Neoplatonism held too strong an interest for others to neglect it.

While Christianity had been gathering followers, Platonic philosophy had taken on an increasingly religious character. This was reflected partly in the nature of its concepts and arguments (see above, pp.9–12); and partly by certain more practical manifestations of religion which, since the time of Plotinus, had become linked with Neoplatonism. Worship of the pagan gods, reverence for the wisdom of the Chaldean Oracles, the practice of theurgy and divination were combined, by men such as Porphyry, with a virulent hatred of Christianity. Such aspects of Neoplatonic religion could not but provoke the hostility of the Church. The internal, philosophical aspects of Neoplatonic religion were little influenced by these external manifestations, and they presented much to attract the educated Christian of the late Empire. The

Neoplatonists' God was strikingly like his own God; but he was described in a sophisticated, abstract language not to be found in earlier Christian writings, and much that was said about him was presented in the form, if not the substance, of rational argument. At the least, Neoplatonism offered the intellectual churchman the challenge of comparison; for the greatest of the Latin Christian Neoplatonists, Augustine, it gave much more.

Augustine's treatment of pagan philosophy

The resemblance between the God of the Christians and the God of Neoplatonists seemed to Augustine especially close. Alone of other sects the Neoplatonists described God as incorporeal, immutable, infinite and the source of all things. In his *City of God*, Augustine devotes a good deal of space (especially in Books 8–12) to praising Platonism above other non-Christian beliefs. He speculates about whether Plato could have had some knowledge of the Hebrew scriptures and suggests that the Neoplatonists talk, though in a confused way, of the Trinity. Their God is, he considers, not merely similar to the true God, but the same. Yet the Platonists cannot reach him. They know where to go, but not how to go there. The Platonist is filled with pride by his knowledge; the Christian must humbly accept Christ.

These views about Platonism were more than theoretical for Augustine. He puts them forward in the chapter of his spiritual autobiography, the *Confessions* (VIII.xx.26), in which he describes how he himself had been led towards Christianity by reading 'the books of the Platonists' (probably parts of Plotinus' *Enneads* in translation). Augustine sees the workings of providence in the fact that he became acquainted with Platonism before his conversion to Christianity. Had he discovered the Platonists' books only after he had joined the Church, he might have thought that they alone could have taught him what he had learned from the Christian faith: his experience showed him that they could not. The Platonists know nothing of Christ; and, in accepting the truth of the Incarnation, Augustine implies, the believer does much more than add another detail to Platonic doctrine: he reverses the very structure of philosophical speculation. For the Neoplatonist, the nature of the One and the real, intelligible structure of the universe, are discoveries made as the result of intensive intellectual speculation. For Plotinus' successors, this speculation might have been learnt from authority rather than based on active reasoning: its results were none the less the arcane reward of the philosopher. For the

Christian, God had taken on human flesh; he had preached to fishermen; and he had left his gospel for the simplest of men to understand. What was not clear in Scripture, his Holy Church had the authority to determine and expound.

Nevertheless, Neoplatonism had a use for Augustine after he had become a Christian; but it was one to which the character of this philosophy as a metaphysical system was irrelevant or obstructive. Augustine did not need to have the authority of Plato or Plotinus to tell him the structure of the universe; as a Christian, he knew it. Moreover, he knew that certain of the central ideas in Neoplatonism were false, because they contradicted his faith: reincarnation, the uncreated status of matter, the almost entirely negative view of the human body and the created, material world. But Augustine found that his own thought could profitably take two things from that of the Neoplatonists: first, certain individual concepts which, detached from their place within the Plotinian system, could be used to explain aspects of the Christian universe; and second, some themes of argument, although not necessary in order to confirm revealed truth, could help the Christian better to understand what he already believed.

This adaptation of Neoplatonic concepts generally involves their separation and simplification. Augustine was willing to understand the relations between the three Plotinian hypostases in a sense nearer to the Christian idea of creation than modern scholars will allow. But his God is not beyond being, like Plotinus' One, but rather true being, on which all created things depend. Augustine has little use for the World-Soul or for Soul as the third hypostasis; but he profits from Plotinus' psychological speculations, using them, in the *De trinitate*, as part of his plan to discuss the Trinity through its analogies in the human soul. The Ideas are held by Augustine to be thoughts in God's mind (*De diversis quaestionibus lxxxiii*, qu. 46; cf. above, p.7). This may suggest that, as in Plotinus, they are to be identified with Intellect, the second hypostasis. But, for Augustine, they are not a level of reality so much as a medium which enables the believer, through his own contemplations, to come into direct contact with God. The emphasis is less on the hierarchy of being, than on man's relation to his Maker.

Augustine's early dialogues, such as *De libero arbitrio*, *De ordine* and the *Soliloquia*, illustrate especially well Augustine's fondness for arguments on themes commonplace to Neoplatonists. The direction of such arguments is to move from self-evident premises, often discovered through observation, to a knowledge of immaterial things and thence to an affirmation of God's existence. What distinguishes Augustine from the Neoplatonists in his treatment of these themes is his emphasis on the form of the argument. For a Neoplatonist, a philosophical argument is intended to reveal some important truth about the structure of the universe: it is the conclusion that is important, and, once that has been established, there is a tendency for subsequent philosophers to forget the questions and arguments which led to it. Augustine, however, knew the most important conclusions about the structure of the intelligible world from his faith: the importance of argument lay for him in the process of reasoning itself. The earlier works of Augustine, with their attention to the logical movement of ideas, their frequent use of the dialogue-form, and their simplification of Plotinian concepts, have as much in common with Plato's own writings as with those of his followers. Few productions of the pagan Neoplatonists (Plotinus excepted) bear so clearly the stamp of a powerful, logical mind. The case should not be overstated: Augustine's arguments must reach a conclusion predetermined by his religion; and, in his later works, whilst the power of his reasoning is nothing diminished, the self-imposed bounds within which it must operate are often narrow. But the rational aspect of Augustine's writing would not be overlooked by the thinkers of the early Middle Ages.

Augustine was not the only Latin Father to read philosophical books; and scholars have analysed the traces of Neoplatonism and the theories of other schools in other patristic writings, notably those of Ambrose. Augustine, however, was alone in the extent of his intellectual involvement with Neoplatonism and the depth and subtlety of his reaction to it. His work, immensely popular in medieval times, eclipsed that of the other Western Fathers in transmitting philosophical ideas and Christian attitudes towards philosophy. One predecessor of Augustine's does demand special mention. Marius Victorinus was a pagan rhetorician who converted to Christianity in the late 350s. He was the first Latin Christian to make extensive use of Neoplatonic writings in his work. His main concern is the nature of the Trinity, and he finds philosophical concepts and arguments of value in explaining orthodox dogma and defending it from heresy. The few early medieval readers of his writings would have found discussion of being nearer to Plotinus than anything in Augustine's thought. God he describes as 'not something that is' (*Ad Candidum*, 13) – meaning, like Plotinus, that the being of God is not limited.

The Greek Christian Platonists

A Christian like Augustine, who knew no Greek, had to depend on whatever translations were available for his knowledge of Greek philosophy. In the Greek-speaking world a whole range of philosophical writing was available, and the educated members of society were more deeply imbued with philosophical ideas than was common in the Latin parts of the Empire. Not surprisingly, pagan philosophy had a far more general and fundamental influence on the Eastern Fathers than on those in the West. In some Greek Christian writing, the framework of theology seems to be borrowed – with some adaptation – from the systems of the philosophers, especially the Platonists.

The extent to which the Greek Fathers contributed to the development of early medieval philosophy in the West is, however, limited. Much of their more speculative work was untranslated; and the writings which were translated into Latin rarely enjoyed a wide diffusion. Intensive study of the Greek Christians was the province of the rare enthusiast, such as the ninth-century thinker, John Scottus (Eriugena) (see below, pp.58 ff).

Christians in the East had brought philosophy to bear on their religious thought by a much earlier period than the Latins. Origen (c. 184/5–c. 254) had been a student of Platonic philosophy under Plotinus' teacher, Ammonius Saccas. His philosophical inclinations led him to doubt that even the devil and his associates could be damned eternally and to argue, along Platonic lines, for the pre-existence of souls. Despite the taint of heresy in some of his ideas, Origen's commentaries on Scripture were widely translated and exercised an important influence on the development of allegorical exegesis in the West. But his more general theories were not very influential, although the West had access to them in his *De principiis*. The *Hexaemeron* of Basil (c. 330–79), translated into Latin by Eustathius, contained some Stoic ideas. Basil's brother, Gregory of Nyssa (c. 330–94), wrote a work on the creation of man, *De hominis opificio*, which John Scottus translated; some of the scientific and philosophical doctrines in this work appeared to have influenced John (see below, p.64), but no other Westerner. The writings of John Chrysostom (c. 347–407), some of which were available in various Latin translations, put forward an optimistic view of Man's nature and capabilities, characteristic in Greek Christian Platonism. The philosophical content of his works was too slight, however, to have a definable effect on early medieval philosophers.

Iamblichus, Proclus and the pseudo-Dionysius

A different form of Greek Christian Platonism is represented by
the writings which made the claim (believed in the medieval West)
to be the work of Dionysius, the Areopagite who was converted
by St Paul. In fact, these treatises cannot have been composed
before the late fifth century, because they show very clearly the
influence of the late Neoplatonist Proclus (*c.* 410–85).

Proclus' Neoplatonism is based on the metaphysics of Plotinus
and Porphyry, but is very different from their philosophy in
method, presentation and detail. One of the concepts to which
Plotinus had given no more than a mystical explanation was that
of emanation. How could a lower hypostasis 'emanate' from a
higher one, without affecting or changing the higher hypostasis in
any way? Iamblichus (d. 326) tried to solve the problem by multiplying the stages in the process of descent from the One. Each
level of the hierarchy is doubled into an imparticipable and a
participated form. The result is to present the Intelligible World as
a series of triads: each form participates in the participated form
above it, which, in its turn, has proceeded from its imparticipable
double. Iamblichus also believed that there was procession within
each hypostasis (as well as from one hypostasis to that below it):
this principle led, in the work of Proclus, to the multiplication of
terms within each hypostasis. Any reality, Proclus argued, can be
considered as permanent, as proceeding and as reverting. Each
hypostasis is thus threefold; and each of the terms of each such
triad can itself be divided into three. In Proclus' second hypostasis,
for instance, there are three orders of triads, amounting to over a
hundred terms. These are used, not merely to expound the structure of intelligible reality, but also to explain the functions and
order of the traditional pagan gods.

The pseudo-Dionysius (as this thinker's pseudonymous publication of his works has led him to be called) took Proclus' hierarchy
of triads and used it to explain the angelic orders of the Christian
heaven and the ranks of the Church. The pseudo-Dionysius' borrowings involved considerable change to Proclus' theories; nevertheless, the structure of Neoplatonic metaphysics provides, in a
direct way, the structure of his theology. But the pseudo-Dionysius' manner of presenting his thought is very different from that
of Proclus. It was one of Proclus' achievements to introduce a
severe logical order into Neoplatonism. In his *Elements of Theology*,
for instance, he tries to show how his theories can be deduced
from a set of axioms which he takes as self-evident. The mystical

aspect of Neoplatonism disappears in the rigid and elaborate hierarchy which separates the thinker from the ultimate source of reality. The pseudo-Dionysius was, by contrast, a mystic, given to assertion rather than argument, who veiled more than his identity in deliberate obscurity.

A complex, metaphysical angelology was not the pseudo-Dionysius' only bequest to the Middle Ages. In two of his works, *On the Divine Names* and the brief *Mystical Theology*, he confronts a problem which was to trouble many a Christian thinker. How can one speak at all of a God who is beyond human understanding and description? The problem was particularly acute for the pseudo-Dionysius because, as a much more faithful Neoplatonist than Augustine, he held that God could not even be described as 'being'. The pseudo-Dionysius turned to the pagan Neoplatonists for help, but the solution which he found was to a problem rather different from his. In commentaries on Plato's *Parmenides*, it had become the practice to apply the series of negations found in Plato's dialogue to the One (whose absolute transcendence had been stressed ever since Plotinus), and the series of positive statements to the hypostases which emanated from the One. Despite his adoption of the Neoplatonic scheme of hierarchies, the pseudo-Dionysius was a Christian, who had to accept both that God was immutable and transcendent, and yet that it was he, directly, who created and who administers the universe. He could not therefore equate God with the positively indescribable One; nor could he directly transfer every description of God to some lower emanation. Consequently, he applied both series of statements, positive and negative, to God himself. God is at once describable by every name, but only metaphorically, by reference to his manifestation of himself in his creation; and he can be described by no name – every attribute may be more truly negated of him than applied to him positively. The doctrine of positive and negative theologies, and the logical contradictions it tended to inspire, was especially influential on John Scottus, whose translation made the pseudo-Dionysius known in the medieval West (see below, pp.61–9); and it had a long history in subsequent thought.

3 *The antique logical tradition*

The rediscovery and development of Aristotelian logic is one of the most important themes in the intellectual history of the Middle Ages. Problems of logic fascinated the ablest minds, and logical distinctions influenced a host of other areas of knowledge – theology, rhetoric, poetic theory, grammar – in a way which has surprised, and sometimes appalled, later times. The importance of logic to the development of early medieval philosophy goes beyond that of providing tools for argument: from the logical tradition come many of the philosophical questions, concepts and theories which most stimulated thinkers in the early Middle Ages.

Aristotle

Aristotle did not distinguish formal logic – the study of forms of argument and their validity – from philosophy in the manner of a modern logician. Nevertheless, much of the material chosen by the ancient schools for his logical corpus is purely formal in its interest. But the two of his logical works available from early in the Middle Ages, the *Categories* and the *De interpretatione*, are perhaps the richest in philosophical discussion.

The philosophical character of the *Categories* is particularly evident. The *Categories* is not a study of arguments, nor even, save indirectly, of the terms used to express arguments. It is an attempt to explore the way in which reality, as represented accurately by language, can be divided and categorized. Aristotle's concern here is with things that can be said 'without combination' ('man', 'runs'; as opposed to 'man runs'). Such things may be divided into ten classes (1b25). Nine of these are self-explanatory: quantity, qualification, relation, place, time, being-in-a-position, having, doing and being-affected. The remaining category is problematic. Aristotle calls it *ousia*, which is usually translated as 'essence' or 'substance'. He has noticed that there are some important logical distinctions to be made when considering nouns and what they signify. For example, a man is an individual – Tom, Dick or Harry; but 'man' can be said of the individual man (1a20) – 'Tom is a man'. Knowledge-of-grammar may be what is said of knowledge-of-grammar ('Knowledge-of-grammar is a mark of a good education') or it may be the individual knowledge-of-grammar which is in the individual soul. In both cases, knowledge-of-grammar cannot be except in a subject, the soul; just as white can be only in a subject, the body. *Ousia*, says Aristotle (2a11), is that which is neither in a subject nor said of a subject, such as the individual man or horse.

Part of Aristotle's purpose in making these distinctions and basing his definition of *ousia* on them may well have been to attack Plato's metaphysics at its foundations. Plato had argued that individual things were dependent on the Ideas. Aristotle states that universals are simply what is said of a subject or what is said of a subject and in a subject. Aristotle allows that what is said of a subject may be called a secondary *ousia*, but he states explicitly that nothing else could exist were it not for the primary *ousiai* (2a34). Universals, then, are either secondary *ousiai*, requiring individual things for their existence; or else they are what is said of what is in a subject – a type of universal which Aristotle also seems to describe as a quality later in the work (8b25). The discussion of *ousia* raises philosophical problems which Aristotle does nothing to resolve in this book. What are the secondary *ousiai*? (A type of word? Concepts? Collections?) What is the relation between the notion of *ousia* and the various concepts expressed by the verb 'to be'? And what is the relation between the category of *ousia* and that of quality? Aristotle gives deep consideration to such questions in his *Metaphysics* and arrives at a rather different concept of *ousia*. But early medieval thinkers, who eagerly debated all these questions, could only base themselves on the *Categories* and on works from later in the antique logical tradition.

The *De interpretatione* is far more of an introduction to the formal study of arguments than the *Categories*. The work is a study of the basic components from which statements are built – sounds, names, words, sentences – and of how statements may be affirmative or negative and can contradict or imply one another. But Aristotle does not restrict himself to formal considerations and passes some comment on the relation between language and reality.

At the beginning of the work (16a3) he sketches a rather vague theory about how language, spoken or written, consists of conventional signs which signify 'affections of the mind'. This raised, rather than resolved, important questions about meaning for his medieval readers. Later, a problem occurs which involves questions about free will and determinism, but concerns, at root, the relation between statements and the facts which they state. It is raised as part of the discussion of affirmation and negation (18a28–19b4). It seems reasonable to think that statements must be either true or false; and that they are true when the case is as they say, false when it is not. The statement 'John is sitting down' is true if, and only if, John *is* sitting down. What, then, about statements concerning future contingent events (events in the future which are subject to will or chance)? If these statements are either true or false, does this not mean that the future has already been determined and so the events are not, in fact, contingent? If, for instance, the statement 'John will sit down tomorrow' is true, then John cannot choose to remain standing all day, otherwise the statement would be false: but it is true. If statements about future events must be true or false, then there can be no future contingents, and therefore no scope for chance or free will. Aristotle seems to take into account an unstated objection to this argument. Some statements, it might be objected, are true or false necessarily; some are true or false contingently. It is a matter of contingent truth, for example, whether or not John is sitting down; but it is necessarily true that, if John is sitting down, then he is not standing up. If, then, it is true or false contingently that an event will take place, then that event may or may not take place. Only after the event has taken place (or failed to do so) can we know whether or not a statement about its happening is true or false; but the truth or falsity of that statement does not limit the role which chance or volition can play in determining that event.

Aristotle counters such a possible objection by remarking that 'what is necessarily is, when it is' (19a23); 'if it is true to say that something is white or not white, then it is necessary for it to be white or not white' (18a39). His point is that, since a statement is true or false only by virtue of the facts in the world being, or not being, what it says they are, then, if it is true or false, events must necessarily be such as to make it so; that its truth or falsity may not be *known* does not affect the issue, so long as it is held that it *is* true or false. Although, then, 'John will sit down tomorrow' is a contingent statement, the statement, 'If "John will sit down tomorrow" is a true statement, then John will sit down tomorrow', is a necessary one; and it is this type of statement which is the cause of the problem. Aristotle considers that the conclusion to which his argument has led him – that chance and volition play no part in determining future events – is self-evidently absurd; and so he considers that he must reject the initial premise, that every statement must be true or false.

Such seems to be the train of thought running through a complex and obscurely expressed passage. For both later antique and medieval writers, the problem here would be linked with metaphysical and theological questions about divine prescience, free will and determinism. It became one of the most philosophically fruitful discussions in Aristotle's logic.

The other logical works by Aristotle are of much less importance for understanding the development of early medieval philosophy. This is partly because they did not begin to be read until after the early decades of the twelfth century (see below, p. 130–1), and were only fully absorbed by medieval thinkers after 1150; partly because the emphasis of these treatises is decidedly formal. The *Topics* is designed to teach skills necessary to public debating: the *topoi* are a set of standard argumentative ploys which can be used whatever the subject of the debate. This involves discussion of a number of terms of importance to the logician, such as definition, property, genus and accident; and a discussion of the rules of argument anticipating the doctrine of the syllogism, which receives its full development in the *Prior Analytics*. The *De sophisticis elenchis* is a study of sophisms: invalid, but superficially convincing, patterns of inference. The *Posterior Analytics*, which contains Aristotle's profoundest discussions of philosophical logic, was not available in the early Middle Ages.

Logic in late antiquity

The centuries between Aristotle and Porphyry bequeathed few logical works to the early Middle Ages. Cicero wrote a *Topics*, professedly based on Aristotle's work on the subject, but probably derived from a later source. The book was quite widely read in the Middle Ages, at the time when Aristotle's *Topics* was unknown. A work attributed to Apuleius, and bearing the same Greek title (transliterated) as the *De Interpretatione* – *Peri hermeneias* – enjoyed a certain vogue among the earliest medieval logicians. For modern scholars, it is a useful source of Stoic logical theories; but its philosophical content is slight.

By the time of Porphyry, however, a development had taken

place in the status, rather than the doctrine, of Aristotelian logic, which would be of great importance for medieval philosophy. Aristotelian logic had been adopted by the Neoplatonists and given a definite place in their programme of teaching. Whereas their use of Aristotle's philosophical works was piecemeal and distorting, his logic was studied faithfully as a whole. Aristotle had rejected the notion of Platonic Ideas; and he had consequently treated genera and species in his logic purely as class-designations for individual things. The Neoplatonists assimilated this approach, which contradicted the very basis of their metaphysics, by limiting the application of Aristotelian logic to the world of concrete things. Stripped of its metaphysical relevance, the tendency was for logic to become more purely formal than it had been for Aristotle. However, the extra-logical aspects of the *Categories* and the *De interpretatione* were too intrinsic to these works to be ignored; and the result was the growth of a body of philosophical discussion and commentary within the Neoplatonic logical tradition, only vaguely related to Neoplatonic metaphysics, and sometimes seemingly antithetical to its principles.

Porphyry himself did more than anyone to establish Aristotelian logic within the Platonic schools. He commented the *Categories* and the *De interpretatione* and wrote a short *Isagoge* ('Introduction') to logic, which quickly became established as a prologue to the Aristotelian corpus. The *Isagoge* is devoted to explaining five concepts which play an important part in the *Categories*: genus, species, difference, property and accident. It illustrates well Porphyry's formal approach to logic; and he avoids a philosophical discussion of the nature of genera and species, listing various opinions, but refusing to discuss them further in a work which is designed as an introduction.

The language of philosophy in the Roman Empire was Greek. The few philosophers who wrote in Latin were of vital importance in transmitting the logical tradition to the Middle Ages, even – perhaps especially – where their activity was limited to translation and paraphrasing. From the circle of Themistius (*c.* 317–88) derives a Latin epitome of the *Categories*, known as the *Categoriae Decem*, much read in the ninth and tenth centuries. This work adds some further remarks, on quantity, space and the relationship between *ousia* and the other categories, to a summary of Aristotle's text. The author begins by treating Aristotle's text as a discussion of speech (133:1–8) – a term he believes should principally apply to nouns and verbs which, unlike other words, designate things (133:11–15). He searches for a word which will include (that is, presumably, designate) all things, and arrives (134:16–20) at the conclusion that this word is *ousia* 'one of the ten categories'. This seems a fair enough conclusion from Aristotle's theory, since every thing is an *ousia* and can therefore be signified by the word *ousia*. But, a little later (145:25–146:2), the author produces a similar definition, but one which this time applies not to the word 'ousia', but the concept designated by it: '*ousia* has no genus because it sustains everything'. The suggestion here is that *ousia* refers, not to the individual thing as in the *Categories* (although this definition is also given by the paraphraser), but to that which every individual has in common by virtue of being something at all. The implication may well not have been intended by the epitomist who, in general, tries to give a faithful impression of Aristotle's text; oversight or not, it proved influential.

Marius Victorinus seems to have been a prolific translator of philosophical and logical works into Latin. Augustine used his versions of the 'Platonists' books' (probably parts of Plotinus and Porphyry); Boethius – whose opinion of him was low – used his adaptation of Porphyry's *Isagoge* in his first commentary on it (see below, pp.30–1); and there is evidence that he wrote a commentary on Cicero's *Topics*. But the only part of his logical work which reached the Middle Ages intact was a brief treatise *De diffinitione*, an aid to studying the Topics.

In the Middle Ages, the *Categoriae Decem* was attributed, wrongly, to Augustine. But Augustine's authentic comments about the Categories, as well as the misattributed work, made him an authority for the earliest medieval logicians. In the *Confessions* (IV.xvi.28), Augustine describes his first contact with Aristotle's treatise, which he found himself capable of understanding without the aid of his teacher. When he came to write his *De trinitate*, he included a discussion (V.ii.3) of a type frequent among the Neoplatonists, about the Categories and their inapplicability to God. But he stated that *ousia* could be applied to God: indeed, that it was God to whom it most properly applied. This idea, fully consistent with Augustine's ontology (see above, pp.15–16), was to influence ninth-century interpretations of the Categories. A short treatise, *De dialectica*, was also attributed to Augustine in the Middle Ages; and most scholars now accept its authenticity. The work is remarkable for its linguistic approach to dialectic. Having separated words into single and combined (1) – as Aristotle distinguishes at the beginning of the *Categories* between things said with and without combination – Augustine devotes most of his energies to discussing single words, how they gain their meaning and how ambiguity is possible. Dialectic includes, says Augustine (IV), the discussion of the truth or falsity of sentences and conjunctions of sentences; but the treatise does not go on to consider this topic.

4 Boethius

Despite these many and various debts, the early medieval West unquestionably owed most in its knowledge of the logical tradition to one remarkable figure: Boethius. Boethius, too, provided a couple of mathematical handbooks; a set of brief theological works of great philosophical influence; and a work in prose and verse – the *Consolation of Philosophy* – which was recognized as a master-piece by thinkers and poets alike.

Boethius was born, shortly after 480, into the Roman aristoc-racy. His wealthy and influential guardian, Symmachus, to whom his education had been entrusted on his father's early death, was a man of learning and intelligence. He and his friends saw no contradiction between the practice of Christianity and the intellec-tual pursuits traditional for cultured Romans, among them the study of philosophy. Theodoric, the Ostrogothic king who ruled much of Italy, treated the Roman noblemen with respect; the Senate retained at least some appearance of power; and many of the kingdom's most influential administrators were drawn from the senatorial aristocracy. Boethius was educated, most probably in Rome, in Latin literature and Greek thought; and his familiarity with the Neoplatonism of the Greek East has led certain scholars to conjecture (unnecessarily) that some of his schooling was re-ceived in Alexandria. In accord with the traditions of his class, Boethius entered upon a career which made him an important, and vulnerable, statesman in Theodoric's service. But he also found time for service to the republic of letters, as translator, theologian, poet and (in the broad sense) philosopher.

The treatises on the arts

Boethius' earliest translations provide Latin handbooks to two of the mathematical disciplines, arithmetic and music. Both offer technical guidance to the theory of the discipline; music being seen as an abstract study of numerical relations, rather than as a performer's art. The *De arithmetica* is very closely based on a work by the second-century Neopythagorean, Nicomachus of Gerasa. An introductory section was of particular interest to medieval philosophers. Following Nicomachus, Boethius defines wisdom as 'understanding the truth about things which are' (7:26–8:1). This definition is less trivial than it at first appears, because only those things which neither increase, diminish nor vary can be said to *be*, according to Boethius. There follows a list of the 'essences' which are said to *be*: qualities, quantities, forms, sizes (*magnitudines*), smallnesses, conditions, acts, dispositions, places, times 'and whatever, although transformed by participation with bodies and changed, by contact with what is variable, into mutable inconstancy, is incorporeal by nature and receives its strength by the immutable reason of substance' (8:4–11). The *magnitudines*, Boethius goes on to explain (8:15–19), are the continuous bodies of which the world is made, such as trees or stones. Collections made of discrete parts (a flock, a people) are multitudes; and it is with the study of multitude in itself, rather than in relation to anything else, that arithmetic is concerned (8:19–9:2).

Boethius also composed handbooks to the other two branches of mathematics: geometry and astronomy. One medieval thinker, Gerbert, may have glimpsed them, but the authentic treatises were probably transmitted no further.

The logical works

Boethius' main work as a translator of Greek lay in the field of logic. He translated the corpus of Aristotelian logic standard in his time – the *Categories*, *De interpretatione*, *Topics*, *De sophisticis elenchis*, the *Prior* and the *Posterior Analytics* (a translation now lost); along with the accepted introduction to logic, Porphyry's *Isagoge*. He also provided a set of logical commentaries: for the *Isagoge* and the *De interpretatione*, two each – one elementary, one more advanced; and a single commentary to the *Categories*, *Topics* (lost since antiquity) and to Cicero's *Topics*. Some glosses to the *Prior Analytics* may be his; but it is doubtful that he commented the *Posterior Analytics*, or the *Categories* for a second time. Boethius also com-

posed a series of short monographs on some technical aspects of
logic. His *De divisione* discusses logical methods of division, a
subject close to that of the *Isagoge* but wider in its scope than the
relation of genus to species. The *De topicis differentiis* is a discussion
of the differences between the Topics in rhetoric and in logic. Two
treatises on the categorical syllogism expound much of the material
in Aristotle's *Prior Analytics*, whilst the *De syllogismo hypothetico*
provides an introduction to a branch of logic mostly developed
since the time of Aristotle: the study of complex propositions (such
as 'if A, then B').

Neither the commentaries nor the monographs are expositions
of Boethius' own, original ideas; Boethius was concerned to make
available in Latin a tradition of learning which had been brought
to him through Greek sources. Aristotelian logic had acquired a
body of commentary by diverse philosophers of antiquity, some
of which Porphyry preserved in his exegetical work on Aristotle.
Boethius made extensive use of Porphyry's first 'question-and-
answer' commentary on the *Categories* and of his (lost) commentary
on the *De interpretatione*. He must also have used commentaries
composed by Neoplatonists of nearer his own time, although it
has not been possible for scholars to decide with conviction who
in particular were the authors of these works. It has been suggested
that Boethius' commentaries were merely a literal translation of
scholia found in the margins of his copies of Aristotle's texts. The
assumption is gratuitous, since it supposes an extreme literality in
the transcription of cross-references and editorial comments; and
no glossed manuscripts of the kind envisaged as Boethius' sources
survive. There is, however, reason to emphasize that Boethius did
not use his sources like a modern scholar, as an historical background to be organized and assessed in the light of his own discoveries. Whether his direct sources were many or few, inherited
wisdom was his material and his task merely to expound it.

Aristotle's logical works raised, but did not solve, a deep problem
about the relation between the terms and concepts of the logicians
and reality. Are the Categories divisions of language or of the
world? Do genera and species constitute another set of real beings,
besides the sensibly-perceptible objects which they classify? In
what way do words, and statements made up from words, represent things? These questions do not belong to the province of
formal logic, in the modern sense; but Boethius followed that
school of ancient opinion which held that logic was not just a tool
for philosophy, but a part of it (*In Isagogen* edition II 142:16–143:7).

He would thus consider it his job to pause over such philosophical issues as arose in reading Aristotle's logical works. But his commentaries suffer, by their very nature, from one grave disadvantage as a philosophical source. Philosophical problems are discussed as and when they are raised by the logical text and often treated in terms suggested by its phrasing. The reader is in danger of being led to accept superficial solutions to individual questions, when a more general and difficult underlying problem remains unsolved.

Boethius apparently worked on his commentaries according to the order in which the treatises were usually studied: *Isagoge, Categories, De interpretatione*. In each of these texts, the problem about the meaning of logical concepts is raised in one of its forms. The solutions advanced by Boethius do not form a coherent whole, partly because he tends to treat in isolation the individual manifestations of the more general problem; partly because the sources are not the same in each commentary; and partly because Boethius' own opinion about the correct approach to certain issues may have changed. The importance to early medieval philosophers of the material on this subject transmitted by Boethius can scarcely be overestimated; and the very diversity of arguments to be found was as much a stimulation to them as a cause of confusion.

In his two commentaries on the *Isagoge*, Boethius restricts his discussion of the meaning of logical terms to that relevant to the solution of three questions raised by Porphyry as an aside. Porphyry had said that he would not pause to consider whether genera and species 'exist in themselves [*subsistunt* in Boethius' translation] or whether they are merely thoughts [*in solis nudis purisque intellectibus posita sunt*]; and whether, if they do exist in themselves, they are corporeal or incorporeal, and exist in separation from sensibly-perceptible things or in and about them' (5:11–14 in Boethius' translation).

In his first commentary (24:3–32:2), Boethius takes these questions to apply to all of Porphyry's five 'predicables' (difference, accident and property, as well as genus and species). His approach is literal and confused, since it fails to distinguish the problem of whether the 'predicables' are meaningful concepts from that of whether they should be hypostatized. In Platonic fashion, he speaks of understanding the universals as a process by which the mind, from the most basic things, reaches a 'higher and incomparable understanding' (25:3–4); but he believes that the 'predicables' are attached to individual things. The genus of an incorporeal thing, for example, would be itself incorporeal and could never be attached to a body; whereas the genus of something corporeal, although itself incorporeal, could never be separated from a body.

In his second commentary (159:10–167:20), Boethius gives a more carefully argued account of the same problems, and offers a solution in accord, so he believes, with Aristotle's theories (though not necessarily with the truth of the matter); and which he says is that of Alexander of Aphrodisias, the great Peripatetic commentator. The discussion begins with an extended *reductio ad absurdum*. A universal is, by definition, what is common to many things (to all members of a given class); and everything, Boethius assumes, which is, must be a single item. But a single item cannot be common to many things. The universal is not shared out piecemeal amongst its individual members. It must be whole in each of them; and yet it seems impossible for anything to be one and many in this way. Universals, then, cannot exist as substances: they must be mere thoughts. But thoughts, Boethius continues, must be based on objects which exist in reality, or else they will be empty.

The solution offered by Boethius to this problem is the following (164:3 ff). Every member of a species bears a likeness to the other members of that species, which the mind, by setting aside the many dissimilarities between each individual member, can perceive. This likeness, 'considered in the mind and truly envisaged' (166:11–12) constitutes the species; in the same way, a genus is made up by the mind's perceiving the likeness between its member-species. Genera and species, Boethius concludes, subsist in sensibly-perceptible things in a way that is sensibly-perceptible, but they are also 'thought as subsisting in themselves and not having their being in other things' (*intelliguntur uero ut per semet ipsa subsistentia ac non in aliis esse suum habentia* – 167:10–12). The difference between this view, which Boethius considers to be Aristotelian, and Plato's, is that Plato believed that 'genera and species are not merely thought as universal things but really are and subsist apart from bodies' (167:12–14). The purpose of Boethius' argument is clear. He wishes to solve the dilemma of the universal as one and many by distinguishing between the sensible likenesses on which species (and, indirectly, genera) are founded, and which are as many as there are sensible objects; and the universal which is collected by the understanding from the sensible particulars and is single. That this way of distinguishing is unsatisfactory is hidden by the ambiguity of Boethius' phrasing. Does he mean that, according to his 'Aristotelian' view, genera and species are *thought* to subsist in themselves, but do not really do so? Or does he mean that the genera and species are thought, quite truly, to subsist in themselves? By the former interpretation, thoughts about universals are empty; by the latter, the universals really are one, and yet it is they which subsist in the multitude of individual things; and so the problem of one and many remains unsolved.

In the commentary on the *Categories*, Boethius touches on the nature of universals while discussing the distinction between primary and secondary substances. Here (183C) he makes collections of like individuals, rather than their likenesses themselves, the basis of genera and species. Boethius justifies Aristotle's treatment of individuals as primary and universals as secondary substances by referring to the supposedly linguistic nature of the *Categories*: the treatise is about words, not as independent objects of grammatical description but 'in so far as they signify', that is, in respect of their denotation (160A). The first person to use the word 'man', Boethius argues (183CD), did not use it to refer to a universal concept collected in the mind from all individual men, but rather to describe a single, individual man; and, because the *Categories* is a treatise about names (*nomina*), the individual sensible things which, supposedly, they were invented to denote must be treated as primary.

The subject-matter of the *De interpretatione* demanded a rather more stringent examination of the relation between words and things. This is most developed in the second of the commentaries Boethius wrote on this text. There Boethius rejects the opinions of other philosophers and follows Porphyry (26:17 ff), who argued that words signify, not things, but thoughts (*intellectus*). Thoughts, he believes, must be carefully distinguished from images (*imaginationes*). Truth and falsehood belong to thoughts and not images, as Aristotle says in the *De anima* (28:3–13; cf. *De anima* 432a11); but there can also be thoughts of simple things, to which distinctions of truth and falsehood are not applicable. There is a thought signified by the word 'Socrates' as well as by the sentence, 'Socrates is a man'. There cannot be a thought without an image; and the action of the intelligence in producing a thought from an image is compared to the colouring in of an outline drawing (28:28–29:6) – perhaps a slightly confusing comparison, since thought is to be distinguished from the confused image by its clarity of definition (29:9–11). Boethius goes on (38:3 ff) to distinguish between thoughts, which are the same among all peoples, and words, which vary between nations. A foreigner will not use the Latin word for a stone; but the same thing will not strike him as a stone and a Roman as a man. Even thoughts of incorporeal things, such as goodness, justice and God, are the same for everyone, says Boethius (42:4 ff). The 'likeness in the mind' of natural good and bad is shared by everybody, even if it is sometimes applied to the wrong object: 'the man who judges that something good is bad cannot do so by forming the likeness of good in his mind' (41:25–7). Thoughts of what is legally right or wrong may vary from nation to nation; but this is because law is a matter of custom.

A little later in this commentary (76:10 ff), Boethius comes to consider a more specific problem of meaning. Words may signify thoughts, but it still remains to determine which thoughts certain troublesome words should signify; and this ultimately involves a decision as to the nature of the reality on which thoughts are based. A particularly problematic word is the verb 'to be'. Alexander (of Aphrodisias), Boethius notes (77:3–13), said that this word is equivocal, since it can be used of any category; and that therefore, by itself, it means nothing. But Porphyry, whose opinion Boethius quotes at length (77:13 ff), distinguishes two uses of 'to be'. Either it may be used simply, as when one says 'Socrates is', which is to be interpreted: 'Socrates is one of those things which are and I include Socrates in the class of things which are'. Or it may be used to indicate participation, as in 'Socrates is a philosopher' which means, 'Socrates participates in philosophy'. The distinction between 'to be' as an indicator of existence, and its use as the copula, would be of great importance to subsequent accounts of the relations between logical statements and reality (see below, pp. 108 ff).

As this passage – along with other remarks later in the commentary (for example, 140:29–141:3) – shows, Boethius interpreted statements of the type, 'Socrates is a philosopher', as indicating the inherence of a universal quality in a particular. When Boethius comes to consider Aristotle's definition of a universal as 'that which by its nature is predicated of a number of things' (17a39), he consequently treats genera and species as the defining qualities of classes: the species of Plato is humanity; his genus animality (136:1 ff). Such an interpretation is required by his theory about predication. 'Socrates is a man' can be interpreted as 'humanity inheres in Socrates', but scarcely as 'man inheres in Socrates'. Whether, as modern logicians assert, this way of talking about universals is preferable to the manner in which Boethius treats them elsewhere, is debatable. In the commentaries to the *Isagoge* and the *Categories* Boethius had, in accord with the texts being discussed, treated universals as the names of classes: the species of Plato was man, and his genus animal. There is nothing immediately objectionable about this position: it is only when the search

begins for some single thing which this name signifies that confusion arises. But a philosopher so inclined can just as easily hy-
postatize the defining quality of a class and then struggle to explain
its relation to the particulars. At any rate, Boethius extends his
consideration of class-qualities to suggest that, just as humans are
distinguished by their possession of humanity, so an individual
such as Plato is distinguished by his possession of 'Platonicity'
(*Platonitas*) (137:6–26). It was left for Boethius' medieval readers
to assess the implications of this not at all straightforward
comparison.

A whole book (III; pp. 185:17–250:16) of the second commentary
to the *De interpretatione* is devoted to the problem of future contingent statements, raised comparatively briefly by Aristotle (see
above, pp.22 ff). The solution actually proposed to the difficulty
Aristotle had noticed is not, however, a very satisfactory one.
Boethius follows and explains Aristotle's scheme of argument: if
future contingent statements are true or false, like statements about
the past or present, then everything must come about of necessity.
But this cannot be the case; and so the initial premise must be
rejected. But Boethius does not interpret Aristotle as saying that
future contingent statements are neither true nor false. The Stoics
interpreted him in this way, he says (208:1–7); but they were
wrong. What Aristotle says, according to Boethius, is that statements about contingent events in the future are not definitely
(*definite*) true or definitely false; and that this indefiniteness is not
a product of human ignorance, but a facet of the statements themselves (208:7–18; 250:12–14). Since it is not definitely true or false
that a particular thing will happen in the future, the role of chance
and free will in the determination of events is, Boethius believes,
preserved.

However, it is hard to see how Boethius' formulation solves the
problem. If, by saying that future contingent statements are not
definitely true or false, Boethius means that they are not necessarily
true or false, then he is merely raising the objection which Aristotle
anticipated in his text (see above, p.22). And Boethius has ruled
out another possible meaning: that we cannot know the truth or
falsehood of statements about contingent events in the future. It
seems that Boethius has wanted to say, in effect, what Aristotle
says – that future contingent statements are neither true nor false
– but, feeling that this cannot be the case, qualifies his position
with an adverb that turns out, on analysis, to be vague or
meaningless.

In the course of Boethius' exposition (230:3–19), Aristotle's arguments that necessity shares control of events with chance and deliberation, and that determinism would render human planning vain, are repeated and expanded. Boethius also touches on another, related subject: the compatibility between divine prescience and human free will. The argument on this point is not very profound. Boethius says (225:9–226:13) that it would be wrong to argue that God knows that all events are to come about necessarily, because some are not necessary; and it must certainly be incorrect to reason that God foreknows what is not the case. In his *Consolation of Philosophy*, Boethius turns to the subjects of chance, free will, determinism and divine prescience, and provides an analysis which better explains how God can foreknow what will be freely decided (see below, pp.40–1).

The 'Opuscula sacra'

In the course of his second commentary to the *De interpretatione* (79:10–80:6), Boethius announces his intention to translate and comment all the works of Aristotle which he can find – logical, ethical and scientific – and all the dialogues of Plato; and to demonstrate the fundamental agreement between these two philosophers. He seems, however, to have done little to realize this project, except to translate the remaining works of Aristotle's logic (probably, by this stage, the *Topics*, *De sophisticis elenchis* and the *Prior* and *Posterior Analytics*). It is hard, indeed, to see how Boethius could have carried out his plan. The fundamental agreement between Plato and Aristotle was a commonplace assumption among Neoplatonists; but it was based on a Neoplatonic reading of both philosophers which depended, especially in the case of Aristotle, on taking certain concepts in isolation from their context. A complete translation of their works would be likely to reveal the great difference in outlook between Plato and Aristotle, rather than to demonstrate their agreement. In the works which occupied him in the last decade or so of his life – the *Opuscula sacra* and the *Consolation* – Boethius united Plato and Aristotle in a less complete, but more feasible way than he had projected. Medieval readers would not have gathered from these books many of the original arguments of Plato and Aristotle; but they gained a good, if partial and in some respects peculiar, picture of a Neoplatonic synthesis based ultimately on the work of both great thinkers.

The *Opuscula sacra* consist of five short treatises, transmitted and studied as a group, but not all of the same character. The fourth treatise, *De fide*, is a profession of dogma, made without rational

argument: its unargumentative character has led scholars, probably
wrongly, to doubt its authenticity. Treatises I, II and V are all
related to the theological controversies of Boethius' time, which
owed much of their complication to the interplay between three
factors: doctrinal differences among churchmen in the East; the
wish, partly inspired by political motives, of the Eastern Emperor,
Justin, and his son, Justinian, to end the 'Acacian' schism which
divided Christians in the East from those in the West; and, in the
short term, the attempt by a group of Scythian monks, who visited
Rome in 519, to gain support for their theology of the Trinity.
Treatise V (probably written between 513 and 518) is designed to
refute the views of Nestorius, who emphasized the distinction of
the two persons, God and man, in Christ, and of Eutyches, who,
by contrast, asserted that Christ was of one nature after the Incarnation. Treatises I and II (probably written between 519 and 523)
are intended to show that, whilst terms such as 'God', 'justice',
'goodness' and 'immutability' may be predicated substantially of
the Trinity, the persons of Father, Son and Holy Spirit may be
predicated of it only relatively. Treatise II is a concise statement of
this doctrine; treatise I, which probably came later, develops and
justifies the position at some length. The main concern of all three
treatises, then, is to use logical and philosophical distinctions to
clarify religious dogma and, by doing so, to ease discord between
ecclesiastical factions. The use of logical terms and methods in
discussing the Trinity was not an innovation: Boethius profited
greatly from his reading of Augustine's *De trinitate*, especially in
treatises I and II; and Augustine himself owed something to Marius
Victorinus. But the clarity and neatness which Boethius brings to
his formulations is novel; and it suggests that he was more concerned to defend a doctrinal position, than to investigate the profound mysteries of the triune God.

   The philosophical passages in treatises I, II and V are incidental
or prefatory. Boethius begins treatise V with a list of the different
definitions of nature (76:1–80:63), drawing on both the Platonic
and Aristotelian traditions. He is then able to move on to analyse
the term 'person'. This involves him in a discussion of universals.
He remarks that 'the understanding of universal things is taken
from particular things' (86:35–88:36); and then he distinguishes
between the mode of existence of individuals, which 'have substance', and that of universals, which 'subsist' (*subsistunt*). Boethius'
terminology has undergone a change since his treatment of universals in the second commentary on the *Isagoge*, and this makes
it particularly difficult to be sure of his meaning. When he trans-

lated the *Isagoge*, Boethius used the word *subsistere* to render the Greek *hufistasthai*, the term used by Porphyry in posing his three questions about the existence of universals. In the commentary, Boethius takes it for granted that individual things subsist (*subsistant*): his problem is to determine whether universals also subsist. In treatise v, however, he says that *subsistere* is the translation for a different Greek verb, also meaning 'to have being', *ousiōsthai*, whereas *hufistasthai* is to be rendered by a different Latin verb, *substare* (88:42–5). This distinction certainly leaves it open to suppose that universals do exist in themselves, in a different way from particulars, although men can only understand them through the individuals. Boethius goes on to apply these different types of being to an individual, such as a man (90:79–87): he has *ousia* or *essentia*, because he is; *subsistentia* because he is not in any subject (that is, he is not an accident, which can only exist in something else); and *substantia*, because he is the subject for accidents. Moreover, he is a person, according to Boethius' definition: 'individual substance of a rational nature'. The whole of this passage illustrates well how antiquity handed to the early Middle Ages no clear Latin terminology for philosophical concepts: the distinctions of vocabulary suggested by authorities such as Boethius gave the illusion of clarity to conceptual confusion.

The second chapter of treatise I, *De trinitate*, contains an extended piece of metaphysical discussion. Boethius begins by dividing 'theoretical philosophy' according to its subject-matter (8:5–10:21). Physics concerns the forms and matter of bodies, which cannot be separated in reality (*actu*); the bodies are in motion, in accordance with ancient physical theory. Mathematics studies the forms of bodies apart from matter, and therefore not in motion; but – as with the objects of physics – the forms, although considered in separation, are really in matter. Theology deals with the substance of God, which is really separate from matter and lacks motion.

Boethius goes on to explain in more detail about the relation between God, form, matter and being (10:21–12:58). He begins by stating that 'all being [*esse*] comes from form' (10:21). Every object is envisaged as a combination of unqualified matter and form, which characterizes it. For instance, says Boethius, earth is unqualified matter characterized by the forms dryness and heaviness: it is these forms, not the matter, which cause it to be; and any accidents are received not by the forms, but by the matter (10:42–12:46). A little earlier in the *De trinitate*, Boethius asserts that 'variety of accidents makes numerical difference' (6:24–5). Taking all these statements together, it would seem that Boethius sees universals somehow uniting with matter, and being separated into numerically different individuals by the accidents sustained in their matter. Such individuals will owe their being to their forms, that is, to the classes of which they are members. But there is a further complication to Boethius' theory. The forms which are embodied in matter and give being to concrete wholes of matter and form are not the real forms, but merely their images (12:51–6). There are therefore two sorts of form, one incorporeal, one only found in bodies. The notion might perhaps owe something to the rather vague distinction, made in the second commentary on the *Isagoge* (see above, pp.31–2), between universals as likenesses in sensible things and universals thought of in separation from bodies.

One of the objects of this examination of form and being is to distinguish between God and all other things. He apparently has in mind two distinguishing characteristics (10:29–40): that God is form without matter; and that God is absolutely unitary – he 'is what he is' (*est id quod est*). The second distinction is not merely a consequence of the first, since Boethius says that everything except for God has its being from its parts: since being comes from form, not matter, the contrast intended must be that God's form is not only immaterial, but also non-composite. However, Boethius offers no explanation of why God is the only non-composite pure form.

The work continues by discussing the relation between God and the ten categories (16:1 ff), and then puts the principles studied to use in resolving its theological problem. The early medieval reader of the *De trinitate* would have glimpsed a metaphysical aspect of ancient discussions on being, the Ideas and objects which is for the most part hidden in the logical commentaries; but he could do so only through an obscure and confusing piece of argument.

Treatise III is of a different character from the other *Opuscula sacra*. It is entirely unconcerned with Christian dogma or controversy and, although fully compatible with Christianity, it is completely Neoplatonic in inspiration. The fact that it is written to answer a query raised by another, lost work of Boethius', the *Hebdomads* or groups of seven, suggests that it was not Boethius' sole attempt at this sort of metaphysical speculation. The problem he sets out to resolve here is this: all things seek for the Good, and therefore all things must be good by nature; but how is it possible to hold this without making all things the same as the Good, and so falling into pantheism? Boethius prefaces his treatise with a set of metaphysical axioms, tersely stated, for which he leaves it to the 'wise interpreter' to find suitable arguments (40:18–42:55).

Taken together, the axioms suggest a train of reasoning which a Neoplatonist would have found familiar. Being (*esse*), being something, and that which is (*id quod est*) are to be distinguished. Everything that is must participate both in being, and in that which makes it something (a man, a horse, a stone). Logically, its participation in being must come before its participation in what makes it something, because it must be in order to be able to participate. Being itself does not participate in anything; and it is therefore distinct from the being of any complex thing, that is, from anything which participates both in being and what makes it something. But in a simple thing (that which is not something) being itself is the same as its being: the one and only simple thing of this sort, Boethius leaves it to the interpreter to note, is God.

Boethius uses this metaphysical position to state the terms of his problem and find a solution. Everything is good in that it is, because the Good is the same as the being by which all things are. White things could not be said to be white in that they are, because they gain their being from one who is good, but not from one who is white. Participation in a given quality is thus quite different from the way in which everything is good by nature, in that it is. However, this should not lead to the identification of everything with the Good. The Good can only be good; but, if one supposed the Good not to be there as the source of being, other things would not then be good in that they were, although they might be good by participation. The Good is not merely good in that it is, it unites being and the good and being good (48:149–150). The identification of true being with the Good, upon which the argument rests, goes back to Plato's *Republic* and was an important notion in the tradition of Platonic metaphysics. It was, perhaps, especially attractive to thinkers such as Boethius, who like Augustine (see above, p.15), tended to reject the Neoplatonic idea that the One is beyond being.

The 'Consolation of Philosophy'

In 522, Boethius' two sons were appointed together to be consuls – a rare honour for their father: and Boethius himself became master of the offices (*magister dignitatis*), an important administrative post in Theodoric's court. Yet soon afterwards Boethius was a prisoner, found guilty of treason and awaiting execution. The immediate cause of his downfall was an attempt to save a fellow senator, accused of conducting a treasonable correspondence with the Eastern emperor. The deeper causes lie in the politics of the time. So long as religious differences separated the Catholics in Italy from those in the Eastern Empire, the Catholic aristocracy of Rome was a valuable and safe ally for Theodoric. Once the Eastern emperors began to make overtures of friendship towards the Italian Catholics, Theodoric could not help but see a threat to his rule. It is difficult to be sure at exactly what time, between 524 and 526, Boethius was killed, and to what extent his execution was brought about by the failure of Theodoric's attempts at ecclesiastical diplomacy with the East; but his death was both a manifestation and a symbol of the sudden deterioration of relations between Romans and Goths.

While in prison, Boethius composed the work which has come to be regarded as his literary masterpiece. Wretched with self-pity, Boethius is visited in his cell by the personification of Philosophy. Having given Boethius the opportunity to protest his innocence of treason and give, to herself and to posterity, his version of the events leading to his imprisonment, Philosophy begins her consolation. Boethius, she says, has no right to blame fortune for taking away the gifts which she freely gave: fortune, by its very nature, is mutable. Moreover, none of the gifts of fortune – riches, honour, power or sensual pleasure – can be enjoyed for long or without alloy; the wise man will not value them highly. For this description of fortune and the nature of its benefits Boethius drew on a long antique tradition, represented by authors such as Seneca, Plutarch and Macrobius. Philosophy then argues that, in their search for the partial, imperfect goods of fortune, men are really searching for the highest Good, although they are misled by their ignorance. This highest Good is to be identified with God (as in treatise III of the *Opuscula sacra*). Despite their seeming success and impunity, those who are evil are powerless and wretched. Evil is, in reality, nothing; and so those who can only do evil are unable to do anything. These arguments derive from the thought of Plato, although it is probably wrong to look for very exact parallels with individual Platonic dialogues, except in the case of the arguments about evil, which are closely related to the *Gorgias*.

Philosophy moves on to discuss fate and providence in Book 4. The universe is subject to the nexus of cause and effect (an Aristotelian theme taken up by the Neoplatonists); a chance event is not one which has no cause, but rather one which comes about from the coincidence of two previously diverse chains of cause and effect. The chain of cause and effect is called fate; but fate is under the control of divine providence, which arranges all so that it is for the best. The nearer that anything comes to God, the more it is free from fate.

In Book 5 the discussion turns to a far more logically intricate problem. One of God's attributes is assumed to be that he foreknows everything: how is such prescience compatible with human free will? The question is one which arose, in passing, in Boethius' second commentary on *De interpretatione* (see above, p.35); and commentators have often pointed to that commentary, or its sources, as the basis for the argument here. Certainly, there are close parallels with the commentary in certain parts of the discussion: the disastrous effect which a supposition of determinism would have on human thought and action; the definition of chance; and the distinction between the necessary truth of statements whenever their truth-conditions obtain, and the necessary truth of certain general propositions about the nature of things – such as that the sun will rise tomorrow. However, when it comes to the nub of the issue, Boethius rejects the solution proffered in the commentary, that God somehow foreknows contingent events as contingent, and he grasps the problem more clearly. Aristotle had thought that statements about future contingents are not true or false; or, according to Boethius' interpretation, not true or false definitely. But God's foreknowledge must be certain, and so Aristotle's theory offers no answer to this difficulty. For a solution, Boethius turns to a view of God's knowledge advocated by Proclus. Different types of being know things in a manner according to their capacities: divine knowledge should not be thought of in the terms applicable to human knowledge. The eternity in which God has his being is not a matter of living for ever, but of being outside the very process of time. He therefore knows all things, which appear to us as past, present and future, at once. His knowledge of a future event is best compared to human knowledge of an event taking place in the present; a type of knowledge which does not imply that the event is not contingent.

It has struck readers of the *Consolation* since the early Middle Ages that there is in Boethius' final work a remarkable absence of explicit references to Christianity. Various explanations have been advanced. Did Boethius avoid doctrinal references for fear of taking sides in the current theological disputes and thus spoiling his chances of a reprieve? Or did he give up Christianity in his last days and turn to Neoplatonism as an alternative religion? Neither suggestion is supported by strong evidence, and it is more fruitful to look at the problem from a different point of view. Nothing in Boethius' earlier work would lead one to expect him to write a personal statement of his religious feelings. In the *De fide* he had expressed his belief in the dogma of the Church, ending with a formal statement about the blissful reward of heavenly life. In the treatises on the Trinity and against Nestorius and Eutyches he had engaged in the details of doctrinal dispute. His statement of faith, once made in the *De fide*, stood in no need of repetition; and the condemned cell was hardly the place from which to engage in theological controversy. The degree of Christian piety and resolution with which Boethius met his executioner is not for the historian to assess; but he should not be surprised, nor impute it to apostasy, that Boethius came to terms with his fate by writing in the philosophic tradition to which his training, taste and work had accustomed him. It is also true that Boethius avoids, in the *Consolation* and elsewhere, much in Neoplatonism that would be incompatible with Christianity. There is no evidence, however, in his work of the conflict which a writer like Augustine recognized between the claims of Neoplatonism and those of his religion; nor of the resulting attempt to adapt Neoplatonic concepts to a wholly Christian metaphysical framework. Boethius censors, rather than adapts. At the very centre of the *Consolation* (Book 3, metrum 9) there is a poem, put into the mouth of Philosophy herself, which epitomizes the *Timaeus*, as seen in the light of Neoplatonic commentary. At the end of the poem, Philosophy prays to God for the power to understand his mysteries: the lines are the most fervently religious Boethius ever wrote, and probably echo Christian forms of prayer. The poem provides a striking example of Boethius' pervasive ability to remain, as a Christian, true to his Neoplatonic heritage.

Part Two

The beginnings of medieval philosophy

5 The earliest medieval philosophers

From Cassiodorus to Alcuin

The execution of Boethius marks the close of an era for the historian of philosophy in a way far more absolute than it could do for the investigator of political or more broadly cultural events. So far from signalling the end of the Roman Empire, Boethius' death may have contributed to the fall of the Gothic Kingdom and Justinian's rule over Italy. Boethius' immediate successor as master of the offices under Theodoric was Cassiodorus, a man of wide reading and considerable intelligence. He retired later in life to found the monastery of Vivarium, a centre which was of great importance in preserving classical texts. Cassiodorus was an historian, a theologian (in a minor way) and the writer of the *Institutiones*, a textbook outlining a basic scheme of education. The work contains a section (109–29) on the divisions of philosophy and logic; but this neither added significantly to the stock of antique philosophical ideas otherwise transmitted, nor showed any originality of thought.

In the early seventh century, Isidore, the Bishop of Seville, had access to a wide range of classical material. His *Etymologiae*, a mixture of encyclopaedia and dictionary, provided (II.xxii–xxxi) a brief epitome of logic and (VIII.vi) information, some of it reliable, about the history of philosophy. Isidore makes no attempt to analyse or connect the other philosophical ideas which he mentions occasionally in the course of his writings.

The seventh and eighth centuries were barren years for intellectual life in most of continental Europe, wracked by the feuds of barbarian kings and deprived, for the main part, of even the remnants of Roman administration. It was once believed by historians that a group of scholars, fleeing the turmoil of seventh-century

Gaul, set sail for Ireland and fostered there a tradition of Latin, and even Greek, culture, which had a direct link with the schools of antiquity. The real, but limited achievements of early Irish Latinity demand no such extravagant explanation. Learning from texts of Augustine and Isidore, Irish scholars set about the interpretation of Scripture with naive enthusiasm. Some grammatical and some literary works of theirs also survive: several demonstrate a fascination for Greek but an ignorance, on their authors' part, of all but a few words of the language. Nothing that might be considered philosophy seems to have been produced.

Philosophical reasoning is equally lacking in what has survived of English culture in the seventh and eighth centuries. Aldhelm displayed learning and, at times, verbal ingenuity in a poem and prose work on virginity. Bede's sophistication as an historian did not involve any abstract analysis of his task; and, as an exegete, he removed metaphysical and scientific digressions from the patristic works he adapted. The figure most closely associated with the revival of philosophical studies on the Continent in the late eighth century was an Englishman, Alcuin, who received his education at York. Although some of Alcuin's brightest followers were also Englishmen, there is no reason to suppose that the interests and methods of the continental school were merely those of York transplanted. Most probably, Alcuin's education at York gave him an excellent grounding in the Latin language, the poetry of Virgil and the Christian poets of late antiquity, a wide range of patristic texts and certain English authors such as Aldhelm and Bede: his interest in more abstract speculations developed only after he had moved to the Continent.

Alcuin's association with Charlemagne began in 781. Returning from a visit to Rome, Alcuin met Charlemagne at Parma and was asked by the king to enter his service. At his palace in Aachen, Charlemagne was patron to a group of intellectuals whose role was both cultural and practical. Alcuin's task was partly that of a schoolmaster, teaching at a fairly elementary level. He prepared textbooks and pedagogic dialogues on grammar, rhetoric, logic and parts of Scripture. He also played an important part in reforming the liturgy. In common with many of his colleagues, he wrote poetry – much of it public verse, eulogizing the king. Charlemagne's intellectual protégés were also involved in presenting an orthodox, royally sanctioned view on matters of faith. The most impressive example of such work is provided by the *Libri carolini*, a treatise in four books issued as the work of Charlemagne himself, in which a moderate position on the question of image-worship is defended in opposition to that held by Christians in the East. Whether Alcuin, or his colleague and rival, Theodulf of Orleans, was the author of this work is a question that has intrigued and irritated historians. But Alcuin's authorship of a couple of treatises directed against the Adoptionist heresy in Spain is certain.

None of these functions which Alcuin was required to perform was that of a philosopher. Indeed, whilst they may have used the word *philosophia* to designate human and divine learning in its broadest sense, neither Charlemagne, nor Alcuin, nor his contemporaries would have recognized philosophy, the rational understanding of the world in abstract terms, as a pursuit separable from theology. Yet in the work of Alcuin and, especially, in that of his close followers, the beginnings of medieval philosophy, in this sense, may be found. In retrospect, the achievements of philosophers between the ninth and twelfth centuries can be seen to have as their base the work of late eighth- and early ninth-century scholars. How did Alcuin and his followers begin to engage in philosophy?

The thinkers of the late eighth century came to philosophy through their interest in a combination of two other subjects: logic and theology. Alcuin seems to have been the first man, after Isidore of Seville, to take an interest in the elements of logic. His *Dialectica* shows knowledge, through Boethius' commentaries, of the *Isagoge* and *De interpretatione*. It draws, not directly on the *Categories*, but on the *Categoriae Decem* – a work which Alcuin may have been responsible for introducing into circulation with its attribution to St Augustine. Alcuin also uses Apuleius' *Peri hermeneias* and Cassiodorus' *Institutiones*; Boethius' commentaries on Aristotle and Porphyry play little part in the text – a reflection both of its elementary and of its formal (as opposed to philosophical) character.

Alcuin found his energies as a theologian employed by Charlemagne, in the service of whom he wrote the treatises against the Adoptionist heretics in Spain. He also composed a non-polemical theological work, *De fide sanctae trinitatis*. It amounts to scarcely more than a summary of parts of Augustine's *De trinitate*, and so it cannot demonstrate Alcuin's own skill at theological argument; but it does illustrate the interest – which he shared with his followers – in one of Augustine's most difficult and philosophically suggestive works.

Alcuin also appears to have been the earliest medieval reader of Boethius' *Consolation of Philosophy*. In a preface 'on true philosophy' (*de vera philosophia*) which he wrote to his *De grammatica*,

Boethius' language and theme of man's search for beatitude is echoed, though transformed: Alcuin's subject is the search for wisdom, and his aim to justify a Christian in the study of the liberal arts.

The circle of Alcuin

If the intellectual life at Charlemagne's palace school could be studied solely on the basis of the works which Alcuin issued complete and named as his own, it would be impossible to argue with any confidence that there was an interest in philosophy there. Alcuin's works show an interest in formal logic, on the one hand, and in theology on the other; the two types of thought are hardly brought together in a manner which might lead towards philosophical speculation. However, there survives a set of material which illustrates more fully the sort of questions which Alcuin and his followers discussed, and the manner of their discussions. (These passages will be referred to by their opening words *Usia graece* . . . following the convention adopted for all untitled anonymous texts and commentaries in this book.)

Only two of the passages – both discussions of the Trinity – are attributed to authors: one (VII) is said to be by Alcuin himself, the other (VIII) by a certain Candidus. It is probable that, although the passages are best regarded not as the work of a single author, but as the record of discussions among Alcuin and his followers, this Candidus was responsible for their compilation. An Englishman like Alcuin, he has often been confused with another Candidus, Candidus Bruun, a monk of Fulda who belonged to the next generation. Candidus was one of Alcuin's most valued followers and may already have been his pupil in England. For most of the time between 793 and 802 he played a subsidiary role in affairs on the Continent, as Alcuin's confidential messenger, as an assistant to Bishop Arno of Salzburg, and as part of Charlemagne's court circle. Evidence for the rest of his life leaves open two possibilities: that he died in the early 800s; or that he went on to become bishop of Trier, only later to be dispossessed of his diocese.

The *Usia graece* . . . passages provide a glimpse of the interests and abilities of the thinkers like Candidus associated with Charlemagne's court. Some of the passages are merely excerpts from antique and patristic writings; others are closely based on an inherited argument; others are more original in content. Both the pieces of inventive discussion and the passages which are merely copied extracts are informative. Indeed, it is wrong to draw too clear a distinction between original writing and copying at this time. The achievement of late eighth-century scholars was to begin to understand certain of the logical doctrines developed in antiquity, and to bring these into a relation with theology which provided the stimulus for philosophical speculation. The choice and juxtaposition of extracts from authors of the past served this end as effectively as more original argument.

The strictly logical of the *Usia graece . . .* passages comprise an extract from Claudianus Mamertus (a sixth-century writer, strongly influenced by Augustine) on the distinction between subjects and accidents (XII); an extract from Boethius' commentary to the *Categories* about substance (*ousia*) (XIII); and two brief pieces (XIV and XV) on space and time, closely based on the *Categoriae Decem*. With these passages, and Alcuin's *De dialectica*, there should be taken a third piece of evidence for the knowledge of logic at the turn of the ninth century. A manuscript (Rome: Bibliotheca Padri Maristi A.II.1), written before about 817 and belonging to Alcuin's associate Leidrad, Bishop of Lyons, contains Porphyry's *Isagoge*, the *Categoriae Decem*, extracts from Alcuin's *De dialectica*, Apuleius' *Peri hermeneias*, Boethius' first commentary to the *De interpretatione*, and Boethius' list of the categories of things which really *are*, from the *De arithmetica*.

These testimonies suggest a special interest in two aspects of logic: the Categories and the concepts associated with them; and the elementary techniques of logical deduction. Certain of the *Usia graece . . .* passages show the application of both these interests to questions of theology. One (I) bases itself closely on the demonstration in Augustine's *De trinitate* that only the first of the Categories, *ousia*, is applicable to God; two (V and VI) use Augustine to discuss the relationship of God with space and time. Another (X) discusses 'how it can be proved that the soul does not have a position in space'. Following Augustine's *De trinitate*, the writer says that the soul can be described as memory, deliberation and will. Memory, deliberation and will, he argues, are not corporeal things, and could not be enclosed in a bodily container. And, if the constituents of the soul are not corporeal and cannot be corporeally contained, then the soul cannot have a position in space. The argument is scarcely rigorous; but it is expounded in a step-by-step manner, which indicates the author's fascination for the procedure of reasoned inference itself, in addition to his interest in the concept of space and the distinction between corporeal and incorporeal things.

Others of the passages are more purely theological, drawing

especially on Augustine's *De trinitate* – as Alcuin does in his *De fide sanctae trinitatis* – and using the supposed structure of the human soul as a way of understanding the Trinity. One passage (IV – summarized by III), however, consists of a dialogue designed to prove the existence of God. The beginning of the argument, in which life, sense, reason and intellect are arranged in ascending order of excellence, is adapted from Augustine's *De libero arbitrio* (II.25–54). But whereas Augustine goes on to show how the intelligible world contains something superior to the human intellect by which it is perceived, and thereby to demonstrate the existence of God, the Carolingian writer argues rather simplistically from the limitations of the soul's powers to the existence of a superior being, who is identified with God. The importance of this passage is not that a demonstration of God's existence implies a need for his existence to be proved by reason as well as accepted according to faith. There is no reason at all to suppose that the author believed this to be the case; and such a position would be completely outside the tradition of patristic and early medieval thought. Rather, the passage shows the Carolingian author, like Augustine, trying to construct a rational argument, the conclusion of which is already known and could not be doubted. It also illustrates the assimilation, through Augustine, of certain broadly Neoplatonic concepts, such as the grading of the powers of the soul. Another passage (XI), based on Augustine's *Soliloquia*, shows the compiler accepting that what is true is true because of truth; and that truth is not a bodily thing. Thus, in a crude sense, the writer grasps the notion of a Platonic Idea.

This picture of intellectual life among Alcuin's circle can be extended a little by some more material associated with Candidus. One manuscript (Munich: Clm 18961) contains most of the *Usia graece . . .* passages, two pieces by Candidus on the Trinity, and some further extracts from antique and patristic writing. The texts from which excerpts are taken include not only works by Augustine, but also Boethius' *Opuscula sacra*, Seneca's *Quaestiones naturales* and Plato's *Timaeus* (in Calcidius' translation). The manuscript itself dates from the second half of the ninth century, but there is a good possibility that all the material derives from the schoolroom of Candidus and his colleagues: a possibility made the stronger by the fact that Candidus seems to use Boethius' *Opuscula sacra* in the *Usia graece . . .* passage attributed to him; and that one codex, at least, of the *Timaeus* can be dated to the reign of Charlemagne. If the collection in this manuscript was compiled by Alcuin's circle, then it shows that, by early in the ninth century, thinkers wished to explore pagan, as well as Christian, sources of the philosophical tradition; and that Boethius' logical approach to theology was already attracting interest.

Another work most probably by Candidus is a passage about the number three, *Omnia tribus constant . . . .* The first part contains a crude but ingenious – and probably original – attempt to show that everything can be analysed into being, being able and willing. Even inanimate things are said to will or not to will, in so far as they facilitate or frustrate the purposes of their users. The piece continues with a parallel analysis into three: all things have a beginning, middle and end. This argument derives from Augustine's *De musica*; whilst the whole idea of finding analogies to the Trinity is inspired by Augustine's *De trinitate*. But, although the Carolingian writer hints by his phrasing that his triads are similar to the Holy Trinity, he does not explicitly say so. The passage is based on concepts and arguments developed by theologians; yet it offers an abstract account of the nature of things for its own sake.

Candidus is not the only one of Alcuin's pupils whose name can be put to a piece of philosophically inclined writing. Fredegisus, like Candidus, was an intimate associate of Alcuin's. In the late 820s, Fredegisus had an angry exchange of letters with Agobard of Lyons about various doctrinal differences. Only one letter, by Agobard, survives from this controversy; but it suggests that, during the intellectually dull years which followed Charlemagne's death in 814, Fredegisus carried on some of the interests of Alcuin and the palace school.

A short work by Fredegisus, *De substantia nihili et de tenebris*, from rather earlier (*c.* 800; but a later date is quite possible) relates to a discussion broached by Alcuin on the meaning of negative concepts. It is of interest because it approaches its subject in linguistic terms, a method not otherwise found in the speculative writings of Alcuin's circle. God, he says, created not just objects but also their names; he made a name for each object; and he instituted no name to which there was not a corresponding object (554:30–2). Every 'definite name' (*nomen finitum*) signifies something, and since, according to grammar, 'nothing' is a definite name, it must signify something (553:8–18): nothing, he concludes, must be a substance which exists. Fredegisus also refers to the concept of universals, but rather inconclusively: the name 'man', he says, designates the universality of men. It is not clear whether he is referring here to some type of abstract concept, or simply to the collection of all individual men.

The achievement of Alcuin, Candidus, Fredegisus and their

anonymous colleagues in the field of philosophy seems very slight, unless it is seen in its proper perspective, as the beginning – and only that – of a medieval tradition of philosophy which is not the direct descendant of the ancient one. The strongest influence on their writings is not that of a philosopher, but of a theologian, Augustine. But the Carolingian scholars have taken the aspects of Augustine's thought which come nearest in their concerns or methods to philosophy: Augustine's examination of the Categories; his analysis of the soul; his simplified Neoplatonic concepts and assumptions, and the rational explanations to which they lend themselves. The strictly theological ends to which these features are used in Augustine's work often disappear, or slip into the background, in the Carolingian adaptations. That this change of emphasis is deliberate rather than negligent is borne out by the many straightforward theological adaptations of St Augustine from this period, including Alcuin's treatises against the Adoptionists and his *De fide sanctae trinitatis*: the scholars of Charlemagne's time could be Augustine's faithful apprentices in theology when they wished. The study of elementary logical texts was one – perhaps the most important – of the encouragements towards the philosophical approach to theological works. The Carolingian scholars searched through Augustine's writings for further information about the concepts they had learned of from the *Categoriae Decem*, itself considered to be one of Augustine's works; and the speculations they found were concerned with metaphysics rather than formal logic. At the same time, their taste for the passages in theological writings most closely and rationally expounded was whetted by an acquaintance with the elementary rules of consequential argument. Whatever could be garnered from the few ancient philosophical texts available was fitted or subordinated to the pattern of interests constituted by this mingling of theology and logic.

6 Philosophy in the age of John Scottus Eriugena

Ratramnus of Corbie and Macarius the Irishman

The philosophical explorations of the late eighth and early ninth century were the work of scholars who had taught or studied at Charlemagne's palace school. By the reign of his grandson, Charles the Bald, advanced learning and philosophical interests were no longer the monopoly of scholars attached to the royal court, although Charles was the patron of the most remarkable philosopher of the day. In the first half of the ninth century, intellectual standards had risen in a number of great monasteries. Alcuin himself had retired from the court to become abbot of Tours in 796; and his successor as abbot was Fredegisus. A catalogue of the monastery at Reichenau from 822 records the *Isagoge*, the *Categories* (in a version of Boethius' translation, rather than the pseudo-Augustinian paraphrase) and the *De interpretatione*, although there is no direct evidence that the works were actually studied there then. The interest in philosophy at Corbie is evident in the monk Ratramnus' contribution to a dispute with an unnamed pupil of an Irishman called Macarius (see below p.54). Macarius' national origins point to another feature of intellectual life in the mid-ninth century. It had been common, for more than two centuries, for Irishmen to emigrate to Europe: some continental monasteries were of Irish foundation; some contained Irish monks, copying texts in their distinctive script. In the middle of the ninth century, however, there are to be found for the first time a number of Irishmen who by their wide learning, intelligence and linguistic ability excelled all their contemporaries. Of these, the three most outstanding were John, Martin and Sedulius (who are all surnamed 'Scottus' meaning – at this period – 'Irishman'). John's work will be discussed in detail (see below, pp.55 ff). In a more general history of culture, Martin, who taught at Laon, and Sedulius, whose activities seem to have had a number of centres, including Liège and the royal court, would merit equally full treatment. But for neither man is there more than tenuous evidence of an interest in philosophy. It is this that makes the ideas of Macarius, as revealed in his pupil's dispute with Ratramnus, of such interest in relation to the thought of John Scottus.

The only evidence for the controversy is a work which Ratramnus wrote in the early 860s, *De anima ad Odonem*. The cause of the dispute was Macarius' interpretation of a passage in Augustine's *De quantitate animae* (XXXII.69). In most of his writings Augustine treats each human soul as an individual thing; but the relationship between the hypostasis Soul and the individual soul in Neoplatonism suggested a unity of all souls which in *De quantitate animae*, one of his earliest works, he was unwilling to reject out of hand. He puts forward three possibilities: that all souls are one; that individual souls are entirely separate from each other; or that souls are both one and many. The first two options he considers unsatisfactory, the last ridiculous; and the problem is left unsolved. Macarius – so far as one can gather from Ratramnus – tried to argue that Augustine had actually chosen the third of these possibilities and asserted that souls are both one and many.

To Ratramnus, who had little way of knowing the Neoplatonic background to Augustine's discussion, the problem in *De quantitate animae* is logical rather than metaphysical: the single, universal soul to which Augustine refers is to be, Ratramnus argues, understood simply as the species to which individual souls belong. Then, using parts of treatise v of Boethius' *Opuscula sacra* and of his first commentary on the *Isagoge* as his authority, he proceeds to deny the real existence of universals more categorically than Boethius had ever done. Not only is 'the understanding of universal things taken from particular things' (*De anima ad Odonem* 71:15–16, 74:8–10; Boethius, *Opuscula sacra* 86:35–88:36); genera and species, he says, 'are formed in thoughts through the understanding of the mind: they do not exist as concrete things' (*in rebus autem existentibus non consistunt*). Ratramnus does not go on to explain in what sense universal thoughts correspond to some feature of reality and so are not merely empty and misleading.

The theory of universals advanced by Ratramnus' opponent is very different. Apparently, he believed that species were ontologically prior to their individual members: the individuals derived from the universals 'like a river from its source or a tree from its roots' (*De anima ad Odonem* 108:37 ff). Other remarks of his – so far as one can gather from Ratramnus' account of them – emphasize the universal form in the particular, rather than the particulars as the source of knowledge about universals. These views have a good deal in common with those of John Scottus (see below, p.67); perhaps they derived from the opponent's Irish master, Macarius. The whole controversy is evidence for the tendency of Carolingian scholars to parade their newly acquired logical knowledge and rely on it to resolve problems scarcely within the scope of logic.

The controversy between Ratramnus and his nameless adversary was one of many theological disputes during the mid-ninth century. The nature of the Trinity; the doctrine of the Eucharist; the virgin birth; and, above all, predestination: all these subjects provoked written debate of some complexity. In most cases patristic authority formed the substance of each opposing view and the discussion was dogmatic rather than speculative. But a scholar could not witness these disputes without an enhanced awareness of the possible conflicts between authoritative writings, and the consequent need for ingenuity, as well as learning, in resolving theological problems. One of the most active participants in doctrinal controversy was Gottschalk (*c.* 805–866/9), a monk of Fulda, then of Orbais, who tried unsuccessfully to gain release from the monastic vows he had been made to take in youth. Besides being a theologian, Gottschalk was also a grammarian and a poet of distinction. His doctrinal and grammatical interests were not distinct, since, for him, the structure of language is a source, though not always unflawed, of theological understanding. The greatest importance of Gottschalk to the historian of philosophy is, however, an indirect one: for he was the instigator of the controversy on predestination, to which John Scottus contributed the earliest of his known works.

John Scottus and the controversy on predestination

Gottschalk argued that divine predestination was of two kinds: of the good to bliss and of the wicked to damnation. This view, he claimed, was Augustine's; and the way in which he defended his case in the various writings devoted to the subject was simply by urging its foundation in scriptural and patristic authority. He did so with enough conviction to gain the support, or at least the acquiescence, of such notable contemporaries as Ratramnus of Corbie and Prudentius of Troyes. But in Hincmar, Archbishop of Reims, he found an implacable opponent, who feared that Gottschalk's theory would discourage believers from any attempt to improve their lives, since it treated damnation as ineluctable for those destined to it. Disappointed in the support of his celebrated fellow churchmen, Hincmar commissioned John Scottus to write against Gottschalk's view. John's role in the controversy is first mentioned in a letter of 851 or early 852, in which Pardulus, Bishop of Laon, refers to him as 'an Irishman at the royal court'. By 852, then, John already enjoyed the patronage of Charles the Bald and resided, perhaps taught, at one or several of the royal palaces in northern France. His work as a teacher of the liberal arts can be known only indirectly (see below, pp.72–7); his writing on theological subjects immediately reveals the character of his thought.

Hincmar looked to John for a decisive condemnation of Gottschalk's opinions, backed by patristic authority; and John's *De praedestinatione* did indeed reject Gottschalk's assertion of double predestination as contrary to both reason and authority, castigating its author as a heretic, madman and blasphemer. But John was unwilling to limit a controversy to the terms in which his contemporaries saw it, or to advance only those assertions strictly required in order to refute his opponent. Already in the *De praedestinatione*, one of the most striking features of John's intellectual character is evident: the tendency to see every problem in the most abstract way possible, and thus to reach back to the logical foundations of every argument.

A discussion of divine predestination must, John considers, be based on an understanding of the special nature of God; or rather – since he held that knowledge about God's nature as such was impossible for men – on a realization of what can and cannot be said about God. Strictly speaking, human language is inadequate to talk of God (390AB); but it describes him 'as if properly' when it adverts to his existence, and to such attributes as his truth, power and wisdom (390C). In so far as God can be described at all, he is known to be absolutely one, lacking in any sort of generic or specific division: any indication that he is divided, in substance or in his mode of being, is at best a metaphor (362A–3A). From this, John argues that it must be wrong to assert that God's predestination is double, because God's predestination and his prescience must be part of his substance, and his substance is absolutely unitary (364C ff). Moreover, John considers that it is misleading to speak of *predestination* or *prescience* at all in respect of God. God exists not in time but eternity; his knowledge has no 'before' or 'after'. The priority of God's prescience and predestination is not in time, but rather that by which God, in eternity, always precedes his creations (392C–3C). Divine predestination, then, not only is not double: in a sense, it is not predestination at all. Gottschalk's theory could hardly be more emphatically rejected.

John's interest in the question of divine predestination went beyond merely showing that it was not double. The very presence of evil and its punishment in a world ordained by an omnipotent and good God was an apparent paradox, needing, he believed, explanation. A Neoplatonic commonplace, adopted by Augustine and Boethius, helped John to find one. God, who created everything, could not have created evil: evil, therefore, is nothing – it is a deficiency of goodness, rather than an existing thing (394C–6C). There are two sorts of evil – sin and its punishment – and both must come from man's will and not from God, since they are not things which are, but rather their privation. Man sins by abusing a free will which is, in itself, a good thing; and the punishment for sin comes from within the sinner himself. In drawing and developing this conclusion (417C ff), John quotes and adapts patristic sources, but goes beyond them to advance a theory which is very much his own. If punishment comes from within the sinner, there can be no physical hell, in which the damned are tortured by worms and fire. Wicked men receive their eternal punishment by being unable to fulfil their own perverse wishes. Their desire is to recede as far as possible from God, who is the source of being: so much so that, were they permitted, they would disappear into non-being. But God has set up a boundary to their evil, preventing them from this ultimate recession into nothingness. The vain struggle to escape into nullity from the restraining power of that which is infinitely good punishes and tortures the malefactor (434AB). On the physical level, John states that the eternal fire spoken of in the Scriptures is simply one of the world's four elements (fire, air, water, earth). Both the blessed and the damned will be sent to it at the Resurrection. But the blessed will have their bodies turned into ether, which will not be harmed by the fire, whereas the damned will have their bodies turned into air, which will be burned by it (436C–8A). There is, then, no hell to blot a perfectly beautiful universe with its ugliness. It is as if – to use John's simile (427B–8B) – a father were to build a house perfectly proportioned and adorned with every splendour. Its beauty would be there alike for his sons and his slaves to enjoy; but the slaves, overcome by greed, would merely suffer at the sight of such magnificence.

John's essay caused more consternation than the writings it had been commissioned to refute. Prudentius of Troyes and Florus of Lyons wrote tracts condemning the work; and Hincmar, trying to evade responsibility as commissioner of the treatise, went so far as to pretend that it was a forgery. This hostility, and the subsequent condemnation of the *De praedestinatione* at the councils of Valence (855) and Langres (859), had as much to do with the politics of the predestinarian controversy as with any comprehending, reasoned rejection of John's ideas. But the extreme nature of some of his conclusions, and his ruthless following of principles founded in patristic authority to conclusions not previously advanced, must have made it all the easier, and more tempting, to stigmatize the work as heretical.

In method and even in scope, the *De praedestinatione* marks a development in Carolingian theology; but how far does its author show himself to be a philosopher? At the beginning of the work John places a statement identifying 'true philosophy' with 'true religion' (357C–8A), which might strike a casual reader as an assertion of the primacy of philosophical forms of investigation, even in matters concerning the Faith. In fact, John is explicitly following Augustine here; and both writers are talking about the identity between true theory and true practice within Christianity, not about the relationship between abstract, rational speculation and Christian dogma. In the *De praedestinatione*, John's investigation is a theological one, which proceeds by linking together concepts inherited from the Scriptures and the writings of the Fathers. Augustine is John's main source (with a few ideas borrowed from Boethius' *Consolation*); and like Augustine, John allows great powers to the divinely illuminated reason in seeking out the truth, but does not in fact use his own reasoning about the world to provide the starting-point for his speculations. John is, however, led by his argument to analyse certain of his concepts in a philosophical manner: for instance, the nature of prescience and predestination, given that God is timeless; or of punishment, given the complete goodness of God's creation. But the purpose of such analyses is to eliminate apparent contradictions and so aid the systematic account of inherited ideas. Philosophical reflection is incidental: the aim of the work is to achieve coherence, rather than to provide any sort of an explanation.

John Scottus and the Greeks

It was a rare chance which transformed John's intellectual horizons and led him to write, in his *Periphyseon*, a work which occupies a unique – and, indeed, somewhat, anomalous – position in the development of medieval thought.

In 827, the Emperor Louis the Pious had been sent a copy of the writings of the pseudo-Dionysius as a gift by the Byzantine Emperor, Michael the Stammerer. The Areopagite (whose authorship of the writings attributed to him was not, at this time, doubted) was identified in the West with Dionysius, the martyred apostle of the Franks. His writings had therefore a special authority and Hilduin, abbot of the church dedicated to the martyr, was commissioned to translate the newly received Greek text. But Hilduin's translation, slavishly following the syntax of the original, was scarcely comprehensible. John was asked by Charles the Bald to prepare a fresh translation. His knowledge of Greek, a rarity at the time, must have recommended him for the task; whilst the *De praedestinatione* shows that John's theological concerns were such as to make him a sympathetic and enthusiastic reader of Dionysius by intellectual inclination and temperament. John duly produced a translation of the Dionysian corpus, styling himself in the dedication by the Graecizing sobriquet 'Eriugena' ('scion of Ireland') which would stick with his works throughout the centuries. He also produced a commentary to one of the works he translated, the *Celestial Hierarchy* – a piece of writing which, though of considerable influence and some theological interest, has little to add to the picture of John's philosophy to be gained from his masterpiece, the *Periphyseon*.

His taste whetted by the pseudo-Dionysius, John went on to produce further translations of Greek Platonic theology: Maximus the Confessor's *Ambigua* (also dedicated to the king), his *Quaestiones ad Thalassium* and Gregory of Nyssa's *De hominis opificio* (both for his own private use). Gregory's work has already been mentioned (see above, p.17); with Maximus one enters the world of early Byzantine theology. Born in 580, his life extended beyond the middle of the seventh century – just two hundred years before Eriugena set to work. Maximus inherited the intellectual tradition of the pseudo-Dionysius (his *Ambigua*, indeed, consist of explanations of difficult passages in the works of the pseudo-Dionysius and Gregory of Nazianzen), but he also showed a considerable interest in Aristotelian philosophy, and this led him to modify many of the ideas he inherited.

John himself summarizes some of the most valuable points which he thought Maximus added to pseudo-Dionysius' theories in the preface to his translation of the *Ambigua*. Maximus taught, he says (1195BC), how God is simple and multiple; of his procession into all things, from the most general genera to the most specific species, and then the reversion of all these into God; and he explained the superiority of what was least divided (1196A). John also credits Maximus with showing how the negative and positive theologies of pseudo-Dionysius are complementary; and he notes in Maximus the theory – widespread in Neoplatonism – that God contemplates all things in their eternal reasons (that is, as Platonic Ideas).

The 'Periphyseon'

Eriugena was not to be a mere translator and commentator. Shortly after he had completed his translations he began his most ambitious work – a treatise putting forward an all-embracing theological system and (according to the best manuscripts) named, appropriately enough, *Periphyseon* ('about Nature'). The work is certainly a tribute to John's studies in Greek theology: an extension of the Greek Christian Platonism of Gregory of Nyssa, the pseudo-Dionysius and Maximus the Confessor. But Western writers are not neglected, and Augustine is as important a source as any of the Greeks. In the first book, especially, John draws important materials from the logical tradition (see below, pp.65–70). Moreover, the scope and generality of the work distinguish it from any of its direct predecessors, Latin or Greek.

At first sight the form of the *Periphyseon* is puzzling. Eriugena begins by declaring his intention to examine the four divisions of Universal Nature: that which creates and is not created; that which creates and is created; that which does not create and is created; and that which is not created and does not create. He goes on to devote the first book to an examination of whether Aristotle's ten categories apply to God – a patristic theme which scholars since the time of Alcuin had discussed (see above, p.49). The four remaining books of the *Periphyseon* are given over to an exegesis of the opening of Genesis with lengthy digressions. The creation of the world and man, and Adam's temptation and fall were subjects which had received special attention from many of the Fathers, such as Origen, Gregory of Nyssa, Basil, Ambrose and Augustine, either in separate treatises or as substantial parts of commentaries on Genesis. Many of Eriugena's immediate predecessors had also written on Genesis and discussed its opening sections in detail – Bede, Alcuin, Hrabanus Maurus, Angelôme of Luxeuil; their work is especially influenced by Augustine. The two forms on which the structure of the *Periphyseon* was based belonged, then, to the common heritage of Carolingian theology: it was their combination and use to form a treatise of such broad scope which was unprecedented. Yet, given the aims of the work, its methods and presuppositions, the juxtaposition of these two formal models in the *Periphyseon* is entirely appropriate; this becomes evident when the structure of John's theological system is analysed.

John's fourfold division of nature is a static representation of a universe which he, like Maximus, finds it more accurate to describe dynamically, in terms of its interrelations rather than its parts. The movement of universal nature which John supposes is described by the Neoplatonic triad of *monē*, *proodos* and *epistrophē* (permanence, procession and return). The *Periphyseon* is organized around this pattern.

As John had realized even at the time of the *De praedestinatione*, God, from whom all else derives, cannot be properly described in human language or known by men's minds. The nearest approach to talking about God directly is to discuss the possibility – or, rather, to argue the impossibility – of doing so. John therefore describes God in his permanence, as that which is not created and creates, by showing how none of the ten categories which embrace all things is applicable to him; and he prefaces this with an account of positive and negative ways of characterizing God, based on the pseudo-Dionysius and Maximus. It was this tradition (see above, p.19) which allowed John simultaneously to assert that God is beyond understanding and yet to venture, metaphorically, through his creation to understand him.

Faithful to the Platonic tradition transmitted by Augustine and the Greek Christians, Eriugena sees the procession of created things from the permanence of God in two stages: as the creation of an intelligible world (that which is created and creates), and then as the creation, from that intelligible world, of the world of sensibly-perceptible things (that which is created and does not create). In looking to the Genesis story as a basis for discussing the creation of the sensible world, John was acting like any Christian of his days; and, in using its opening sentences to treat of the creation of the intelligible world, Eriugena was following, although greatly extending, a patristic tradition of exegesis. Genesis also provided a starting-point for a discussion of return – the third term of the triad, which is represented statically by the fourth division of nature, since God as final cause, that to which all things return, is that which is not and does not create. A grammatically dubious interpretation of one of the verses in the account of the Fall (3:22 – which is taken to mean that the descendants of

Adam *will* ultimately eat of the tree of life and live eternally – *Periphyseon* 859D–62A) makes it into a prophecy of the end of the universe and the return of all things to God.

The structure of the universe which John describes according to this scheme is based on that of Neoplatonic speculation, as modified by the pseudo-Dionysius and Maximus the Confessor to accord with Christianity. God is beyond all description and determination and, indeed, beyond being itself. The implicit qualification within much of Greek Neoplatonism, that it is *finite* being which God is beyond, has been lost: for Eriugena it is truer to say of God that he does not exist than that he exists, although God's not-being is through excellence, not through privation. This God – indescribable, immutable, non-existent – is also the creator of heaven and earth, the redeemer of mankind (as Christ) and the ultimate judge of all creation: like the pseudo-Dionysius, John must apply the positive attributes, traditionally predicated of the second hypostasis, as well as the negative characteristics, predicated of the One, to his God. The requirements of his system make John's God, by the criteria of logic, a self-contradiction.

The intellect, or world of Ideas, cannot be identified with the second person of the Trinity, because this would make the Son less than equal to the Father. By following patristic precedent and saying that the primordial causes (concepts which play a role similar to that of Platonic Ideas) were created in the Son, John avoids this problem. For the enumeration of the primordial causes, and the order of their effects, John relies quite closely on the pseudo-Dionysius (622A–4B).

Soul, for Eriugena, is the human soul. There is but the faintest echo of the concept of the World-Soul (476C–7A); and nothing which could be described as an exposition of Soul as the third hypostasis. The discussion of the structure of the human soul is substantially based on Maximus (572C ff). The soul has three motions: of the intellect, the reason and the sense. The motion of the intellect is about God himself and beyond the very bounds of nature; the motion of the reason is responsible for impressing on the soul a knowledge of the primordial causes; to the motion of the sense belongs knowledge of particular things, both as passed to it from the sensible world by the exterior senses, and as derived from the knowledge of primordial causes handed down by the motion of the reason.

The soul shares with the third hypostasis of Neoplatonism the responsibility (or at least the partial responsibility, for this is not the only explanation given) for creating all that lies below the intelligible world. The soul creates its own mortal body (580B); and the reason why man was created as one of the animals was so that the whole of nature lying below him could be created in him (764C–9D). The basis for these assertions is a theory which makes knowing into a kind of defining, considers that true definition is essential definition, and essential definition that which makes a being what it is (485A–6A). This theory owes much to Maximus.

Just as the rest of nature is created within the soul of man, so man is created within God's mind (770B): 'Man is a certain intellectual notion, eternally made in the divine mind.' This telescoping of Idea with object, in the case of both human and divine cognition, has two opposite effects. Each lower order seems to disappear into the higher – nature into man, and man into the divine intellect; but also, each lower order becomes a manifestation of the higher. The whole universe is both a divine act of knowing, and a way of knowing God. The concept of 'theophany', which John found in his Greek sources, helped him to express this view, which emerges as a consequence of his system. A theophany is an indirect manifestation of God. According to Eriugena, none of God's creatures can ever perceive God, except in a theophany; and the whole of God's creation is itself a theophany.

As this sketch indicates, in the *Periphyseon* John produced under the influence of the pseudo-Dionysius and Maximus, a Neoplatonic system which reflects, in an altered and somewhat incoherent form, the patterns of thought which had obsessed Platonists from the time of Plotinus, but had almost vanished from the tradition of Western Christian thought. In many respects, the *Periphyseon* is an historical curiosity: a new construction built by a skilful and sometimes imaginative craftsman from elements of Neoplatonism neglected in the West: the first and only attempt in the early Middle Ages to put the systematizing, cultivated by so many followers of Plotinus, to use in expounding the principles of a Christian universe. Yet John's masterpiece is more than the product of its Greek sources, embellished with themes from Augustine. Three elements especially preserve the individuality of John's approach: his attitude towards history; his use of the Bible; and his interest in logic. Looking at the first two helps to show the great extent to which, despite his philosophical terminology, John worked with the aims and methods of a theologian; the third, by contrast, provides an opportunity to see the moments where John is neither reviving a metaphysical system, nor expounding Christian texts and dogma, but tackling genuine problems of philosophy.

A by-product of the Neoplatonists' indifference to the sensible world was their disregard for history: the aim of the philosopher was to free himself from the world of time and change and enter the changelessness of eternity. Some features of the *Periphyseon* suggest that John shared this attitude, and preferred to ignore the more literal and historical interpretations of Genesis which he could have found in the Latin patristic and medieval tradition. Certainly, John had a fondness for allegorical interpretation (see immediately below) and, at times, the historical details about Adam, Eve and Paradise disappear into a welter of metaphorical exegesis (for example, 822A ff – an allegorization of the topography of Paradise to represent man's soul, taken from Ambrose). However, throughout the *Periphyseon* the great pattern of sacred history – creation, fall, redemption by Christ, and resurrection at the end of time – is clearly visible. It is a counterpart, on a historical level, to the scheme of permanence, procession and return, advanced on the plane of metaphysics. John's use of his primordial causes to stand both for the Platonic Ideas and Augustinian 'seminal reasons' (*rationes seminales*) – immanent principles of reproduction and evolution in created things – helps, at the cost of a little unclarity, to emphasize the historical, physical aspect to the story of creation. And the return to God becomes neither a moment in the metaphysical analysis of nature, nor the mystical goal of the sage, but rather – in a way which reflects the thought of Gregory of Nyssa – a physical process, involving all things and bringing them, at the end of time, back to God. From the point of view of God in eternity, the state of the universe now and after the return may be identical; and this perception is shared to some extent by a man such as Paul, rapt in his ecstasy to the third heaven (683CD). But Eriugena's exposition follows the order of sacred history, its beginning marked by the creation, the end by the return.

To the modern reader, the exegetical framework of Books 2–5 of the *Periphyseon* may seem an encumbrance; but to John the fact that these books are a commentary on Scripture is their very justification. For all that he was, indirectly, influenced by a tradition of Neoplatonic philosophizing in which the thinker's unaided speculations provided one route to an understanding of metaphysical reality, John's ideas about the sources and scope of human knowledge were shaped by a Christian humility which was even accentuated by his contact with Neoplatonic formulations of God's ineffable superexcellence. The indescribability of God was not a discovery which John came to at the end of his reasonings, but rather the premise on which the manner of his investigation was founded. Once he had set forth this position at length, in the first book, John was left with a problem about what else he could say, since every attempt to understand the universe seemed bound to end in the realm of the inexpressible and incomprehensible. The Scriptures came to the thinker's rescue. They are the very word of God – truth's secret dwelling-place (509A) – expressing truths in themselves ineffable in a way which can be understood by their human readers. For this reason, their mode of expression is not literal; nor is there necessarily a single meaning for any set of these divinely inspired words. As Eriugena says at one point: the words of the Bible are open to infinitely many understandings; the short-est passage contains numberless meanings, just as the smallest part of a peacock's feather contains an innumerable variety of colours (749C). This does not entitle the exegete to interpret in an arbitrary or cavalier way. Even in his most extravagantly allegorical in-terpretations, John displays a scrupulous regard for the linguistic detail of his text. Every nuance of phrasing, every omission (for in a perfect, divinely inspired text, every omission is deliberate, every absence meaningful) is used as evidence by the interpreter.

It should, therefore, cause no surprise that in Books 2–5 of the *Periphyseon* Eriugena tries to arrange into a coherent whole con-cepts and theories inherited from the past and to show that this system can be derived from the story of Genesis, but that he attempts no independent philosophical justification of his ideas from first principles. Created nature, John believed, was a mani-festation of God; and the words of the Bible God's own speech in the language of man. By finding in the account of creation in Genesis the elements of the system he had inherited in part from the Greeks and, to a lesser extent, from Augustine, John founded the system in the only rational way he could.

In a work like the *Periphyseon*, dedicated to proposing a meta-physical, theological system, it is surprising to find, especially in the first book, so evident a preoccupation with logic. John's wide and unusual reading did not isolate him from the dominant inter-ests of his own day; and the concepts he gathered from the *Isagoge* (and Boethius' second commentary to it) and the *Categoriae Decem* play an important role in his masterpiece. However, Eriugena differs from contemporaries such as Ratramnus of Corbie by the extent to which he uses and interprets logical ideas in the light of his metaphysical and theological aims. For this reason, though he may be the most sophisticated logician of his age, he is also one of the most confused.

The ten categories are used in a straightforward way, based on Augustine and Boethius, as a means of analysing the relation between God and universal nature: because John's God is entirely beyond description and understanding, none of the ten categories, which embrace all created things, is applicable to him. Three of the categories receive further, elaborate metaphysical treatment – *ousia*, place and time.

Eriugena's handling of *ousia*, the first of Aristotle's categories, is bound up with the use he makes of the generic tree and shows very clearly how different was his manner of approach to logic than that of his antique sources and most of his medieval successors. Logicians of the antique tradition – even those who, as metaphysicians, were Neoplatonists – had considered the hierarchy of genera and species very much as Aristotle had done: it was a tree of classes, the least general of which had individuals for their members. To individuals – this man, that horse – Aristotle gave the name of *ousiai* ('beings') in his *Categories*. By this term his ancient followers took him to say nothing about the manner or cause of the individuals' being: that question they left to the separate field of metaphysical inquiry. As logicians, both Aristotelians and Platonists accepted the reality of individuals as the basis for their hierarchy of classes.

Eriugena's knowledge of the antique logical tradition was wide enough for him to know about the concepts of *ousia*, species and genus, but too narrow for him to suspect that he should isolate these notions from his metaphysics. For John the ten categories were a tool, second in importance only to the Scriptures, for analysing the relation between God and his creation: why should he suspect that an order of priorities so clear in his patristic sources – one before many, creator before created, intelligible before sensible – should be reversed when dealing with the concepts of logic?

On the contrary, John strived to incorporate the concept of a generic hierarchy into his metaphysical system, and he fashioned his treatment of *ousia* accordingly. The hierarchy of genera and species is for him real, and what reality the individuals have depends on their relation to it. The relation between genus and species is frequently represented as parallel to the creative relation of primordial causes to their effects; and the creation of universal nature is seen as the unfolding of the logical hierarchy, whilst the return of all things to God is a telescoping of species into genus, and genera into *genera generalissima*. So unimportant is the variety of accidents which numerically differentiate individuals, that Eriugena is willing to advance the surprising assertion (470D–1A) that, according to reason, there is no difference between an individual and the species to which it belongs: the species is 'whole and one in its individual members, and these members are one individual in the species'. Individuals are real in so far as they are strictly representative of their species; and, as such, John can place them at the bottom of his generic hierarchy. Porphyry and the logical tradition had placed them below the logical tree; but for Eriugena this would have been altogether to cut their link with reality.

In putting the view that individuals derive their being from their species, and species from their genera, John turns to the concept of *ousia* as it was used in metaphysics as opposed to logic. Here it meant not the individual (as in logic), but rather that by which the individual has being. To Platonists, it became a universal, separate from individual things, in which they must participate in order to be (just as good things must participate in goodness in order to be good). Eriugena found this use of *ousia* in the pseudo-Dionysius and Maximus the Confessor, and also in Augustine's *De trinitate*, where it is employed in the discussion of God and the ten categories, the main subject of Book 1 of the *Periphyseon*. Eriugena says that *ousia* is like a spring from which the genera and species flow (493B). He refers to the same concept when he speaks of a 'universal essence' in which all things participate but which belongs to no single one of them (506BC).

However, John does not simply, as these statements might suggest, turn the logical hierarchy upside down in order to make it accord with his metaphysical preconceptions, making *ousia* – as a Platonic universal – the *genus generalissimum*, from which the genera, species and individuals derive. The relation between *ousia* and the logical tree is more complicated than this, according to Eriugena; and the reason for the complication is, in part, a confusion in the writer's mind. John had learned from his logical and metaphysical sources of two different types of universal: on the one hand, universals like 'man', 'horse', 'animal' – the classes of individuals, and then of species, which constitute the generic tree; on the other hand, universals like 'goodness' or 'beauty' which refer to the quality of things. (According to Aristotle, universals of the former variety would be said of a subject, whereas those of the latter would be said of a subject and in a subject; but a Platonist would not accept that 'goodness' or 'beauty' could only be within a subject.) The logical tradition was, for the most part, concerned with universals of the former type; and the problem of universals, debated by antique logicians and transmitted to the Middle Ages by Boethius (see above, pp.30–2), centred on a characteristic of this type of universal: that whatever distinguishes the species must be present wholly in each of its members – no man, for instance, is any less a man than any other man. Platonic metaphysics, by contrast, made especial use of the 'qualitative' universal which, in this respect, behaved quite differently from the 'type' universal: all good things, for instance, need not be equally good; and, for the Platonist, no good thing except for goodness itself has goodness in its entirety.

The metaphysical use of *ousia* tended to make the concept into a 'qualitative' universal: it is a commonplace of Neoplatonism that things participate in being to greater or lesser extents. But, when John decides to make *ousia* the source of reality for the generic hierarchy, he is led towards talking about it as if it were, like the member-classes of the logical tree, a 'type' universal. Thus he produces the paradox (506D–7A) that universal essence is participated in more by some things and less by others – as if it were a 'qualitative' universal, but that it remains 'one and the same in all its participants . . . whole in the individuals and in itself' – just as if it were a 'type' universal. The two contrasting positions each receive emphasis at different moments in the work. At one point (472C), Eriugena says that *ousia* 'is naturally within' the genera, species and individuals, where it 'subsists entirely as if in its natural parts'. This language suggests that here he is thinking of *ousia* in relation to the generic hierarchy in the way one would of a genus in relation to its subordinate genera and species: they contain it entirely, and their individual members belong to it simply by virtue of being members of a class subordinate to it. (For instance, it is clearer to say that Plato is an animal because he is a man, than that he is a man and an animal: he has no characteristics which make him an animal which are not among those which make him a man.) When John speaks in this way, the bottom level of his generic hierarchy is formed by what he calls individuals (*atoma*). Quite frequently, however, John wishes to treat the relation between *ousia* and the generic hierarchy differently. Instead of being entirely contained within the hierarchy of genera and species, so that by being an individual something is necessarily an *ousia*, Eriugena speaks as if it were a 'qualitative' universal, which is participated in directly, rather than contained by its subordinate classes: everything which is must therefore be what it is (a man, horse, stone) and also have *ousia* if it is to be real.

The confusion is at its greatest when Eriugena talks not of things having *ousia*, but having an *ousia*, treating the concept, which is only directly applicable to individuals if it is a 'qualitative' universal, as a 'type' universal. Perhaps the texts of the logical tradition, which made *ousiai* (in the sense of individuals) into the members of the lowest classes of the logical hierarchy, helped John towards this muddlement. Speaking in this way, John distinguishes having an *ousia* from having a body (489B–94C), but says that every individual must have an *ousia* if it is real: for instance, a mere geometrical figure will not have one (493CD). *Ousia* is the mysterious centre-of-being in each individual – incomprehensible and imperceptible in itself (471B) and known only by the categories which surround it. Behind the apparent world of individuals, Eriugena has discovered another, mysterious one of *ousiai*. Not only has he made the logical hierarchy into part of his metaphysics: from the confusion which resulted from his attempts to place *ousia* in relation to this hierarchy, he has derived a new concept – neither the *ousia* of the logicians, nor that of the metaphysicians, but rather a mystical notion, which fits his theological scheme all the better by being indefinable and epistemologically redundant. It is not, therefore, surprising to find John bringing theological authority and arguments to the support of this notion:

> Gregory the Theologian proves . . . that no visible or invisible creature can understand by intellect or reason what any substance or essence is. For just as God in himself is above every creature and is understood by no intellect, so, considered in the most secret aspect of the creature made by him and existing in him, he is incomprehensible. (443B)

Eriugena's treatment of the categories of place (*locus*) and time is more directly guided by his theology. The word *locus* is used to designate three different concepts, never properly distinguished from one another. First, it can represent *locus* as defined in the *Categoriae Decem*: the limits within which an object is enclosed – its space rather than its place (484B). Second, *locus* is considered, along with time, in very general terms borrowed from Maximus: place and time cannot exist without each other, and must precede the universe, which is subject to time and has a place (481B–2A). Third, the idea of *locus* as enclosing limits is extended to immaterial things: the *locus* of each thing is its definition (474B–89B) (see above, p.63). These three different concepts, advanced in Book 1, reappear in Book 5 of the *Periphyseon*. Augustine, unlike Maximus, had thought that place and time were created at the same time as the world, rather than before it, and that they must end with the world too. When John discusses the return of all things to God, he moves towards Augustine's point of view (888A–9C). Then, realizing that he runs the risk of contradicting what he has said earlier, he adds that he does not mean that *locus* meaning definition will perish; it will remain always in the mind. But *locus* in the two other senses (which he does not distinguish) and time will end with the world (889C–90A). Later (970D), John says that at the end of the world *locus* and time will return to their 'eternal reasons' – a term usually synonymous with primordial causes. It is not made clear what variety of *locus* is meant, nor how such concepts as place and time can have eternal reasons. In short, Eriugena seems to handle these two concepts just as the demands of his system require; and his unclarity over their exact significance does not even issue from the rather sophisticated logical confusion which shaped his concept of *ousia*.

The discussion of logic, then, is similar to the other aspects of the *Periphyseon*: John follows the forms, interests and techniques of his contemporaries, but his purpose is different. He wishes not only to adapt the systematic metaphysics of Neoplatonism to Christianity, but to use them – as neither Augustine, nor Boethius, nor any thinker in the Western tradition had attempted – to provide the structure for a Christian view of intelligible reality. This purpose was suggested to John by his Greek Christian sources, but he pursues it far more thoroughly and systematically than they do, with the help of the theological and logical methods of the Latin tradition. The *Periphyseon*, therefore, although only in a limited sense a philosophical work, is of great interest in the history of philosophy: it presents a unique experiment in Christian Platonism – a path in the history of thought which was never followed further and which could hardly but have led to the creation of elaborate, but philosophically unilluminating, metaphysical systems. Yet, although the *Periphyseon* lacked imitators, it did not lack influence: it is difficult to say what would have been the course of medieval philosophy, had it not been for the work of Eriugena.

7 The aftermath of Eriugena: philosophy at the end of the ninth and the beginning of the tenth century

The influence of Eriugena

It is one of the commonplaces in the history of medieval thought that Eriugena's work was largely ignored by the thinkers of his time but had an important influence on more sophisticated readers in the twelfth century. Neither side of this statement withstands scrutiny. The *Periphyseon* did have one or two devotees in the twelfth century (see below p. 105), but there is no convincing evidence that any of the outstanding thinkers of that time, such as Abelard, William of Conches or Gilbert of Poitiers, were influenced by John's work. The textual parallels advanced by some scholars are not close, whilst ideas and arguments which twelfth-century texts share with Eriugena can generally be explained by reference to a common tradition of Platonism. By contrast, there is ample evidence for the effect which John's thought had on his own generation and the succeeding one. The *Periphyseon* was read – as is witnessed by the multiplication of manuscripts, and it was excerpted in florilegia. Most of the early, close followers of John remain anonymous, but one known figure, Heiric of Auxerre (841–c. 876), was perhaps his pupil and certainly one of his disciples. Heiric's life of St Germanus contains several borrowings from the *Periphyseon*, and one of his sermons uses both John's major work and a homily he had written on the prologue to St John's Gospel, summarizing some of the main features of his system. However, the most far-reaching aspect of Eriugena's influence was exerted through a different channel; and its instruments were not merely the *Periphyseon* and John's other literary works.

Much of the most valuable information about the thought of the second half of the ninth century is to be gained not from self-contained literary works, but from glosses written in the margins of textbooks such as Martianus Capella's *De nuptiis*, Boethius' *Consolation* and *Opuscula sacra* and the *Categoriae Decem*. The earliest such glossed manuscripts which survive date from the later years of Eriugena's life, and many of them show connections with the philosopher himself, his immediate circle or his ideas. How much of the surviving gloss material goes back to Eriugena himself, and what was his part in introducing this method of studying secular texts into the medieval schools? An examination of the various glosses to each of the important textbooks can go some way towards answering these questions, but any very definite answers are made impossible by the very nature of glosses as evidence.

Glosses are not literary works; they are the records of teaching and learning. The spaces in the margins and between the lines of textbooks may have been first annotated for one (or more) of three reasons: by a teacher, in order to expound the text to his students; by a student, copying down his teacher's remarks; or by a reader, noting down his attempts to understand the text. These glosses were not treated with the respect to authenticity, integrity and verbal detail accorded to literary texts. A glossed manuscript might have more glosses copied into it from another source; and a scholar, wishing to annotate an unglossed manuscript, might obtain several glossed copies of the work and select those glosses which most interested him – perhaps adding material of his own – to enter into his own book. The more conscientious an annotator, the less likely his set of glosses to be exactly similar to any set already in existence. Early medieval sets of glosses can, therefore, be sorted only into rough groups, each united by a loose family-resemblance rather than the stemmatic relationships usual between copies of the same text; and different groups of sets of glosses to the same work will often have some annotations in common. It follows that the annotations in any given manuscript will usually derive from the work of more than one scholar and that, as often as not, they will represent neither completely nor accurately what their originators wrote or said. When it is added that glossators rarely signed their work, it will be seen that it is not usually possible to be sure that a particular thinker composed glosses to a particular work and, if he did, to know which of the annotations in the various surviving manuscripts best represent his teaching.

The late ninth-century sets of glosses do not merely throw light on the work and influence of Eriugena. They illustrate in especial three aspects of thought at this time important in the development of medieval philosophy: interest in pagan religion and philosophy and its relation to Christianity (in the notes to Martianus and

Boethius' *Consolation*); interest – not matched by understanding – in the metaphysical ideas Boethius brings to theology (in his *Opuscula sacra*); and the way in which logical doctrine was discussed and assimilated (in the glosses to the *Categoriae Decem*).

The traditions of glosses to school texts

The only work to which glosses survive which, in all probability, derive directly from Eriugena's own annotations, is the *De nuptiis* of Martianus Capella. Found in only a few manuscripts, the Eriugenian ancestry of these glosses (incipit *Martianus in isto libro . . .*) is especially well evidenced for Books 1, 2 and 9. The *De nuptiis* is not a work of philosophy. It offers a basic introduction to the seven liberal arts, but even its discussion of logic is technical and elementary – the glosses it is given say little about any philosophical issues. The first two books of the *De nuptiis* are a pagan religious allegory; and it is their paganism which seems to have been of especial interest to the early annotators. Not only did Martianus' mythological and astronomical allusions require learned exegesis; moments in the allegory provided an opportunity to expound aspects of Platonic thought and religion, as gathered from Macrobius' *Somnium Scipionis* and Calcidius' translation of and commentary to the *Timaeus*. Thus glosses discuss the Platonic view of the purgation and fall of souls (Lutz 21:32 ff; Jeauneau 130:3 ff), the World-Soul (Lutz 10:16 ff; Jeauneau 121:24, 149:15 ff) and of reincarnation (Lutz 22:9 ff; Jeauneau 122:12 ff). These views are explicitly recognized as pagan and unacceptable – the 'ravings of the poets'. The interpretation of Martianus' allegory sometimes, however, results in theories which, except for the pagan terms in which they are couched, correspond to notions acceptable to Platonically–minded Christians. Time is described as an imperfect form of eternity – a Platonic theory picked up by Boethius (Lutz 10:28 ff). The pagan gods are said (falsely insists the annotator) to be beyond human understanding (Lutz 37:28 ff; cf. Jeauneau 147:8 ff), in much the same way as Christian philosophers truly assert the human incomprehensibility of the one, true God. At certain points, the glossator develops some philosophical ideas of his own, Platonic in character, but neither pagan, nor peculiar to the Christianized Neoplatonism of the *Periphyseon*. One gloss (Lutz 27:15 ff) argues that the arts are naturally innate in every soul, although the foolish do not use them properly. Another gloss, to Book 9 of *De nuptiis*, presents a philosophical interpretation of the myth of Orpheus and Eurydice (Lutz 192:28 ff). Eurydice stands for 'the art of music in its profoundest reasons', and Orpheus represents beauty of sound – music in its sensible manifestation. Just as Orpheus tried to rescue Eurydice from the underworld, so the musician must go down into the depths of the discipline of music to rediscover 'the rules of the art according to which the sounds of music are arranged'. And, like Orpheus, the musician is not able to bring back his prize with him: he compares the 'transitory, bodily sounds' with the 'intention of the profound art' and is left unhappy, having 'the sound of music without its reason'.

The adventurous imagination showed by these glosses – which may well be a direct reflection of John Scottus' approach to pagan thought – made them unsuitable for common use as a guide to a classroom text. Another set of *De nuptiis* glosses (incipit *Titulantur hi duo . . .*), in which basic information predominates and the interest in paganism is less pronounced, was far more popular in the late ninth and tenth centuries. This set, which displays the variations, omissions and additions from one manuscript to another typical of the transmission of annotations, has some glosses in common with the other. It may well have been produced in an attempt to adapt the work of John Scottus and his immediate circle to more general use.

Boethius' *Consolation* posed ninth-century glossators with a rather different set of questions about paganism from those raised by Martianus. Boethius, they knew from his *Opuscula sacra*, was a Christian; yet the *Consolation* not only fails to make explicitly Christian references, it also puts forward ideas on occasion which, if literally interpreted, seem to contradict religious orthodoxy.

There are two sets of glosses to the *Consolation* from the late ninth century, neither of them associated with Eriugena. One (incipit *Carmina cantus delectabiles . . .*) is found, badly damaged, in a single manuscript; many of the notes are in insular script and a Welsh origin has been suggested. The other (incipit *Iste Boetius . . .*) is found in four manuscripts, between which there are very considerable variations. No full account of the relations between the manuscripts has been given, but two of them are from St Gall, which suggests a connection between these glosses at some stage in their development and that monastery. Much of the material in both sets of glosses is purely literal explanation and factual information (or misinformation). But when they came to gloss metrum 9 of Book 3, the famous epitome of the *Timaeus*, the annotators were faced by cryptic, poetic allusions to Neoplatonic doctrine which demanded explanation and which seemed, taken literally, to go against Christianity. What can be read of the *Carmina cantus delectabiles* . . . glosses suggests that their author understood few of the allusions in this metrum. He enters into an elaborate astrological discussion, equates the World-Soul with the sun and goes on to quote from the Bible, as if to prove his point. The text has provided him with an opportunity to talk at length about the stars and their properties, yet the pagan nature of this discussion does not dissuade him from treating the *Consolation*, so far as one can see, as an explicitly Christian work. In the manuscripts of the *Iste Boetius* . . . set, glosses are to be found which show a clearer attitude to Boethius' seeming tolerance for paganism. Either the interpreter makes the text explicitly Christian – so, for instance, the personified figure of Philosophy is explained as representing God's wisdom or Christ – or he makes clear where Boethius fails to write as a Christian should. In Book 3, metrum 9, for instance, he considers Boethius' reference (6.19) to fitting pre-existent souls to light chariots a metaphor, but still, a pagan one; and he notes Augustine's disapproval of the notion of the World-Soul. In the present state of research it is impossible to say whether these two different attitudes represent the uncertainties of a single annotator or the combination of glosses from different sources.

Problems about paganism did not arise in annotating Boethius' *Opuscula sacra*; they were replaced by problems of comprehension. The ninth-century glosses to this work display a certain familiarity with Eriugena's thought, but nothing to justify the opinion once held by their editor that John himself wrote them. Rather, the glossator turns to Eriugenian ideas, as well as patristic ones, when he wishes to say something about his text but cannot understand it because Boethius has assumed an acquaintance with Neoplatonic assumptions which he lacks. So, for instance, in glossing a statement from Treatise III (see above, p.39) that 'being itself is not yet', the annotator remarks that the being of, for instance, a man, 'is not yet' when it lies hidden in God's providence; it starts to be when it emerges into genera and species (51:25–30). This is a definite echo of Eriugena's blending of logical and creative processes, which quite misses the point of what Boethius had to say. At other times when he is baffled by Boethius' argument, the annotator simply sticks to literal explanation of words and phrases. But, for much of Boethius' text, these notes provide a useful guide to the novice reader. Lack of recent research makes it impossible to say exactly how this set of glosses developed. During the tenth century it was revised and new material was added; and the earliest version in which it has survived may well have been an edition made at the turn of the tenth century by Remigius of Auxerre (see below, pp. 78–9).

The *Categoriae Decem* was the most intently studied logical work in the ninth and tenth centuries. Notes were copied into manuscripts of it from the late ninth century onwards, and no set is entirely the same – or entirely different. However, among the earlier manuscripts, three (Milan: Ambrosiana B 71 sup. (ninth century); St Gall 274 (ninth century); Paris: Bibliothèque Nationale 12949 (tenth century)) are remarkable for the amount of Eriugenian material they contain. This consists of direct, but unattributed, quotations from the *Periphyseon*, including some of John's discussion of essence and universals; of references to characteristically Eriugenian doctrines, such as the return of all things to God and non-being through excellence; and of a tendency to the metaphysical and theological elaboration of logical ideas. In this third respect, the glosses are more extreme than anything to be found in the *Periphyseon* itself. A discussion of incorporeal accidents, for instance, is transformed into a comment on the relationship between man and God and divine and human virtue (197–8:XV); at another point, the difference between the individual and the species is examined in terms of Christ, 'the good shepherd', and other shepherds – a decidedly anomalous case which the glossator uses to throw this logical distinction into confusion (202–3:XXIV). Eriugenian echoes are not entirely absent from the glosses in other manuscripts, but they are fewer and more directly relevant to the text. Despite the interest of the three 'Eriugenian' manuscripts, as testimony that John's method of thought, as well as his particular ideas, survived among followers, it is the mass of standard glosses found elsewhere (and also in one of these three codices, in addition to the Eriugenian material) which, dull in itself, is of the greater importance for the history of medieval philosophy. It represents an attempt to assimilate, more thoroughly than Alcuin had done and more carefully than is evident in the *Periphyseon*, an elementary part of ancient logic; and, as the thought of the tenth, eleventh and twelfth centuries will show, their increasing grasp of the technicalities of logic led scholars to greater subtlety, range and clarity as philosophers.

Ninth-century attempts to understand the techniques of logic are also illustrated by another set of work. It consists, not of glosses, but of notes and brief treatises found in several manuscripts all written at the monastery of St Gall. The different pieces are impossible to date with precision, but they seem in general to date

from the second half of the century. The pieces in these manuscripts are not for the most part found elsewhere, but there are
two exceptions: two of the *Usia graece . . .* passages (XII and XIII)
are reproduced as one; and a *Categoriae Decem* gloss (I) forms the
basis of a little passage on the meaning of 'nature'.

The scholars at St Gall wished to achieve as wide a knowledge
as possible of the different branches of formal logic. The most
extended of the treatises, a *Dialectica*, discusses the various books
in the ancient logical canon and includes a description of syllogistic
reason, taken most probably from an intermediate source rather
than from Aristotle's or Boethius' logical monographs. A letter
from a certain Master L. (perhaps Liutbert, a master at St Gall who
became archbishop of Mainz in 863) discusses the distinction between a whole and its parts and a genus and its species on the basis
of Boethius' commentary on Cicero's *Topics*. It goes on – in a
manner which might, superficially, seem reminiscent of Eriugena's
approach to logic – to answer a question about the immortality of
the vegetative part of the soul (one of the three parts distinguished
by Boethius in his commentaries on the *Isagoge*) by reference to a
biblical quotation. What in fact the writer does is to employ his
scriptural authority in a neat syllogism: he uses logical technique
to clarify a theological argument without in any sense confusing
logic and theology.

Along with the interest at St Gall in the technicalities of logic
there went an awareness of the links between logic and language.
According to the *Dialectica* 'dialectic is the branch of knowledge
about how to dispute well: to dispute well is to affirm or deny
things correctly' (lvi). Logic, then, was concerned with reality –
it dealt with how things actually are – but reality as represented in
statements, which had necessarily to be formulated in language.
Although these scholars did not try to gather any further philosophical implications from this line of thought, their concern with
argument in language led them on occasion to compare logic with
grammar, in a way which foreshadows some of the most important
developments in the thought of the eleventh century. One little
treatise, for instance, is a 'classification of all types of nouns according to Aristotle's categories' (lxxv-lxxxix); whilst, in the *Dialectica*
(lviii) it is remarked that the grammarian's proper names (*propria*)
correspond to the dialectician's individuals, the grammarian's
type-names (*appelatiua*) to the dialectician's genera and species. In
the mid-twelfth century, Gilbert of Poitiers would still find the
same parallel between logic and grammar of importance.

Remigius of Auxerre

The characteristic of the late ninth-century thought examined has been the anonymity and instability of the texts in which it is found. With Remigius of Auxerre, the historian reaches a figure whose place and time of work is known and to whom definite writings can be attributed, even if his authorship of them consisted more in compilation than original thought or composition.

Remigius was born in the early 840s and became a monk of St Germain of Auxerre. Among his teachers were Servatus Lupus, one of the most widely learned of ninth-century scholars, and Heiric of Auxerre, a follower, and perhaps pupil, of Eriugena (see above, p.71). In 893 Remigius took charge of the cathedral school at Reims and in about 900 he went to teach at Paris. Like his predecessors, Remigius taught by means of explaining and elaborating on authoritative texts. He was an indefatigable commentator: his work includes expositions of the grammarians Donatus, Priscian, Phocas, Eutyches; of Bede (on metre); of Terence, Juvenal, Caelius Sedulius and the *Disticha Catonis*; of Genesis and the Psalms; as well as of Martianus Capella, Boethius' *Consolation* and perhaps also his *Opuscula sacra* (see above, p.76).

The expositions of especial interest to the historian of philosophy are those on the *De nuptiis* and the *Consolation*. Unlike the efforts of his predecessors, these are commentaries rather than glosses – separate texts (sometimes copied in the form of marginal scholia) recording Remigius' teaching on a given work. They are not, however, in any sense original works. The commentary on *De nuptiis* makes extensive use of material from both types of ninth-century glosses. Remigius leaves aside some of the longer discussions of pagan philosophy and religion found in the *Martianus in isto libro . . .* glosses, but makes use of many of the explanations and pieces of information found there. The commentary on the *Consolation* draws on the *Iste Boetius . . .* glosses; on one or more other sets of glosses which are lost or undiscovered; and makes use of material that Remigius had gleaned from the *Martianus in isto libro . . .* glosses when he had been commenting the *De nuptiis*.

Much of Remigius' *Consolation* commentary is given over to grammatical explanation, literal exegesis of Boethius' argument and historical and mythological information – in each case fuller and more thorough than in any earlier surviving interpretation. Remigius' tendency is to Christianize possibly pagan ideas more determinedly than his predecessors. In his discussion of metrum 9 of Book 3 this tendency is especially evident; but it is balanced by Remigius' wish to use the little he knows about Platonism – learnt from the Fathers, from the *Martianus in isto libro . . .* glosses and perhaps from the *Periphyseon* – to interpret Boethius' allusions. Thus the 'perpetual reason by which the world is governed' is identified with God's wisdom, as is the 'form of the highest good'; and God's wisdom is said to be the same as the Son (51:53). Clearly, Remigius is trying to bring this metrum into line with the opening verses of the Gospel of St John. But he also explains the 'form of the highest good' as meaning the Ideas, the exemplar according to which God created the sensible world (53–4). He distinguishes this interpretation from the other one proposed, and so avoids the heresy of equating the world of Ideas with Christ. Yet he seems to have given little thought to the possible difficulties raised by such a juxtaposition of Platonic and Christian explanations.

The stability of the texts of Remigius' commentaries should not be exaggerated: that to the *Consolation*, in particular, was revised several times during the tenth century. To a great extent, however, Remigius was responsible for gathering the work of ninth-century scholars into the form in which it continued to influence the school tradition right into the twelfth century. The next chapter will concentrate on the new material that was studied and the new ideas developed in the tenth and eleventh centuries; but the reader should not forget how much of any student's educational grounding in these centuries was based on ninth-century scholarship, often as collected and arranged by Remigius.

8 Logic and scholarship in the tenth and earlier eleventh century

The most important intellectual developments are not always the most obvious, or the most exciting. The tenth century produced no philosopher to compare with Eriugena in the ninth, or Abelard in the twelfth. But the increase in philosophical clarity and sophistication, and in range of intellectual reference, which separates Abelard from Eriugena is based, to no small extent, on the unspectacular work of tenth-century scholars. For the most part these scholars were monks of the great Benedictine houses, such as Fleury on the Loire, and St Gall. No king made his court the pre-eminent centre for learning that the palaces of Charlemagne and Charles the Bald had been; but the career of Gerbert, who became Archbishop of Reims and then Pope, set a pattern, often followed in the next two hundred years, of ecclesiastical promotion gained through scholarly reputation. The thinkers of the tenth century made their greatest contribution to philosophy through the development of logic, especially formal logic; and, by the middle of the eleventh century, these developments in dialectical technique were having an important effect on the manner of theological debate and its philosophical implications. The scholars of the tenth and eleventh centuries also continued the work – begun in the ninth century – of absorbing, understanding and reacting to the antique philosophical heritage.

Tenth-century logic

For thinkers from the time of Alcuin to that of Remigius of Auxerre, the most important work on logic had been the pseudo-Augustinian *Categoriae Decem*. By the beginning of the eleventh century the picture had changed: the *Categories* were studied in a version of Boethius' translation and interest in the pseudo-Augustinian paraphrase was beginning to fade; the *De interpretatione* was becoming more widely known and Boethius' logical monographs, as well as his commentaries, were used by the most advanced teachers. It is not possible to chart the course of these developments as they took place in the tenth century: records are few, and manuscripts of this period notoriously difficult to date with precision. But more than twice as many copies of the *De interpretatione* and Boethius' first commentary on it have been dated to this century than to the one before, and the earliest manuscripts of the more advanced second commentary date from this period. Probably in the middle of the century, a writer who is known by only four letters of his name – Icpa – glossed the *Isagoge* in a manner which, despite a reference to the *Periphyseon*, was largely technical and, indeed, derivative from Boethius. The glossed manuscripts of the *Categoriae Decem* suggest that, from about 900 onwards, scholars were less and less interested in the extravagant metaphysical comments which Eriugena's immediate followers had foisted on their logical text, and concentrated their attention on understanding Aristotle's doctrine: this tendency could hardly but lead them to exploit Boethius' direct translation of the *Categories*, which had been available (but hardly used) in a few libraries since the ninth century.

There is much more evidence about the logical teaching of three scholars at the end of the tenth century: Notker Labeo, Abbo and Gerbert. The range of texts which they used and understood was the result both of the work of the preceding decades and of their own contribution to the subject.

Notker Labeo (d. 1022) was a monk at St Gall, a monastery distinguished even in the ninth century for the study of logic (see above, pp. 76–7). His main work was as a translator of Latin textbooks into German: Boethius' *Consolation*, Martianus Capella's *De nuptiis* (Books 1 and 2) and two works of Aristotle's logic – the *Categories* and the *De interpretatione*. Notker chooses the Boethian translation in preference to the pseudo-Augustinian paraphrase of the *Categories*; he wishes to introduce his students to the difficult *De interpretatione*; and, in order to elucidate each of these works, he turns to Boethius' commentaries. Notker also composed his own Latin treatise on syllogisms, basing himself on Martianus Capella and Boethius' commentary on Cicero's *Topics* (but not his logical monographs).

Abbo (d. 1004), of the monastery of Fleury, had before 986 shown his grasp of more advanced formal logic than Notker's in his *Enodatio* ('explanation') of the categorical and hypothetical syllogisms. He uses Boethius' monographs on the syllogisms (sometimes followed very closely), his *De differentiis topicis* and *De divisionibus*, and Apuleius' *Peri hermeneias*; the more formal sections of Aristotle's *De interpretatione* seem to have been the starting-point of Abbo's inquiry. Abbo's *Quaestiones grammaticales* do not take up any of the philosophical problems so often raised in grammatical works from the eleventh century onwards. But there is a record of Abbo's views on at least one, important question of philosophical logic. He is led to discuss the subject by a text in a computistical work which he is commenting: 'the unity from which all multitude of numbers proceeds'. The phrase is decidely Platonic in its implications. But Abbo uses it to advance the argument that everything that exists is one in number, that is to say, an individual; and then to draw the most unplatonic conclusion, that universals, which must be whole in many things at the same time, cannot therefore exist in reality. Man may be thought of universally, but only individual men, each one in number, exist.

Like Notker and Abbo, Gerbert was a monk, first at Aurillac and then, as abbot, at Bobbio. However, he resembles many a scholar of the twelfth century, in having spent a period (937–82) as master at a cathedral school, in Reims, before he became archbishop there and, finally, Pope, and it was through a journey to northern Spain in the late 960s that Gerbert gained the basis of his exceptional knowledge of mathematics and astronomy. The width of his scientific and literary interests is better documented than that of his contemporaries. His letters mention, or request, manuscripts of Statius, Caesar, Cicero, Pliny and Eugraphius; and, as a teacher he discussed the work of Virgil, Statius, Terence, Juvenal, Persius and Lucan, and lectured on the heavenly motions with the aid of a spherical model, and on arithmetic with the aid of an abacus.

At Reims, his logical teaching embraced the *Isagoge, Categories, De interpretatione*, Cicero's *Topics* and the full range of Boethius' logical monographs; he is said to have used Boethius' commentaries for the *Isagoge* and Cicero's *Topics*; and he knew at least one of Boethius' commentaries to the *De interpretatione*. This set of works would provide the basis for study of logic until the mid-twelfth century, although Gerbert's successors would gain a more intimate knowledge of Boethius' commentaries. And, although Aristotelian logic might seem desperately incomplete without the *Topics* and *Analytics*, some of the basic technical material from these works could be mastered by way of Cicero's *Topics* and Boethius' two treatises on the categorical syllogism.

Gerbert left one logical work of his own, the *De rationali et ratione uti.* Although the discussion is inclined to strike the modern reader as an unnecessarily elaborate analysis of an easily solved problem, the treatise is fascinating for the way in which it shows Gerbert assimilating his new logical sources. In the *Isagoge* (22:1–2) and Boethius' commentaries on it (edition I, 104:20–105:15; edition II, 294:10–21) the terms 'that which is rational' and 'to use reason' are discussed: 'to use reason' is a differentia of 'that which is rational', since something can be rational when it is not actually using its reason. Why then can 'to use reason' be predicated of 'that which is rational' (as when one says 'That which is rational uses reason'), when the scope of 'to use reason' is the wider? This is the question which Gerbert sets out to answer. He solves it, very simply, at the end of his treatise (XV:308–9) by making use of what he has learnt from Aristotle and Boethius about the different types of syllogism. When 'to use reason' is predicated of 'that which is reasonable', it is to be understood of *some* reasonable thing, not *all* reasonable things; just as when one says that 'man is a philosopher' (*homo philosophus est*), this means that some man, not every man, is a philosopher.

Gerbert does not proceed to this conclusion by a direct route. His discussion takes in the notion of act and potency, which he derived from the *De interpretatione* and Boethius' commentaries on it (the application of the distinction to generic relations is made in his commentaries to the *Isagoge* – edition I, 92:5–93:22; edition II, 262:14–265:12) and alludes to the psychological discussion with which Aristotle begins his treatise. Gerbert tries to combine this material with a metaphysical hierarchy he learnt from the beginning of Boethius' first commentary to the *Isagoge* – a text to which he also turned when setting forth a division of philosophy during a scholarly dispute. Knowledge (the concept which is understood) may be considered as an act of the mind; thoughts (the understanding of the concept) are, in Aristotle's phrase from the *De interpretatione*, the 'affections of the mind'. A concept may also become attached to what is corruptible, losing its immutability through contact with bodies (XI:305–6: cf. Boethius *In Isagogen* edition I 9:2–6); it then becomes a potentiality which may be realized in act. As a concept, that which is rational is always in act (and therefore no narrower in scope than the concept 'to use reason'). In contact with bodies it may or may not be realized: the individual person, who is rational, may or may not actually be using his reason. Like Abbo, Gerbert has formed his views on universals from reading Boethius; but, whereas Abbo had taken him at his most Aristotelian, Gerbert seems to choose the most Platonic of his theories.

Antique philosophy and the Christian scholar

The attitude of scholars in the tenth and earlier eleventh centuries to the antique philosophical heritage is illustrated by two types of evidence: glosses and commentaries (as in the ninth century) and certain explicit discussions, generally of a critical nature, about the value of studying ancient philosophy, as opposed to Scripture or theology. During the years from about 850 to 910 glosses and commentaries had been produced to a wide variety of school texts, including antique philosophical works. As a result, tenth- and eleventh-century scholars were often content to use or revise their predecessors' work, rather than devise their own comments. But this rule has some exceptions: the *Timaeus*, which was not apparently glossed in the ninth century; Macrobius' commentary on the *Somnium Scipionis*; and Boethius' *Consolation*, which, despite the work done on it in the ninth century, continued to exercise the minds of commentators in the tenth and eleventh.

In the ninth century the *Timaeus* had been read by a few, quoted occasionally, but hardly studied. Some readers in the tenth century recorded their attempts to understand Plato's difficult work (along with Calcidius' even more difficult commentary, which usually followed it in the manuscripts) – and passed on their results – by composing brief marginal notes, merely giving the main subject of the section of the text they accompany. A slightly more ambitious series of glosses is found in at least eight further manuscripts of the tenth and eleventh centuries, some of which have annotations in common. One of their features is the use of quotes from metrum 9 of Book 3 of Boethius' *Consolation*: Boethius' epitome could clarify Plato, just as the *Timaeus* was used to clarify Boethius (see below, p.86). Other more familiar authors were also mentioned by the glossators in their effort to connect a new text with their framework of knowledge: for instance, a note in at least two manuscripts (Paris: Bibliothèque Nationale 2164 and 6282), compares the views on formless matter advanced by Calcidius with those of Augustine. At the end of the text of the *Timaeus* in another manuscript (London: British Library Add. MS 15601) there is a note recalling Augustine's view (put forward in his *De doctrina christiana*; but denied in the *De civitate dei* – a fact not mentioned by the annotator) that Plato learned monotheism from the teaching of Jeremiah, which he encountered on a visit to Egypt. Some of the readers of the *Timaeus* in the tenth and eleventh centuries seem, then, to have been ready to accept its compatibility with Christian doctrine; but their understanding of Plato was too faint to allow any strong assertion of such a view.

So little work has been published on glosses to Macrobius that it is difficult to say anything about them with assurance. Some sporadic notes are certainly found in ninth-century manuscripts of his commentary to the *Somnium Scipionis*, but it may not have been until later that the work was more thoroughly annotated. Many of these glosses are of an encyclopedic nature – quotations from other authorities on the scientific matters discussed by Macrobius. Despite the importance of Macrobius as a source for Neoplatonic ideas, his work had to wait until the twelfth century for a more philosophically-minded commentary (see below, pp. 120 ff).

The case is very different for Boethius' *Consolation*. Ninth-century scholars had passed on a body of mainly literal, grammatical and factual exegesis; and indeed, as a complete commentary, Remigius' book was not replaced, although it was variously revised. But ninth-century scholars also passed on a dual challenge posed by the *Consolation* and not convincingly met by them: to explain the Neoplatonic allusions, and then to consider the extent to which they were acceptable for a Christian. Both aspects of the problem were posed in their acutest form by metrum 9 of Book 3; and in the tenth and eleventh centuries a succession of scholars composed commentaries devoted exclusively to this poem.

One of these commentaries (incipit *Expositio rationem . . .*) is very close to Remigius' text on the metrum; most probably it is a revision of Remigius, although it might possibly be based on an unknown source which Remigius also followed. It reads like a sensible abbreviation of the material in Remigius' work, but adds hardly anything to it.

Another commentary on this metrum is the work of Bovo, who was abbot of Corvey, the sister house of Corbie, and died in 916. Whereas other commentators tackled the question of Boethius' pagan material indirectly, either Christianizing it or ignoring its incompatibility with Christianity, Bovo begins by raising the problem. This metrum and the *Consolation* as a whole contain, he says, 'much which turns out to be contrary to the Catholic Faith' (384:44). Boethius was indeed the author of a work on the Trinity and a work against the heretics Eutyches and Nestorius; but in his *Consolation* 'it is certain that he did not wish to discuss Christian doctrine but rather, that he wished to reveal to his readers the doctrines of the philosophers, especially the Platonists' (384:50–3). Bovo's clear recognition of Boethius' Platonism enables him to be remarkably successful in explaining his text. Using Macrobius, he explains Boethius' allusions to exemplars, the World-Soul and the pre-existence of human souls with a clarity due in no small part to the absence of attempts to equate these doctrines with Christian ones; the two latter, indeed, he roundly condemns. But Bovo's recognition of the unacceptability of pagan philosophy does not obscure his lively interest in it.

Another commentary on Book 3, metrum 9 (incipit *Inuocatio haec philosophiae . . .*) – written, like Bovo's, in the early tenth or possibly at the very end of the ninth century – goes a stage further in using Platonic material to explain the *Consolation*, and draws directly on the *Timaeus* to explain Boethius' epitome of it. Otherwise it is a much more perfunctory examination than Bovo's, similar to it in that it treats Boethius as a Platonist, different in that it offers no condemnation of the *Consolation* for ignoring or contradicting Christian dogma.

The most elaborate of these commentaries on Book 3, metrum 9 was written by Adalbold, Bishop of Utrecht at the beginning of the eleventh century. Adalbold's work is at a far remove from the glosses of the ninth century, being written in an accomplished rhetorical style, and paying a great deal of attention to the supposed logical structure of Boethius' arguments. His approach is in an important way the diametrical opposite of Bovo's. So far from condemning Boethius for deviating from Christianity into Platonism, he praises him for his ability to reveal truths hidden to the Platonists but open to him as a Christian (409–10). Since the metrum is, in fact, an almost wholly Platonic piece of writing, Adalbold must Christianize it to prove his point. Whereas Remigius had been content to offer Platonic and Christian interpretations of terms like 'perpetual reason' and 'form of the highest good' as alternatives, Adalbold combines them, suggesting the heterodox view that Christ, the wisdom and mind of God, is equivalent to the Platonic world of Ideas, which provided the exemplar for the sensible world. Adalbold notices that, later in the metrum, Boethius seems to imply the pre-existence of souls: wishing neither to condemn his text, nor to approve a position that might be regarded as heretical, Adalbold says that he, like Augustine and Jerome, prefers to profess himself ignorant on the question of the soul's creation: he knows *that* God created it, but not *how* (422:332–41). For the 'light chariots' he proposes, like his predecessors, a metaphorical reading which turns Boethius' Neoplatonic allusion into orthodox Christian sentiment (422:341–423:355). With regard to the World-Soul, Adalbold rejects the opinion of those who attribute to it the power of giving life and so worship it as if it were a God, but accepts it as being that through which God imparts life (420:265–75). As these instances illustrate, Adalbold's Christianization of the metrum does not take from its Neoplatonic character, but rather, by slightly modifying or qualifying Boethius' words, it turns them into a statement of Christian Platonism.

There were, however, many in the eleventh century who could not accept Adalbold's view of an easy union between pagan and Christian thought. Often, this view amounted to no more than a general statement of priorities: why study secular texts when the time could be spent on studying sacred ones, and when it is possible that the secular texts might lead a reader away from orthodox belief? Such strictures are found in the writings of Otloh of St Emmeram (*c.* 1010–*c.* 1070), Peter Damian (on whom, see below, pp.91–4) and Gerard of Czanad (d. 1046).

Far more interesting is the detailed attack on pagan thought made by Manegold of Lautenbach in his *Liber contra Wolfelmum*. Born in about 1045 and still alive at the beginning of the twelfth century, Manegold may have taught about pagan philosophy before he became a monk; but he is probably not to be identified with the Manegold who taught William of Champeaux and is treated by twelfth-century chroniclers as one of the forerunners of the intellectual life of their time. Manegold's *Liber*, stimulated by its recipient's interest in Macrobius, is a detailed list of the various errors made by pagan philosophers – especially those found in Macrobius' commentary. Like Bovo of Corvey, Manegold has a wider and clearer idea of Platonic and Neoplatonic thought than most of those contemporaries who championed it. Manegold does not think that everything put forward by pagan philosophers is to be rejected: he knows that 'holy men' have accepted some, whilst other of their statements, he says, not without irony, are too subtle for his understanding (44:1–6). But the philosophers were mere humans, working without divine guidance; they trusted too much in reason, which is easily deceived; and much of what they say is in error. He is especially critical of the doctrine of the World-Soul and of philosophical discussions of the human soul, holding the former up to ridicule and listing the various, dissentient opinions of different philosophers about the latter. With the error, uncertainty and disagreement of the philosophers, Manegold contrasts the certain knowledge of the Christian, from faith, about God, the creation and the glory of eternal life.

The various reactions to pagan philosophy in the tenth and eleventh centuries – whether in commentaries or general discussion, whether enthusiastic or hostile – illustrate the difficulty which early medieval philosophers experienced in using the heritage of ancient philosophy as a basis for their own thought. The tradition reached them not as a collection of abstract questions and arguments, but as a set of metaphysical concepts and systematic relations. As such, it necessarily involved a view about the structure of the supra-sensible universe, which could be compared with that put forward in Christian sources. When scholars found that the two views were not ostensibly the same, they were faced with a problem. To ignore its differences from Christianity, and treat pagan philosophy in its own terms, was a course which, although occasionally fol-lowed (as in the *Inuocatio haec philosophiae* . . . commentary to Book 3, metrum 9 of the *Consolation*), was unsatisfactory, since it provided nothing which justified its value to the Christian thinker. A scholar might condemn pagan philosophy as misleading, in so far as it contradicted Christian doctrine, but this left him with little reason to pursue his study of the antique texts, however clear his understanding of them. Bovo of Corvey is not entirely convincing in the excuse he gives for examining a piece of Neoplatonic philo-sophy in such detail; whilst Manegold, more careful to practise his principles, restrains himself from providing the detailed exegesis of Macrobius and Plato which would, it seems, have been within his powers. A different approach was to argue that the differences between Christianity and pagan metaphysics, as evident from the texts of Boethius, Plato and Macrobius, were apparent rather than real – a position which was especially convincing in the case of the *Consolation*, since its author was in fact a Christian. This method, adopted by Remigius of Auxerre and Adalbold of Utrecht, had two great disadvantages: it produced distortions of both Christ-ianity and Platonism, unacceptable to whoever looked clear-head-edly at either doctrine; and, taken to its extreme, it accepted pagan metaphysics only at the cost of making them useless, since they would always turn out to accord with what the Christian already knew by his faith. Thus whichever attitude he adopted to his pagan material, the early medieval thinker was faced by the severest problems in justifying his interest in it.

The difficulties for an early medieval scholar, as a Christian, in using and developing the antique philosophical heritage had a pro-found effect on the way in which philosophy evolved in the early Middle Ages. Reading of the growing familiarity of thinkers in the ninth, tenth and eleventh centuries with the *Timaeus*, Macrobius' commentary, Boethius' *Consolation* and Martianus' *De nuptiis*, it is easy to imagine that ideas gleaned from these works formed the basis of the philosophical achievements of the twelfth century. In fact, the tradition of ancient philosophy, as passed on by these texts, contributed to the development of early medieval philosophy (as opposed to early medieval cultural life, in a broader sense) only in a subsidiary way. The ancient texts were indeed studied in the twelfth century, with more understanding and enthusiasm than before; but the outstanding twelfth-century expositors either concentrated on the scientific material in these works, or else used Platonism to propound a metaphorical, poetic picture of the world.

It was the ancient logical tradition, enriched by its contact with theology, which provided the foundation for what is most remarkable in the philosophy of the late eleventh and twelfth centuries, as it had done in the late eighth and ninth. This tradition had not been broken; the developments of logical technique in the tenth century led, even at the time, to the consideration of certain philosophical questions, and they made the way open for many more. But there had been a threat that it would be overshadowed: first from Eriugena's revival of Greek Christian Neoplatonism; and then, more widely, from the increasing interest in pagan philosophical texts. The threat was never realized and, as a result, those thinkers who wished to discuss abstract questions, rather than scientific ones, turned to the philosophical issues raised by logical texts, and discussed by the ancient commentators, or to the philosophical passages in theological texts such as Boethius' *Opuscula sacra*. Whereas the liveliest minds of the twelfth century might have merely become the expositors and elaborators of ancient systems (as Eriugena had been of the metaphysics of the Greek Christian Neoplatonists), they had – and took – the opportunity to become philosophers in a stricter sense.

9 *Logic and theology in the age of Anselm*

Dialectic and its place in theology

It is sometimes argued that in the eleventh century logic was treated with a hostility similar to that shown, in some quarters, towards pagan philosophy. Indeed, historians have often written as if the one sort of hostility were indistinguishable from the other, and under the name of 'anti-dialecticians' classed a group of thinkers – among them Manegold of Lautenbach, Peter Damian, Otloh of St Emmeram and Lanfranc of Bec – who asserted the claims of faith over secular reasoning, whether this took the form of logical subtlety or reference to ancient philosophical texts. This classification is misleading because it ignores an important distinction. To assert the claims of religion over pagan philosophy (as the first three thinkers listed did) amounts to a rejection of the pagan texts, except where they happen to coincide with a Christian's belief; but to put religious claims above those of logic merely involves objecting to an inappropriate application of logic to theology. Logic does not, like pagan philosophy, offer a system of ideas which rivals those of Christianity. It provides a set of tools for thought. The complaint of some eleventh-century scholars was, not that these tools were in themselves harmful or even valueless, but that they were being used for a job to which they were unsuited: that many of the mysteries of faith were beyond rational comprehension and so closed to logical analysis. In the two eleventh-century thinkers who put forward such views in detail, this awareness of the limitations of logic is balanced by an interest in logical methods and a respect for their powers.

Lanfranc (1010–89), abbot of Bec and then Archbishop of Canterbury, wrote a work on logic (now lost) and had a philosophical interest in grammar (see below, p.106); but he is known as a

thinker almost only through his part in a controversy with Berengar, a teacher at Tours, over the Eucharist. Berengar questioned
the belief that the consecrated bread and wine really became the
body and blood of Christ on grounds not of a sophisticated ra-
tionalism, but rather of 'naive realism', as a modern philosopher
might call it: he refused to believe in something that went so
decidedly against the evidence of his senses. In his *De corpore et
sanguine Domini*, Lanfranc defends orthodoxy against Berengar's
attacks. He believes that Berengar has made use of logical techniques where they are inappropriate: 'you desert the sacred authorities and take refuge in dialectic' (416D–7A). Lanfranc would
prefer, he says, to answer Berengar simply by reference to the
authority of patristic and biblical writings, but he recognizes that
the matter under discussion can be best explained by the use of
logical methods; and he justifies his use of them by pointing to the
example of Augustine, who praised dialectic as a tool for investi-
gating Scripture and used it with Aristotelian subtlety in refuting
heresy. Lanfranc, then, resents – or affects to resent – Berengar's
intrusion of logical techniques into the field of dogma; but, since
the nature of the discussion has been thereby transformed, he must
use logic himself in order to answer Berengar.

Berengar replies to Lanfranc in his *De sacra coena* and defends his
initial use of dialectic in considering the Eucharist. To use dialectic
in order to make evident the truth is not, he says, 'to take refuge
in dialectic'; or, if it is, then Berengar professes himself glad to
have done so. Dialectic contradicts neither God's wisdom nor his
strength but, rather, refutes his enemies. Indeed, 'to take refuge in
dialectic is to take refuge in reason, and whoever does not take
refuge there, loses his honourable status as a creature made according to reason in the image of God' (101). Berengar's position, then,
is little different from Lanfranc's. Both men are trained logicians,
ready to put their techniques to the service of theology when
necessary. Berengar believes that the accepted doctrine of the
Eucharist is mistaken, and that his skills are required to reveal this
error; Lanfranc considers that it is Berengar who is misled, and
that he must use his skills to combat Berengar. Both men refer to
Augustine in support of their use of logical methods; and, although
Berengar places greater emphasis on the importance of man's
reason, this theme, and the manner in which it is developed, is also
Augustinian.

Peter Damian (1007–72) was an advocate of ascetic Christianity,
and one of the eleventh-century thinkers who considered pagan
philosophy useless, at least for monks. Historians have frequently

imagined that this contempt for secular learning extended to dialectic, and have interpreted his *De divina omnipotentia* as a thoroughgoing condemnation of the application of logical criteria to theological questions. On closer examination, this work turns out to be a subtle examination of the extent to which human logic can be used to talk of an all-powerful God, which anticipates in the questions it raises thirteenth- and fourteenth-century discussions of divine omnipotence.

Damian begins from the question of whether God could restore her virginity to a girl who had lost it. There are problems, he realizes, in talking of what is or is not possible for an omnipotent God. He constructs the following argument (54): if God cannot do what he does not wish (which must be the case if he is all-powerful), then he only does what he wishes, and so what he does not do, he cannot do. This conclusion is, to Damian, self-evidently absurd, and it points to a mistake in understanding what it means to say of God that he cannot do or that he does not know something. God does not know and cannot do what is evil, not from ignorance or incapacity, but because his will is always righteous. This divine will is the cause of all things, visible and invisible, created or as yet awaiting their manifestation (62). Damian's answer to the question of the virgin is therefore that God could restore her maidenhead, but that he would not choose to do so unless it accorded with justice.

Damian then moves on to consider an even trickier question about God's omnipotence: could God bring it about that what has already happened did not happen (70)? Damian begins by admitting that it seems to be the case that what has happened, when it has happened, cannot not have happened. This, he says, is true also of the present and the future: 'whatever is now, whilst it is, without doubt must by necessity be' (76), and 'if it is going to rain, then it is entirely necessary that it will rain and thus entirely impossible that it will not rain' (76). However, it is clear, Damian argues, with regard to future events that such necessity is not of an absolute sort concerning the events themselves. There are many events in the future which may or may not happen. To say 'if it is the case that it will happen, then necessarily it will happen' is to insist on a necessity merely according to 'the consequence of statements' (*consequentia disserendi*): that is – to clarify Damian's point – to insist that, even in the case of a contingent statement, if it is true, then necessarily the facts must be such as to make it true. Damian goes on to apply what he has said about the future to the present and the past. If something is, then, whilst it is, it must be; but only according to the necessity of 'the consequence of statements'. Similarly, it is only according to this sort of necessity that it is impossible for whatever has happened not to have happened (78). But, says Damian, it is quite wrong to think that God's power is limited by a necessity which is merely that of the consequence of statements. If it were, then God would be absolutely powerless, since statements about the present and the future have a similar type of necessity.

Feeling that this explanation might not be completely satisfying, Damian adds a more direct answer (82 ff) to the question about God's power. Basing himself on Boethius' argument in Book 5 of the *Consolation* (see above, p.41) to show the compatibility of divine prescience and human free will, Damian points out that God should not be thought of as if he were in time. In the ever-presentness of his eternity he sees past, present and future in a single glimpse. There is no past for God, as there is for man, and so the whole question of his ability to alter the past is inapposite – a case of inappropriately using human terms to discuss what is divine.

One aspect of Damian's argument is of particular interest. It is, for him, no accident that the examples of logical reasoning about the past, present and future which he produces demonstrate only 'the consequence of statements', not anything about the nature of reality. For him, it is the very nature of logic to be concerned merely with the consequence of statements: the art of dialectic, he says (82), is of relevance neither to the quality (*virtus*) nor nature (*materia*) of things, but 'to the manner and order of making statements and the consequence of words'. Damian uses this judgment as part of his polemic against the misuse of logic. As a purely verbal art, its place is in secular (not monastic) schools, and it should not be used in discussing the sacraments of the Church. However, this opinion – here derogatory – of dialectic as an art of words reflects a growing interest in the connections between language and logic.

In the mid-eleventh century, then, especial attention was paid by thinkers to logic in connection with theology. In the late eighth and ninth centuries, a conjunction of these two disciplines had led scholars to ask certain philosophical questions and develop some philosophical ideas. Part of this process had consisted of making logical concepts metaphysical ones, or developing theological implications from them; and the result had sometimes been to confuse logic, metaphysics and theology in a manner superficially exciting, but ultimately meaningless. Increased knowledge of logical con-

cepts and techniques kept eleventh-century thinkers from perpe-
trating such confusions. Familiarity with some aspects of the *De
interpretatione* and Boethius' monographs on the syllogism had
made the eleventh-century logician a master of argument. The
theology of the time uses logic as a tool and recognizes its separ-
ateness as a discipline. Nevertheless, the contact between logic and
theology in this century was no less productive philosophically
than it had been in the ninth. By having to define the appropriateness of dialectic as a tool in theology, thinkers came to reflect
about the nature of logic itself. And Damian's view of logic as an
art of language was one which, put to different use, was to have
an important part in twelfth-century thought.

Anselm

At Bec, Lanfranc had a pupil, Anselm (born in Aosta in 1033),
who followed closely in his footsteps, becoming abbot in 1078 and
succeeding him as Archbishop of Canterbury in 1093. Unlike
Lanfranc, Anselm produced, from about 1070 until near to his
death in 1109, a series of treatises which have survived to modern
times. Most of Anselm's work is not directly connected with
contemporary doctrinal controversy; and, whilst the vicissitudes
of his life as archbishop may have hindered his intellectual activity,
they did not obviously affect the character of his thought. As a
thinker, Anselm's reputation outstrips that, not only of his contemporaries, but of every philosopher in the early Middle Ages.
His works have been translated into many languages; critical and
philosophical studies of them abound; and Anselm, placed between
Augustine and Aquinas in the row of 'great thinkers of the past',
is presented as having made a decisive contribution to the development of early medieval philosophy. More clearly than any of
his medieval predecessors, he defined a role for reason within his
theological speculations and used rational methods in conducting
them.

There is no reason to challenge this judgment about the nature
of Anselm's work itself. On the one hand, the manner of his
writing is rational: he proceeds by clear, logical arguments from
stated premises to his conclusions, taking care to refute whatever
counter-arguments he imagines might be made. On the other
hand, Anselm openly discusses the role of reason in his theology.
Reason can in no way provide a substitute for faith – 'I do not
seek to understand in order to believe, but I believe in order that
I might understand' (*Proslogion* 1; 1.100:18) – but, by the use of

reason, the Christian can gain an understanding of what he already believes.

Anselm is, in short, a rational, speculative theologian, but does this merit him the place in the history of philosophy which he holds in the common estimation? Many historians have believed that before the assimilation of Aristotelian and Arabic thought in the thirteenth century there was no such thing as medieval philosophy, in the strict sense of the word, but only theology. If the philosophical developments of the later Middle Ages had any antecedents in the earlier part of the period, they could be found, they considered, in the work of those theologians who gave reason an important and explicit role in their investigations. Anselm's writings fulfil these qualifications; and so his importance in medieval philosophy is evident on this view of the development of the subject. But is this view correct? The argument of this book is that it is not; that, although scholars were never just philosophers, nor books devoted exclusively to philosophy, in the early Middle Ages philosophical speculation did go on: sporadically and often confusedly in the ninth, tenth and eleventh centuries, with more sustained assurance in the twelfth. Anselm's originality, imagination, clarity and, in many respects, enduring interest as a speculative theologian do not, therefore, in themselves guarantee him a place in the history of early medieval philosophy. Nor do they necessarily exclude him from one. Philosophical discussion can occur during the course of a work theological in its aims; and Anselm's canon includes some pieces devoted entirely to logical analysis of concepts, with no direct theological reference. The following discussion will therefore have two goals: first, to substantiate and clarify the picture of Anselm as, primarily, a speculative theologian and, second, to examine which aspects of Anselm's work might justly be regarded as philosophical.

Where Anselm's work is not straightforwardly dogmatic, its purpose is thoroughly in accord with his motto that 'he believes in order to understand'. He wishes to demonstrate, by rational arguments, a religious truth which is already known. The argument will be as logically convincing as Anselm can make it; but he will have devised it in order to reach the conclusion it does, rather than having been led by it to its conclusion. The procedure is particularly clear in the *Monologion*, *Proslogion*, *Cur Deus Homo* and *De concordia*. The first two are both designed to argue, from premises Anselm takes as self-evident, that there exists a God who has the various attributes of the Christian God – infinitude, immutability, omnipotence and (in the *Monologion*) triunity. The *De concordia* has the avowed aim of showing how divine prescience, predestination and grace are compatible with human free will. There is no question that God might lack foreknowledge or the power to predestine human activities, or that his grace should not be necessary for salvation. Nor does Anselm contemplate the possibility that the human will might not be free. Anselm's task is to show *how*, not *that*, they are compatible.

In *Cur Deus Homo*, Anselm announces his method most explicitly. Why did God become Man? The Christian knows through his faith that he did, but he must search for an explanation, if what he believes is also to delight his understanding (i.1; ii:47–9). Moreover, this explanation must be of a particularly stringent kind. Anselm begins by arguing for the Incarnation simply on the grounds of its appropriateness: since humankind was damned through the sin of a man, it was appropriate that a man should restore it, and that the devil, who had vanquished a man, should himself be defeated by a man (i.3; ii.50:3–13). Anselm's interlocutor in the fictional dialogue refuses to treat such arguments as more than pictures painted on an insecure foundation, which would not convince those who did not believe in the Incarnation anyway. What is required is the 'solidity of reasonable truth': an argument which shows the necessity of God's becoming incarnate (i.5; cf. ii.8; ii.51:16–52:11; cf. ii.104:13–15) – necessity not in the sense of compulsion, but of how the Incarnation follows as a logical consequence of what is self-evidently true. The argument which follows, although not entirely flawless, is a brave attempt to prove just such necessity. God intended man for beatitude, but original sin was a harm against God which could not be repaid simply by man's obedience to God, since that is owed to him, as man's creator, already. Indeed, no satisfaction that a man could offer would be adequate to recompense a harm done to the Deity. And so it seems that God's purpose has been frustrated. But God's purpose cannot be frustrated. An adequate satisfaction can be offered only by one who is a man (because the satisfaction is due from man) but is a God (because of the extent of the satisfaction required). It is therefore necessary for there to be a God-Man: God must become incarnate.

The logic of the argument in *Cur Deus Homo* is powerful; and would have seemed especially so to Anselm's contemporaries, who would have been less likely than a modern reader to query the relevance of coherence of Anselm's concept of satisfaction. Anselm certainly wished each step of his argument to be regarded as accordant with reason; and most probably he hoped that it might convince those – like the Jews – who shared his assumptions about God's purpose and man's sinfulness, but did not already believe in the Incarnation. Nevertheless, the conclusion of Anselm's argument is determined, and the writer's task is solely to work out its stages; moreover, in this work, Anselm's starts from premises which are themselves theistic, although not specifically Christian. He is explaining, rationally, not reality as perceived by the senses and intellect of any human being, but the truths which the faithful know already through their faith.

Anselm's resolve to exercise his reason only within the limits and to the ends dictated by his faith is further illustrated by his attitude to scriptural authority. Like many an outstanding theologian, but unlike most of his contemporaries, Anselm did not feel that he had to have the support of his human predecessors for all his theories: he recognizes, for instance, that the *Cur Deus Homo* goes beyond anything said by the Fathers (*CDH* I.1; II.49:7–13). The case is not at all the same with regard to Scripture, the word of God. Nothing that he proposes, says Anselm (*De concordia* III.6; II.271:26–272:7), which is of value to the salvation of the soul, is not contained within Scripture. This does not mean that Scripture literally says all that he does. If what he has discovered by reason is neither contradicted by any scriptural truth, nor supports any falsehood censured in Scripture, then he considers it to be supported by the authority of the Bible. But, he adds, 'if Scripture clearly contradicts what we think to be the case, then, even if, to us, our reasoning seems irrefragable, it should not be thought to contain any truth'.

One facet of Anselm's work which, in addition to his prevalent use of rational argument, has sometimes been taken as evidence that he was of importance in the history of philosophy is his Platonism. Anselm is certainly a Platonist in two respects. He treats universals as real existents on which particulars depend. For instance, in his discussion of truth in *De veritate* and of free will in *De libero arbitrio*, he treats rectitude and justice as real existents, by virtue of which things are right or just. Moreover, he uses the basic principle behind Plato's doctrine of Ideas, that the cause of the various appearances of a quality is that quality in its pure form. This method of argument is particularly evident in the *Monologion*, where, by arguing on the basis of unity as the cause of multiplicity, the endless as the origin of the bounded, the immutable of that which changes, Anselm is able to demonstrate the existence and attributes of the Christian God.

Such Platonism, however, so far from attaching Anselm to a philosophical tradition, serves only to make clear his debt, and his similarity in aim, to one of the great speculative theologians of late antiquity. It derives neither from the *Timaeus* nor the work of Macrobius, which Anselm seems not to have read, but from Augustine. Like Augustine, Anselm has no use for the systematic metaphysics of the Neoplatonists, except where it happens to accord with Christianity – and even here it interests him far less than it did Augustine. But individual Platonic concepts and ways of arguing were of value to Anselm, especially in the form in which Augustine presented them to him, stripped of many of their Neoplatonic developments and closer to their origins in Plato's thought than, say, to Plotinus. And, like Augustine, it was especially to Platonism as a *method* of argument that Anselm looked: for both Christian thinkers, the *conclusions* to their arguments were determined by their faith.

It is within the context of Anselm's Augustinian Platonism that it is possible to understand much that is otherwise puzzling about his most famous argument, the so-called ontological proof of God's existence. This proof, put forward in chapters 2 and 3 of the *Proslogion*, has been rather misleadingly extracted by generations of philosophers from the framework of the single argument which runs through the whole of the work. As in the *Monologion*, Anselm's purpose is to demonstrate, rationally, the existence of a God with at least some of the attributes of the Christian God (in the *Proslogion* Anselm does not try to prove that God is triune). He wishes to do so, as he says in the prologue (1.93:6–7), by means of *one* argument. His method is ingenious. He chooses a definition of God which seems self-evidently, apart from any Christian dogma, to describe what God would be, if he existed: 'that-than-which-nothing-greater-can-be-thought'. He then sets about proving, first, that this definition is really instantiated, that something corresponds to it in reality; and second, that that-than-which-nothing-greater-can-be-thought must, as a matter of logical consequence, have various of the characteristics of the Christian God. It is the first stage of this proof which has come to be known as the ontological argument.

Anselm's train of reasoning in chapter 2 is the following. Even the man who denies that God exists can understand the concept that-than-which-nothing-greater-can-be-thought. This concept, therefore, exists in his mind. But, Anselm argues, it is 'greater' to exist both in reality and in the mind, than in the mind alone. If,

then, that-than-which-nothing-greater-can-be-thought were to exist only in the mind, something could be conceived greater than
it, sharing its characteristics, but existing in reality and in thought;
but this cannot be the case, if it is that-than-which-nothing-
greater- can - be - thought. Therefore that - than - which -nothing -
greater-can-be-thought must exist both in the mind and in reality,
otherwise it would not be that-than-which-nothing-greater-can-
be-thought.

The logic of this argument has fascinated philosophers ever since
Anselm's day, chiefly because, in criticizing it, one is forced to
explore a series of very profound and difficult questions about the
relationship between the concept or abstract definition of something, the thought of it, and its existence in reality. But the ontological proof was not for Anselm what, for many, it has since
become: a sophistical argument which, by its falsehood, reveals
important truths about the concepts used in stating it. For its
originator, the ontological proof was obviously true, not just in
its conclusion, but in its order of argument: it was a sudden and
it seemed to him God-given insight, granted at the end of tortuous
and painful reflections. It was Anselm's Platonism which made his
proof seem to him so strikingly convincing and spared him from
many of the doubts felt even by those less Platonically-inclined
philosophers who have, in some form, accepted his argument.

The Platonic tradition, as conveyed by Augustine and Boethius'
Opuscula sacra, did not merely suggest to Anselm that existence
was an aspect of the perfection or greatness of something, and so
the greatest thing that could be conceived would, of necessity,
exist in the greatest possible way. It also made the transition from
understanding a concept to asserting the instantiation of that concept in reality a far less disturbing step than it must seem to most
modern readers. For Anselm, as a Platonist, the most real things
are those which are contemplated by the mind, rather than by the
senses. What a thinker with a different view of universals would
describe as mere concepts – thoughts in the mind not instantiated
in reality – are to him real beings which can only be perceived by
the intellect. Justice and rectitude, for instance, really exist: they
are not a mental construction derived from individual instances of
justice and rectitude: on the contrary, there would be no just thing
without justice; nothing right without rectitude. Moreover, as a
Platonist, Anselm might not distinguish very clearly between perceiving justice-in-itself and forming a concept – arriving at an
abstract definition – of it: by understanding what justice is one
perceives it as a real thing, just as one perceives a man by seeing

or touching him. Anselm, then, begins with the assumption that that-than-which-nothing-greater-can-be-thought is the sort of thing – like justice-in-itself – which can only be grasped by understanding in the mind what it is. But he grants that the mind can form definitions to which nothing at all outside the mind corresponds. The very nature of the concept that-than-which-nothing-greater-can-be-thought shows, he argues, that it is not one of these: when the mind grasps it, it cannot be grasping what is in the mind alone.

The argument of chapter 2 of the *Proslogion* is, then, a brilliant development of Anselm's Platonic assumptions for his theological purposes (the rational proof of what he already accepted by faith), but not in any sense an analysis or vindication of these assumptions. Yet Anselm did not remain totally uninterested in the philosophical questions raised by the argument he had devised. Shortly after he wrote the *Proslogion*, Gaunilo, an otherwise unknown monk of Marmoutier, produced a critical, though respectful, reply. The strongest and most interesting of Gaunilo's criticisms questions the meaningfulness of that-than-which-nothing-greater-can-be-thought as a concept. One cannot know, he says (IV; I.126:29–127:24), what sort of thing it is, and so one understands it rather as a set of words to which one tries to put a meaning without ever succeeding. In his reply to Gaunilo's criticisms, Anselm never produces a totally satisfactory answer to this point; but he is led by it to consider the relationship between knowing the definition of something and actually thinking about it. He makes explicit one of the assumptions in the *Proslogion*: that, since we can make various deductions about the logical nature of that-than-which-nothing-greater-can-be-thought, we must be able to understand it and so in some way have it in our mind (I–II; I.130:3–133:2). Later (IX; I.138:4–27), he argues that, although it may be impossible to have a clear concept of God, this does not make the expression that-than-which-nothing-greater-can-be-thought, which refers to God, itself incomprehensible. He illustrates his point with an example: we can think of 'what is inconceivable' although we cannot, by definition, think of that to which the concept applies. These insights into the differences between concepts and the reality to which they refer might, if taken further, have led Anselm to question some of the assumptions which made the argument of *Proslogion*, chapter 2 so convincing for him.

In fact, perhaps because he was unsure whether the reasoning of that chapter could stand scrutiny, Anselm devotes much of his reply to developing an argument put forward in chapter 3 and hardly mentioned by Gaunilo. In chapter 3, Anselm had argued that that-than-which-nothing-greater-can-be-thought cannot even be thought not to exist, because what cannot be thought not to exist is greater than what can be thought not to exist. In the plan of the *Proslogion*, this argument was a continuation of that of chapter 2, not an alternative to it: not only, Anselm wished to show, does God exist, but he exists in a special way, so that he cannot even be thought not to exist. In his reply to Gaunilo, this argument is often used as an alternative to the proof of chapter 2; and it is linked to a further argument (I–III; 1.130:20 ff) that that-than-which-nothing-greater-can-be-thought must be something which has no beginning; and what has no beginning exists necessarily. Anselm engages in a good deal of discussion which investigates the logical workings of these two principles. Sometimes this falls into sophistry: for instance, he argues (I; 1.131:6–17) that because, if the concept that-than-which-nothing-greater-can-be-thought were a real thing, it would be a thing which could not be thought not to exist; it must exist, if it is thought to exist, otherwise, if it does exist, it might be thought not to exist. However, even the complication of such a confusion shows the sophistication with which Anselm has begun to handle his terms. Anselm's interest in the logic of possibility and necessity might well result from a study of Aristotle's *De interpretatione* and Boethius' commentaries on it: his knowledge of these works is evident elsewhere in his writings. By applying the logic of possibility to the concept of God, Anselm manages to reveal an important set of differences between the way in which God might be said to exist and the way in which anything else exists or does not. Anselm's aim is always to use this discovery for his theological purpose of demonstrating rationally God's existence. Nevertheless, he has succeeded in establishing an important philosophical point about the logical nature of divine existence; here, as opposed to the argument of *Proslogion*, chapter 2, subsequent philosophical discussion has really derived from Anselm's thought, rather than from the unseen implications of his text.

In the *Proslogion* and the reply to Gaunilo, Anselm allowed himself, in the course of his theological discussion, to explore two sets of philosophical problems: the relation between language, concepts and reality; and the nature of possibility and necessity. Anselm explores both of these problems elsewhere in his work.

In his first work, the *Monologion*, Anselm distinguishes between three sorts of words (x; 1.24:30–25:27): written or spoken signs of things (normal speech); written or spoken signs considered in the mind (thinking in words); and a type of words which, following Boethius, he describes as natural – the images or definitions of things which are contemplated in the mind's eye. In his second commentary to the *De interpretatione* (see above, p.32), Boethius had argued that, although the words of speech differed from people to people, the thoughts to which these words refer are the same: the thought or concept of a horse, for instance, is the same among all peoples, although there are many different words for it. At times Boethius refers to these thoughts as a kind of speech – a usage Anselm follows, because it is helpful for the theological argument he is engaged in making. Although, then, Anselm's discussion of thought and language here is derivative, it shows him mastering a text which would become very important in twelfth-century work on language and universals (see below, pp.136–9).

Another treatise also shows Anselm as a precursor of twelfth-century linguistic philosophy. The *De grammatico* is the only complete monograph of Anselm's to deal with a non-religious subject. It concerns a problem which the scholars of Anselm's day debated in connection with the work of Priscian, the late antique grammarian (see below, pp.105–9). Priscian had said that every noun signifies both a substance and a quality: he seemed to have in mind that, for instance, a man is both something – an object one can point at – and a particular sort of thing. Anselm begins his work by taking up this point, but with regard to a very special sort of noun. He chooses the word '*grammaticus*', which can mean either a grammarian or grammatical. To ask, therefore, whether *grammaticus* is a substance or a quality is to take a very difficult case as the basis for examining Priscian's statement, since *grammaticus* is not only substance and quality in the sense that a grammarian is both something and a particular sort of thing, but also in the sense that grammatical is a quality which must qualify something. This double meaning allows Anselm to construct a series of paradoxes which illustrate, among other things, the difference between logical and grammatical propriety. His position becomes clearer in the later part of the work (XIV ff; 1.159:13 ff). Here he turns for a while from exploring the connection between reality and a very problematic noun to that between reality and a common adjective. What does an adjective such as 'white', used in connection with a white horse, actually stand for? Anselm makes an important distinction between what such an adjective signifies (*significat*), which is 'having whiteness', and what it is appellative of (*appellat*), which is the white horse. But he does not draw out the philosophical implications of such a distinction; indeed, he tends to treat the subject-matter of *De grammatico* as if it purely concerned formal logic, a set of paradoxes in argumentation which might be resolved by clearer definitions within a formal system.

The interest in the logic of possibility and necessity shown in the reply to Gaunilo recurs in at least three other of Anselm's works. In a fragmentary discussion, designed to elucidate some concepts used in *Cur Deus Homo*, Anselm discusses the definition of 'being able' in a technical way. In the *De concordia* and the *Cur Deus Homo*, Anselm deals with the relationship between divine certainty and human freedom in terms which derive from Boethius. The problem arises indirectly in *Cur Deus Homo* (II.16–17; II.120:2–126:4). In order to bear Christ, the Virgin Mary had to be pure, and she could become pure only by believing in Christ's future death (and thus the redemption of man). Does this not mean that, in order to be born by the Virgin Mary, Christ had of necessity to be going to die to redeem man, otherwise Mary's faith would have been mistaken and she could not have been purified? Anselm looks at the problem from two points of view. So far as Christ is concerned, to say that he had to die means that he had to will to die; but no necessity can constrain the divine will. God can choose to do whatever he wishes; however, once he has chosen a course of action, he will fulfil it. To carry out a promise does not, Anselm argues, mean to submit to constraint. So far as Mary is concerned, her faith in Christ's future death was indeed justified because his death would take place; but the necessity which this imposes is, Anselm says, with an explicit reference to Aristotle, merely conditional necessity. This is the term Boethius uses (*In De Interpretatione* edition II 243:26) to describe the type of necessity identified by Aristotle as purely logical (see above, pp.22–3). It obtains between a true statement and the facts that make it true: if something is the case then, when it is the case, it must necessarily be the case; but this in no way limits the freedom of human agents to determine what the case should be.

In the *De concordia*, where Anselm tackles the problem of divine prescience directly, he also relies on Boethius, but he adapts his argument. He mentions the notion of God's timelessness, as in the *Consolation*; but it is not for him, as it is in that work, the mainstay of his vindication of human free will. The distinction between conditional and strict necessity serves this function for Anselm, who places Boethius' purely logical conditional necessity within a wider class of necessity which does not constrain by force. His first example of such necessity (1.2; 11.247:8) is not logical, but theological: it is necessary for God to be immortal. Earlier, he had followed Augustine in suggesting that God's prescience cannot be said to impose necessity on the human will, because, by the same token, it would impose necessity on God's will. Anselm is not so much using logic to explain what seem to be difficulties concerning the idea of an omniscient God (as Boethius had done), as employing the special kinds of logic required by the existence of such a God to explain the relationship between the divinity and his creation. In *Cur Deus Homo* and *De concordia*, then, Anselm manifests an interest in the particular logic of divine necessity, which is seen at its most developed in the reply to Gaunilo; but in each case, the interest is strictly contained within the framework imposed by his theological aims.

The preceding paragraphs do not – and do not attempt to – do justice to Anselm, either as a theologian or as a formal logician. He enters into philosophical discussion when he brings logic into conjunction with his theology; and it is these moments which have just been examined. They are brief and few, precisely because Anselm was so accomplished and clear-headed, both as theologian and logician. His theological aims were definite and explicit; he felt no temptation seriously to deviate from them. His talent as a logician kept him engaged in the formal construction and analysis of arguments. Unlike Peter Damian, he had few qualms about the applicability of logical techniques to theology; and, as a result of this confidence, he was not led to any profound investigation of the nature of logic itself. For these reasons, and in spite of his brilliance and originality, Anselm's work plays a significant, but secondary part in the story of early medieval philosophy.

Anselm's pupils and influence

In the limited amount of work produced by followers strongly under Anselm's influence, there is even less philosophical speculation than in his own writings. It was Anselm's theological method which seems to have impressed his disciples, and which they took as a point of departure. The products of three identifiable pupils of Anselm's illustrate this point.

Gilbert Crispin, abbot of Westminster from about 1085 to 1117, had been a fellow monk of Anselm's at Bec and became a close friend. In a couple of dialogues – one between a Christian and a Jew, the other between a Christian and a pagan – he developed the apologetic aspect, implicit in Anselm's method and especially evident in *Cur Deus Homo*. If Christian dogma was capable of rational demonstration from self-evident premises, then it should be possible to prove the truth of the faith to the unfaithful. Gilbert's attempts to do this show notably less flair for rational argument than Anselm's own productions.

A certain Ralph (probably a monk of Caen, who came to England with Lanfranc and died in 1124) has left a collection of work in a single manuscript. In three dialogues and a meditation, Ralph follows Anselm's method of rationally demonstrating what a Christian already believes; and he states the justification for this position in terms that are a crude imitation of Anselm's. The Christian believes all that he learns from Scripture, 'but it is in a certain way sweeter for us if we can understand rationally those things which we believe to be so and which cannot be otherwise than as faith teaches them to be'. Ralph combines his arguments with a more systematic presentation of items of dogma than Anselm had attempted.

The third of these followers was the most productive and, as to his life, the most obscure. Honorius Augustodunensis was possibly of Irish origin and, by 1125, he was probably a monk at Regensburg. In no sense a philosopher, he was interested in collecting and expounding truths about every detail of the faith. One of his favourite sources was the *Periphyseon* of John Scottus, a work which he knew more thoroughly, but understood no better, than any of his contemporaries. In some of his writings, the influence of Anselm is also apparent, especially in the widely read *Elucidarium* and in a set of revisions to his *Inevitabile* – a monograph on free will – which derive from the *De concordia*. But Honorius makes no attempt either to reconcile the arguments of his various sources, or to analyse their differences.

Logic and grammar at the end of the eleventh century

One of the most important developments in eleventh-century thought was the beginning of speculation on philosophical problems raised by Priscian's *Institutiones grammaticae*. In the ninth century scholars at St Gall had noted some of the parallels between grammatical and logical description, and the ninth-century thinker, Gottschalk, had used grammatical analysis as a tool in his theology (see above, pp. 55; 76–7); but grammatical study had not, to any notable extent, influenced philosophy, then or for the next two hundred years. In the middle of the eleventh century, scholars interpreting Priscian began to notice that in a few passages he used

terms, or touched on problems, which were similar to those discussed in the *Categories*, *De interpretatione* and Boethius' commentaries. They explored the implications of these passages using their
knowledge of logical texts and bringing a weight of thought to
matters which Priscian had mentioned in passing.

The best record of these eleventh-century discussions on matters
raised by Priscian is found in an anonymous commentary to the
Institutiones. Several factors suggest that the work was probably
composed towards the end of the century, the date of its earliest
manuscript. One copy of it adds a note on the opinions of various
masters about the nature of the verb 'to be'. Among the thinkers
mentioned is Archbishop Lanfranc, whose views are also noted,
though not attributed, in the commentary itself. Lanfranc's ideas,
as they are represented, lack the sophistication of those which the
commentator himself develops. Lanfranc's generation was, then,
perhaps the first to explore the questions suggested to philosophers
by the *Institutiones*; and the commentary the product of the generation succeeding. This view would make it roughly contemporary with Anselm's *De grammatico*, which treats similar questions in
a manner at once more sophisticated logically and less philosophically inquisitive.

The commentator's philosophical remarks are sparsely scattered
among his grammatical ones: the most substantial are those which
try to apply notions about the relation between language and
reality, suggested by Priscian, to ideas about universals, gathered
from the logical tradition. They are discussions remarkable for the
questions they raise, rather than for any conclusions or coherence
which they achieve.

Whereas the name of an individual corresponds in a seemingly
unproblematic way to a single real object (the individual that it
names), there is no such obvious correspondence with reality in
the case of words naming types of thing, such as 'man' or 'horse'.
One approach to the problem, inherited from the grammatical
tradition and adopted, at one stage, by the commentator, is simply
to distinguish between the way in which names of individuals and
the way in which type-names refer to reality. The names of individuals are 'proper' (*propria*) – they refer to just one thing; the
names of types are 'appellative' (*appelativa*) – they refer to a collection of things which have some property in common. But, the
commentator debates (d$^{viii\ r-v}$), is there nothing to which a type-
name, like 'man', refers to properly, rather than appellatively? He
puts forward two such possibilities: that it might be a proper name
for a single, 'universal nature' in all men, which, though shared,

is a unique thing; or a proper name for a likeness, formed by the rational mind and existing only in the rational mind, of what is common to all men. These two possibilities each represent different aspects of Boethius' view on the nature of universals. The commentator, however, rejects both these suggestions, using two different kinds of argument. Against the first suggestion, he says that names must always be judged according to the 'nature of their invention' (*natura inventionis*) and not any of their 'manner[s] of signifying' (*modum significationis*). Whoever first invented the word 'man' had before him not an abstract species, but a particular man, which he perceived with his senses (compare Boethius' commentary on the *Categories*, above, p.32). To him, and to all others which shared the same qualities definitive of man, he gave the name 'man'. 'Man' is thus by the nature of its invention appellative, designed to refer to more than one thing. Against the second suggestion, he argues that a likeness in the mind of what is common to all men is neither an individual substance nor quality, but what is common to many; what refers to it is not, therefore, a proper name.

The commentator's own view is subtler than the suggestions he rejects. Basing himself on Priscian's observation, that names signify both substance and quality, he makes a distinction (d^(vi r)) between the substances to which names refer – what they 'signify by imposition' (*significat per impositionem*) – and what names mean – what they signify 'by representation' (*per representationem*). Reference is a matter of 'imposition': a name refers to the substance which its inventor intended it to designate. Thus a proper name, like 'Socrates', refers to a substance which is discrete from all other substances because of certain properties; and a type-name, like 'man', refers to a substance which, by similarity of property, is common to many things. Here the commentator's phrasing might seem to suggest that type-names refer to universal essences; but this does not seem to be his meaning, since he goes on to explain what 'man' refers to ('signifies by imposition') as 'the thing of Socrates and of other men' – an awkward set of words which seems to be chosen precisely to make it clear that the reference of type-names is to a collection of things, not to a single essence.

As well as *referring to* a collection of substances, a type-word also *means* a quality: the word 'man', for instance, marks out a certain substance as having the qualities of rationality and mortality, and thus represents that substance as a man. If there is a certain vagueness in the commentator's analysis of both the reference and meaning of type-words, it is perhaps because he tries to bring together, without fundamentally rethinking, a theory of universals which treats the classification of individuals as fixed by nature and a theory of language which puts the whole process of naming (not merely the choice of words) into the power of man. However, the commentator is able to make his distinction far more clearly in the case of type-adjectives like 'white'. They refer 'by imposition' to the objects qualified by the adjectives; and so the reference of the word 'white', each particular time it is used, will be the thing in question which is white. But 'by representation' such adjectives mean the qualities for which they stand in the abstract: the meaning of 'white' is whiteness. Here the commentator has arrived at a distinction almost identical to that in Anselm's *De grammatico* (see above, pp. 102–3).

One of the problems which had engaged even the earliest eleventh-century interpreters of Priscian was the nature of the verb 'to be': it was unlike other verbs in that it did not indicate any specific sort of action or being-acted-upon; and it seemed, as Boethius had pointed out (see above, p. 33), to demand a different analysis when used absolutely, to signify existence, and when used as the copula in a statement. The commentator has well-thought-out views on the subject (Hunt (ed.), 226:32 ff). One of the functions of the verb 'to be' is to indicate that something exists: 'Socrates is' means that Socrates is among the things which exist. This function, he argues, makes the verb suited to performing its other role of joining together two terms of a statement such as 'Socrates is an animal'; for what it does here is simply to couple the 'thing which is Socrates' and 'the thing which is an animal'. His analysis of 'Man is an animal' is similar: it means that 'that thing which is a man is that thing which is an animal'. But what about a statement such as 'Socrates is white'? It would be nonsense to maintain that white and Socrates were the same thing. The commentator is able to draw on his earlier analysis of the meaning and reference of type-adjectives to overcome this difficulty. In statements like 'Socrates is white', the verb 'to be' can either be treated in the way he has just explained (as what he calls 'the verb substantive') and the adjective analysed in terms of its reference: the meaning of the example would therefore be 'That thing which is Socrates is a white body'. Or the verb 'to be' can be taken to predicate white – in respect of its meaning, not its reference – of Socrates: in which case the example means that whiteness inheres in Socrates.

The commentator also applies this twofold analysis to a statement in which the verb 'to be' links a word to a definition of the meaning of the word. '"Dog" is an animal which barks' can be analysed as meaning either, he says, that that thing which is an animal which barks is one of the meanings of 'dog' (where 'is' has the function of the verb substantive); or (where 'is' has the force of predication) that the two phrases – 'dog' and 'an animal which barks' have the same meaning; or, alternatively, that this thing – an animal which barks – is what is meant by the word 'dog'. Here the commentator seems to have become confused, since it is difficult to see how this alternative analysis of 'to be' used predicatively of definitions differs from the analysis of it used as a verb substantive in such statements. And, more generally, there are serious oversights in the commentator's analysis of statements: most notably, that he seems not to take into account that it is possible to make statements about what does not or could never exist. But the sophistication of his approach to language and meaning opens up philosophical possibilities which, within fifty years, would be penetratingly explored.

Language and logic are connected in a different way by two other thinkers of the late eleventh century, both of whom, in dealing with traditional logical material, suggest that they are dealing not with the nature of things, but with the nature of words and statements in language. Garland, a master who produced a *computus* some time before 1088, was the author of a *Dialectica* which is of considerable importance in the history of formal logic, as an early attempt to bring together, in an independent treatise, what had been learnt from the antique logical textbooks about the analysis of argument. For Garland, the subject of logic is not reality, but argument as expressed in language: logic is a science of speech and disputation (*sermocinabilis vel disputabilis scientia*) (86:4). Consequently, he refuses to treat concepts such as universals as being more than linguistic entities. This view of the nature of logic is not, however, the result of thought about the problem, but simply a convenient way of disposing with questions that might, otherwise, have obstructed him in his task of formal, technical explanation.

Garland has been almost forgotten; but the name of Roscelin has lived on in the histories of philosophy as the first thoroughgoing exponent of nominalism – the view that universals are neither things nor concepts, but merely words. The details of Roscelin's life are hazy, and his ideas are known only at second hand. Born in about 1050, he was brought before a council in 1092, accused of propounding a heretical doctrine of the Trinity. Later, he taught logic to Abelard at Loches, earning – like most of Abelard's teachers – the bitter enmity of his pupil; a loathing reciprocated in

Roscelin's only certain surviving work, a letter to his former student. Roscelin's nominalism seems to have been a doctrine he held early in life. The various references to it merely make it clear that he thought that universals were words, not in the sense of words with a meaning, but – as Anselm put it in an attack perhaps aimed at Roscelin (*De incarnatione Verbi* II; II.9:21–3) – of breaths of air. Roscelin may have taken this physical analysis of words from Priscian (I.1); but there is no solid evidence of his having produced a theory of language which would explain how, if universals are just words, they are nevertheless meaningful ones. (For a treatise possibly recording Roscelin's views, see below, pp.134–5.)

In his *Dialectica*, Abelard records (554:37–555:9) another of Roscelin's theories, according to which nothing was made of parts, but parts, like species, were merely words. Roscelin reasoned that, since a whole is no more than the sum of its parts, then what is a part of the whole must be a part of itself. Abelard (554:10–12) neatly refutes this argument, by observing that a part of a whole indeed is a part of itself, but not of itself alone, rather of itself in conjunction with the other parts that make up the whole. Possibly the thought behind Roscelin's notion was that all classification – whether into parts and wholes, or individuals and species – is made by language and therefore amounts, in some sense, merely to words. But the argument he used to make his point seems flimsy, if not, perhaps, as Abelard describes it, 'insane'.

Part Three

1100–50

10 *Masters and schools*

Had Eriugena or Gerbert or Anselm awoken one morning to find himself in the 1130s or 1140s, the world of philosophy would in many respects have seemed to him familiar. The most important sources had not changed, and the fundamental problems were, in the main, those which had fascinated scholars of the three preceding centuries. Only after 1150, when the later books of Aristotle's logic had been absorbed and translation from the Arabic provided a new range of scientific materials, would the perspectives of medieval thought begin to alter. The change which characterized the first half of the century was one in the method of teaching and learning. Eriugena, Gerbert and Anselm had all been teachers; but their instruction took place in the leisure afforded by royal patronage, high ecclesiastical office or monastic seclusion. They had learned friends and learned enemies, but neither professional colleagues nor competitors. In the twelfth century teachers proliferated, and ambitious pupils were no longer content to be taught by a single master: in different disciplines they turned to different specialists; and even within one area of study they sought variety of opinion and approach. These external developments were not without influence on the manner of speculative thought. Logic, grammar, theology and physical science each began to develop a distinctive method, vocabulary and set of assumptions. Yet many a teacher interested himself in more than one of these areas; and the influence of logic on grammar, grammar on logic, and both logic and grammar on theology moulded the form of each of these disciplines.

In the twelfth century, as before, philosophy was not explicitly recognized as a separate subject, but was pursued within the various specialized branches of learning. Since the *Isagoge*, *Categories* and *De interpretatione*, all of them works rich in metaphysical problems, were still the logicians' most valued sources, the link between philosophy and logic remained especially strong; the more so, because differences of a more than merely formal nature were the stuff of controversy between rival dialecticians.

It will be clearest to examine philosophical problems as they were raised within each discipline: physical science; grammar and logic; and theology. But first a more general framework – biographical, chronological and geographic – will be sketched.

By 1100, northern France was undoubtedly the centre of higher learning in the West. It owed its pre-eminence no longer to the monasteries such as Bec and Fleury, but to the cathedral schools; and the most outstanding of these schools gained much of their reputation from the celebrity of their masters. In Laon, a town where scholarship had flourished in the ninth century, but declined in the tenth and eleventh, a certain Anselm began to teach sometime after about 1080. By 1100 Anselm had turned Laon into a leading centre of theology. Students thronged the small town and followed so closely their masters' methods that it is very difficult, now, to be sure exactly what writing is authentically Anselm's. The school at Chartres was already of considerable distinction in the eleventh century; at the beginning of the twelfth, it had a master who won for it new pupils. Bernard, who was chancellor of Chartres between 1119 and 1124, and taught there from 1114 and perhaps before, specialized in grammar and, like many of his contemporaries, interested himself in Priscian; he also had leanings towards the more metaphysical aspects of logic and established for himself a reputation as a Platonist.

Between them, Anselm and Bernard had as pupils many of the brilliant thinkers of the next generation; but the education of these pupils shows that Laon and Chartres were not the only influential schools at the turn of the century. Gilbert of Poitiers was taught first in his native Poitiers by a Master Hilary, then by Bernard at Chartres, and finally at Laon by Anselm and his brother, Radulf. William of Champeaux had as his teachers Manegold (probably not Manegold of Lautenbach) and Anselm of Laon. William of Conches appears to have been Bernard of Chartres's pupil. Adelard, an Englishman born in Bath, came to France during the 1100s in search of knowledge. He went to Tours and Laon before his curiosity led him to journey far further afield. One of Anselm's pupils in the years shortly before his death in 1117 was Abelard; but Abelard had been restless as a student, just as he would be restless as a teacher. Roscelin – Anselm of Bec's old adversary –

was teaching at Loches, and Abelard, probably still a teenager, went to study with him. He progressed to Paris, where William of Champeaux was now master at the cathedral school of Notre Dame.

Abelard had himself been a teacher for some years before he went to study at Laon. Abelard's career is in many respects the peculiar reflection of his personality: recklessly brilliant; quite lacking modesty yet strangely without self-confidence; hypercritical but unable to bear criticism. But it also set a pattern of independence, which more and more teachers would follow in the coming decades. Abelard, so he says, proved himself William's superior in argument, arousing his teacher's dislike. In 1104, when he was only twenty-five, Abelard decided that he would set up his own school of logic. He taught pupils at Melun, then, nearer Paris, at Corbeil; finally he tried to become the master at Notre Dame, as William (now a canon of St Victor) had been. William frustrated his efforts, and, after teaching again at Melun, he set up a school on Mt Ste Geneviève, just outside the city of Paris. Only after he returned from Laon, which he had left when Anselm refused to allow him to give his own theological lectures, did Abelard succeed in becoming a teacher at Notre Dame. The career of a contemporary of his, such as Gilbert, proceeded more smoothly: from a canonry in Poitiers (*c.* 1121) to one in Chartres (*c.* 1124), where, in 1126, he became chancellor. But Chartres did not remain the centre of Gilbert's activities as a teacher; and, even in the 1120s, he may have combined his official position there with freelance teaching in Paris.

When John of Salisbury journeyed from England in 1136 to study in France, he made straight for Paris. The Mt Ste Geneviève had now become an important place of study in its own right, the place for which a student anxious to learn about logic would head. Abelard was back there briefly, having become a monk after the violent end of his romance with Heloise (1118), founder of his own monastery (1122) and then abbot of a particularly unruly house in Brittany (1125). Abelard's place on the Mont was soon taken by two logicians of the next generation: Alberic and Robert of Melun. Another of John's teachers, probably on the Mont, was Thierry, a Breton who had seemingly been teaching in Paris for some time and who, by the 1140s, enjoyed an outstanding reputation. John studied rhetoric with Thierry; but Thierry – like so many famous masters of the time – was also a logician.

By the 1140s, the centre of Paris, as well as the Mont, offered the student a wide variety of lectures. In the bishop's hall, Gilbert of Poitiers would lecture in logic and theology before an audience three hundred strong. When he went to the see of Poitiers in 1142, his theological teaching was taken over by Robert Pullen – a master whose *Sentences* contain many Abelardian ideas; and, in 1144, by Simon of Poissy. An Englishman, Adam of Balsham, purveyed his particular brand of logical instruction at a school near the Petit-Pont. Richard 'the Bishop' – none of whose work has survived – taught on a wide range of subjects, including grammar and rhetoric. At the Abbey of St Victor there had been a tradition of learning ever since its founder, William of Champeaux, continued his lectures there. Under Hugh, teaching at St Victor came to be less concerned with logic, and more with the other liberal arts and theology. After Hugh's death in 1141, the study of theology at the abbey was continued by Achard, Richard and Andrew. A student might, it seems, study both at St Victor and under a freelance teacher: Clarembald of Arras, for instance, had as masters Thierry the Breton and Hugh of St Victor.

Pupils themselves soon became teachers. Peter Helias, who, like John of Salisbury, had attended Thierry's lectures, was himself lecturing on rhetoric by the late 1140s. John, back again in Paris, went to the lectures of Helias among others; but he also became a private teacher to the children of noblemen.

Outside Paris, cathedral chapters kept a far closer hold on teaching, and teachers lacked the freedom to solicit students on payment of a small fee. The reputation of a provincial school depended to a great extent on the quality of the master who happened to be there. Bernard Silvestris, author of perhaps the finest twelfth-century cosmological poem, was teaching at Tours probably from the 1130s. William of Conches (who seems, by 1138, to have been neither at Paris nor Chartres) doubtless lent lustre to wherever he taught, if, indeed, he still practised public lecturing. Chartres is associated with two eminent thinkers: Gilbert of Poitiers and Thierry the Breton. Thierry became chancellor there in about 1142; Gilbert had held the post until 1137, and perhaps for longer. Both these men are known to have taught at Paris, and it is very difficult to assess at what stage and to what extent they lectured at Chartres. It seems to have been quite common for a master, teaching independently in Paris, to hold an ecclesiastical position elsewhere: Richard 'the Bishop', for instance, was archdeacon of Coutances; Thierry himself was probably archdeacon of Dreux whilst he taught in Paris. The diocese of Chartres was a very large one, stretching to the left bank of the Seine: a position in the cathedral chapter might have been thought an excellent concomitant to a distinguished teaching career in Paris. Yet one cannot be sure that Gilbert and Thierry did not spend distinct stages of their careers at Chartres and at Paris; and there is no evidence that Thierry went on teaching at all after he had become chancellor.

For a certain type of inquisitive scholar, interested in cosmology, physics and biology rather than logic or theology, neither Paris nor the other schools could satisfy his curiosity. Before 1109, Adelard of Bath had set out on a journey which lasted for seven years and took him to Salerno, Syracuse, Tarsus and Jerusalem, bringing him into contact with Arabic learning without his having to leave the area of Christian rule. For later scholars in search of Islamic knowledge of the sciences, Spain was a more obvious destination. Hermann of Carinthia was one of the earliest northerners to make his way there and set about translating from the Arabic into Latin. He had contacts with the scholars of northern France, as he demonstrated by dedicating his translation of Ptolemy's *Planisphere* to Thierry in 1143. In the second half of the century, the Spanish centres of translation would attract scholars from all over Europe; and men such as Robert of Chester, Hugh of Santalla and Gerard of Cremona would provide the Latin world with new sources of scientific and mathematical knowledge.

As teachers and students flocked to Paris and elsewhere to pursue secular learning and theology, a very different vocation stirred the minds and changed the lives of some of their contemporaries. The austere Cistercian order gained new members and new influence under the sway of St Bernard. A very distinctive type of mystical theology, literary in its expression and wide-ranging in its use of patristic sources, was developed by Bernard and his follower William of St Thierry. However, the strongest impact which Bernard and William had on the higher intellectual life of the time was through their violent opposition to ideas which they thought heretical. Three of the leading masters of the time were subject to their attacks: William of Conches, Abelard and Gilbert of Poitiers. William was criticized by William of St Thierry for remarks in his *Philosophia mundi* (*c.* 1122) which were supposedly contrary to Scripture; Abelard and Gilbert were challenged by Bernard over their views on the Trinity. The grammarian of Conches took into account at least some of William's criticisms when he revised his work about twenty years later. Abelard, who had already been forced to burn a copy of his work on the Trinity by the council of Soissons in 1121, made a sudden decision not to plead before the council which had been assembled at Sens in 1140, but to appeal to the Pope. Undefended, Abelard's work was condemned as heretical without being read; and the Pope merely ratified the decision of the council. Gilbert's appearance at the council of Reims (1148) had a rather different outcome. Gilbert's subtlety and learning impressed the assembly; and conceding perhaps more to his opponents than he really believed, Gilbert managed to substitute, for the condemnation they demanded, an undertaking that he would correct his book in accordance with an agreed profession of faith, if it needed correction.

Gilbert's impressive performance at Reims is one of the latest testimonies to his brilliant generation. Already Abelard, sick since the Council of Sens, had died (1142/4) under the care of Peter the Venerable, abbot of Cluny. Gilbert lived until 1154. And in that year William of Conches was still alive and enjoying considerable celebrity; but after this time he too disappears from the historical record. A few years before, Thierry had given his books to the library of Chartres and, renouncing the title of 'doctor', retired into monastic solitude. A younger generation of masters would absorb and develop the new material, for which their teachers' work had made them ready.

11 *The antique philosophical tradition: scholarship, science and poetry*

The sources for the antique philosophical tradition had hardly changed between the ninth and twelfth centuries: Plato's *Timaeus* with Calcidius's commentary, Macrobius' commentary on the *Somnium Scipionis*, Boethius' *Consolation of Philosophy*. But the careful, scholarly attention which these texts began to receive from some of their readers, is new; and it is accompanied by a degree of respect – at times, indeed, reverence – for Plato, which is unparalleled even in the most enthusiastic Platonists of the earlier Middle Ages.

The result of this detailed attention to the sources of Platonism was not the development of a form of Platonic philosophy. The antique texts contained little that could inspire genuinely philosophical speculation: they indicated the outlines of a metaphysical system, without providing the arguments to support it; and they contained a vast store of scientific information. In the tenth and eleventh centuries, scholars concentrated, though not exclusively, on the metaphysical ideas in the ancient works; the more thorough readers of the twelfth century were preoccupied by their scientific aspect. The work of William of Conches illustrates this approach and the reasons behind it.

William of Conches

John of Salisbury describes his master, William, as a grammarian. The term is appropriate not only because of William's work on Priscian (see below, pp.129–30), but also on account of his characteristic scholarly method. Whatever the text, William approaches it with a grammarian's care and thoroughness. He is at the service of his authors; and, whether he is providing a word-by-word gloss, discussing the meaning behind what he takes to be a metaphor, or explaining more broadly a theory advanced, his task is seen as helping others to understand an authoritative text. When he had already glossed Boethius' *Consolation*, Macrobius' *Commentary* and, perhaps, Martianus Capella, he produced an independent work, the *Philosophia mundi* (revised later as the *Dragmaticon*, 1144–9). But its purpose was not to replace the antique authorities, but rather to aid their comprehension. It is indicative of this attitude that, after writing the *Philosophia*, William returned to the *Timaeus* and rewrote an earlier set of his glosses to this work.

William's great respect for his ancient authorities, and his wish to expound them thoroughly and in detail, posed him a serious problem. From patristic times Christians had had to choose whether to reject Platonic metaphysics as incompatible with their faith, or, by adapting and selecting them, to preserve many concepts and theories developed by Plato and his followers. But there was little chance, in a word-by-word commentary on the *Timaeus*, to refashion pagan metaphysics into a system coherent and yet fully compatible with Christianity: the text was too close to allow such freedom of movement. And, whilst Boethius and even Macrobius caused fewer problems, Plato was William's revered authority; and he realized that the *Timaeus* provided a key to much in the other ancient texts.

William tackled this problem from two directions. He admitted that his pagan sources were pagan; that they could not always be expected to tell the truth; and that it would be wrong to follow them into heresy (for example, Glosses to Macrobius II.xvii.13; *Dragmaticon* 18). But this attitude of scholarly detachment merely provided an 'emergency exit', the chance for the exegete to preserve his Christian orthodoxy when every other means failed. William was no mere antiquarian: his interpretative enterprise would have seemed to him futile, had it produced only a set of interesting falsehoods. For the most part, then, he adopted a very different stance, and asserted – indeed most probably believed – that the divergences between Plato's teaching and that of Christianity were, with few exceptions, apparent rather than real. The casual reader of the antique authorities might be misled by the manner of expression and by metaphor into finding doctrines contrary to the faith: it was for the skilled and faithful interpreter, like William, to correct him. Such syncretism was novel, not in its concept, but in the extent of its application; for William was thereby committed to interpreting the letter of patently pagan philosophical texts in a Christian sense. (A precedent might be sought in the exegesis of classical *literary* texts; but these presented different problems, and offered different rewards.) William's method produced dissimilar results, with respect to the two most important aspects of his authorities. The scientific material could be expounded literally and elaborated from fresh sources; the meta-physical ideas were interpreted in such a way as to make them both unobjectionable and uninformative. This sacrifice of Platonic metaphysics is not one which William would have found difficult to make: his cast of mind inclined him towards physical, rather than abstract explanations; and his interests in science, and in an-tique authorities, can hardly have been separate or coincidental in their development.

A few examples will show how William deals with metaphysical notions in his text which do not, at first sight, appear to accord with Christianity. Sometimes William need only point out an implicit qualification which he assumes his author to be making: when, for instance, Plato talks of a final return of sinners to a blessed state, he is not uttering heresy, since he means to refer only to the souls in purgatory (*Timaeus* glosses 219–20). Sometimes William can look to a long tradition of Christian–Platonic syncre-tism to help him: the Ideas are interpreted by him as thoughts in the mind of God – a view convenient for a monotheist which goes back at least to Philo, the Alexandrian Jewish exegete (*c.* 25 B.C.–*c.* A.D. 50) (*Timaeus* glosses 126). Or when Boethius, following Neoplatonic interpretation of the *Timaeus*, talks of pre-existent souls being placed on light chariots and sown through heaven and earth (*Consolation* III.m.ix:18–20), William is able to follow a meta-phorical interpretation suggested already in the tenth century by Remigius of Auxerre: 'by the reason of his soul man transcends the stars and finds his creator above them' (*Consolation* glosses 77). The supposition that his authorities used *integumenta* – extended metaphors or meaningful myths – is one of William's most valuable exegetical tools. He can use it to find a deeper meaning to mythological allusions; or it can help to explain away embarrassing metaphysical concepts, such as the World-Soul.

When William first came upon the concept of the World-Soul in glossing the *Consolation*, he felt that he could identify it with the Holy Spirit, thereby avoiding any danger of divergence be-tween the Platonic and the Christian universe. But this, he soon realizes, is not without its own problems, since there is a danger of suggesting that the third person of the Trinity is not uncreated. In his glosses to Macrobius, William tries to guard against such a possibility by speculating, rather uneasily, that his author is using words in an unusual way. In the *Philosophia mundi* he falls back on quoting a number of alternative opinions, without giving his approval to any one in particular. The extended treatment of the World-Soul and its functions in the *Timaeus* makes it impossible for William to avoid discussion of the concept in his glosses to this work (144 ff). He will 'neither affirm nor deny' that it is the Holy Spirit. Plato's description of the World-Soul is, he considers, an *integumentum*. As such, it can have a number of meanings; and all those which William discovers avoid anything that might be metaphysically embarrassing for a Christian. In describing the World-Soul, Plato is really describing the world and its inhabitants: referring to the different degrees of life – vegetative, sensitive and rational; or to the differences and similarities between species; or to the motions of the universe. When, much later (1144–9), William came to revise his *Philosophia mundi* as the *Dragmaticon*, he decided that he could follow the simplest course of all in dealing with the troublesome concept of the World-Soul: he omitted it entirely.

The physical and cosmological parts of his antique texts presented William with no such difficulties. And the *Timaeus* provided him with exactly the sort of scientific material in which the Genesis story of creation was so deficient. Whereas the Church Fathers had embroidered their commentaries on the beginning of Genesis with whatever physics and cosmology they knew or thought appropriate, William could present the story of the creation through a text far superior in its detail, and only slightly less venerable in its authority. William's physical account of the creation of the universe is his outstanding intellectual achievement, and it forms a central theme in the *Philosophia mundi* (48D ff) and the *Dragmaticon* (68 ff), as well as in the glosses to the *Timaeus*. The explanation of how heaven, earth and their inhabitants came into being is especially ingenious, if naive. There were, initially, the four elements: at the top fire, then air, then water and then earth. The water entirely covered the earth and consequently was pushed up into the greater part of the air. The fire, air and water were all thicker than they have since been; and so some earthy and watery substances inhered in the thickness of the air and fire. When these had been dried and coagulated by the warmth of the fire, they formed the stars. The stars, being of a fiery nature, began to move, and their movement heated the air. From the air, the water was heated and produced the birds and fishes. The consequent diminution of the stock of water caused spots of earth to appear in the midst of the waters. The earth had been made muddy by the water and, when this mud boiled in the heat, the various types of animal, including man, were created from it; but man's soul, William is careful to add, was created directly by God (*Timaeus* glosses 119–22; substantially the same account in *Philosophia mundi* and *Dragmaticon*).

This is not a philosopher's reading of Plato: the concern is entirely with physical cause and effect rather than abstract analysis. William's predominant interest in scientific explanation is also demonstrated by his devotion of the greater part of the *Philosophia mundi* and the *Dragmaticon* to physical, cosmological, geographical and meteorological subjects. And it is perhaps most strikingly evident when William has to tackle the question which might seem least suited of any to a scientific approach: how can one know that God exists? William replies by asking how the body, which is naturally heavy, can move: there must be a spirit which moves it. But heaviness is repugnant to the spirit; and therefore there must be some wisdom which joined the spirit to the body and which keeps it there. Whose is this wisdom? It cannot be that of a creature, and so it must be the Creator's. This argument (*Philosophia mundi* 41A–C; *Timaeus* glosses 101; *Dragmaticon* 308–9) moves from a physical premise through a series of deductions from cause and effect. The impression of flimsiness it gives is perhaps due to the inappropriateness of such scientific reasoning to the manifestation of God.

If, outside his work on Priscian, William is at any time a philosopher, it is when he finds himself obliged to answer questions about the scope of scientific investigation. For, whilst he is willing to make almost any sacrifice of the metaphysical elements in his authorities which faith might demand, he believes that a large area of scientific explanation is compatible with Christianity. Nature cannot operate without God's willing it; but it is no derogation of the Creator's powers to suggest that he works *through* natural processes (cf. *Timaeus* glosses 122). Scripture says that certain things were made: how can it be thought a derogation of its authority, asks William in the *Philosophia mundi*, to explain the manner in which they were made? 'In every case', he says, 'one should look for a reason, and continue enquiring, whilst remaining in the Catholic faith; then one should seek help; and only then, if that fails, say that one accepts something on faith' (*Philosophia mundi* 56C). But is it not always a good enough explanation to say: 'God made it'? Absolutely not, says William. God has the power to perform miracles, but he does not in general use it: he does not do what he could do. The investigator must therefore demonstrate how things are, or for what reason they are as they are (58C). William admits that, at times, God does work directly, as in his first creation of the elements of all things from nothing, and in occasional interventions in the course of things. But, in general, he allows nature to serve him, creating in its own way one similar being from another (*Consolation* glosses 128). The position has the patristic precedent of Augustine's *De Genesi ad litteram*; William articulates its consequences more explicitly, and uses them as the justification of his whole scientific enterprise.

A discussion in the *Dragmaticon* shows with especial clarity William's view of the scope of science being put to use. Basing himself on the *Pantechne* of Constantine the African (an eleventh-century translator), William has argued that, physically speaking, the elements consist of small particles, which cannot be further subdivided, and, though corporeal, cannot be seen except in quantity. The elements of traditional Platonic and Aristotelian physics – water, earth, air and fire – are not elements but 'elemented things'. When this theory is put forward by the Philosopher in the *Dragmaticon*, the Duke, his imagined interlocutor, suggests disparagingly that it seems like Epicureanism (27). The Philosopher replies by stating that no sect is so wrong in everything as not to be right in something. The Epicureans were correct in believing that the world is made up of atoms, but wrong in thinking that the atoms were without beginning. Scientific explanation, William is suggesting, can be taken right back to the most fundamental constituents of things; but beyond them it is to God that the thinker must look.

Minor cosmological works

William was not alone in his scientific reading of antique philosophical texts, or in the special interest in the creation of the universe which it stimulated. The *De mundi constitutione* – once, and certainly wrongly, attributed to Bede – most probably dates from the beginning of the twelfth century; its incoherence suggests that it was a compilation, rather than an integral work. Heavily influenced by Macrobius, the writer dwells mostly on scientific matters: the stars and their motions, the lands of the earth, the weather and its causes. But he includes a section on the soul, which offers as a possibility a far more literal interpretation of the World-Soul than William had ever countenanced.

Thierry the Breton, so his pupil Clarembald of Arras reports, wrote a short work on the six days of the Creation in which he showed 'how, according to physical reasons alone, the exemplary form operating in matter produced all things'. Some scholars have thought that Thierry's work is preserved, intact, in a letter of Clarembald's; it is far more probable that the letter contains only Clarembald's own little treatise, which he says he has based on his reading of Thierry's. Through Clarembald's adaptation (if it is this), Thierry's discussion appears as one which – written perhaps ten years after the *Philosophia mundi* – places William's type of scientific account of creation into relation with the Genesis story, rather than the *Timaeus*; and there is some evidence that, in Thierry's original, the links with Scripture were even closer. Thierry has some points directly in common with William, such as the explanation (559:16–18) of the appearance of earth among the waters by a diminution in the stock of water; although, for Thierry, the water has been vaporized to form, first, the waters above the firmament (cf. Genesis 1,7), and then the stars. Thierry's views about the creation of the fishes, birds, animals and man remain unknown, because Clarembald's adaptation tails off, rather inconsequentially, into a discussion of the Trinity (see below, p.146).

Bernard Silvestris

The one twelfth-century work which used the *Timaeus* to present an account of the creation very different from William's (or Thierry's) scientific analysis, is the *Cosmographia* of Bernard Silvestris. Here, however, Platonism is set out in literary and imaginative terms which favour the presentation of a metaphysical system rather than philosophical arguments.

Bernard was not the first twelfth-century scholar to present a discussion of Platonic inspiration in distinctively literary terms, although his predecessor, Adelard of Bath, displays neither Bernard's detailed knowledge of the *Timaeus* nor his talent as writer and poet. Adelard wrote his *De eodem et diverso* in about 1116, perhaps just after his return from Sicily, Greece and the Holy Land. In this little treatise he describes the apparition of two maidens, Philocosmia (love of the world) and Philosophia (love of wisdom), the former accompanied by representations of wealth, power, honour, fame and pleasure, the latter by figures of the seven liberal arts. Philocosmia tries to draw Adelard away from the pursuit of wisdom, pointing out to him the many disagreements among learned men, and their lack of worldly success. Philosophia rebuts her arguments, and proceeds to give brief descriptions of each of the liberal arts. The veneer of allegory is therefore very thin; and, although Adelard mixes poetry with his prose, the two metrical interludes are brief. The title is Platonic, referring to the Sameness and Difference which go into the constitution of the World-Soul; and Plato appears to be Philosophia's preferred thinker, although she emphasizes that his theories do not contradict Aristotle's: Aristotle based his reflections on composite, sensible things, whereas Plato tried to understand things from their origins, before their embodiment (11:6–11; for Adelard's theory of universals, see below, p.132). However, Martianus Capella's *De nuptiis* provides more of a model for Adelard than the *Timaeus*; and the defence of learning is too general to leave room for the details of any given metaphysical system.

Bernard Silvestris' *Cosmographia* is an allegorical presentation of the metaphysical and physical story of the creation. Bernard writes in a mixture of verse and close-textured prose, using a Latin rich in suggestive subtlety and often striking by its lexicographical inventiveness or its purposeful liberty of syntax. In the first part of the work, the *Megacosmus*, Bernard follows the basic lines of Plato's cosmogony: the world is ordered by the imposition of form on unformed matter. He expresses this in dramatic terms. Natura begins the poem by complaining to Noys (the world of Ideas) of the rough formlessness of Silva (matter). Noys responds by imposing order, stage by stage, on Silva, until, by the end of the *Megacosmus*, the heavens, the earth, the animals, plants and fishes have been created. Bernard also introduces the World-Soul or, as he usually calls it, Endelichia, which is said to emanate from Noys. Its purpose is not, as in the *Timaeus*, to be used for an elaborate cosmological metaphor; rather – in the manner of the Neoplatonic hypostasis of Soul – it is an intermediary between Noys and material things, helping to bring the irregularity of Silva into harmony and bringing life to the sensible world.

In the second part of the book, the *Microcosmus*, Bernard describes the creation of Man. He begins, however, by sending Natura on a journey through the heavens, to search for two helpmates in this task: Urania, the principle of heavenly existence, and Physis, the principle of earthly existence. This journey and the return from it allows Bernard to discuss the heavenly spheres and their influence on human character and destinies: a motif suggested by Macrobius but greatly elaborated. Urania, Natura and Physis set about constructing Man, each of them provided with a special tool: Urania with a mirror, in which the metaphysical aspects of the universe – the Ideas, Silva, Endelichia, the forms – are shown; Natura with a tablet recording all the events, from the initial ordering of Silva, which will make up the history of the world;

and Physis with a book about the physical constitution of the world and of man. Combining the work of Urania and Physis, Natura forms Man; and his physiological composition is then discussed in some detail.

From such a summary it is impossible to gain an idea of the *Cosmographia*'s great interest and value as literature; of the imaginative qualities which made it a widely read poem in the Middle Ages and gave it great influence on the development of both Latin and vernacular poetry. Yet the rough outline of Bernard's poem does show why the *Cosmographia* should be considered as a work which uses metaphysical ideas, rather than as an independent contribution to philosophy. Bernard's aims are not those of a philosopher – even a bad philosopher. He does not analyse or argue; nor does he seek economy or particular coherence in his use of metaphysical concepts. His task is indeed the same as a philosopher's: to explain the nature of reality. But the explanation which he offers is in the terms of poetic metaphor. At the summit of Bernard's universe is God, indescribable and, directly, unknowable by any lesser being. The various personifications through which God operates, and the story of creation in which they act, are indirect attempts by Bernard to express truths about the divine ordering of the universe. The *Cosmographia* does not provide an alternative to the story of Genesis, but rather an aid towards understanding the same ineffable truth as that presented by Scripture. Unconstrained by the need to put forward what was literally true, Bernard could use the *Timaeus* and Macrobius with fewer Christian scruples, and thus less need for learned reinterpretation, than William of Conches. And the *Timaeus*, for so long and so inappropriately used as a source-book for Platonic philosophy, is employed in a way perhaps closer to its author's intentions, as basis for the elaboration of a myth.

12 *Grammar and logic*

Grammar

Grammar and logic had produced their profoundest philosophical consequences in the eleventh century when most closely combined; they would do so again, in the twelfth, in the work of Peter Abelard. Abelard was certainly not the only thinker to be interested in both grammar and logic, but most of his contemporaries tried to separate these two disciplines as much as possible.

An explicit example of this is provided by William of Champeaux's views on the grammatical and logical meanings of statements, recorded by Abelard (in the glosses to *De differentiis topicis* from the commentary *Ingredientibus* . . . pp. 271:38 ff). For the grammarian, a statement such as 'Socrates is white' is to be analysed as saying that 'Socrates' and 'white' are names for the same thing; Socrates is that thing which is affected by whiteness. And the sentence 'Socrates is whiteness' would, similarly, identify Socrates with, not the thing that is white, but whiteness itself; it would thus, for the grammarian, have a different meaning from 'Socrates is white'. But not for the logician: for him both sentences mean that whiteness inheres in Socrates. Every statement, then, has two meanings: for the grammarian, according to the 'joining of essences' – saying that one thing and another are the same; and for the logician, according to 'simple inherence'. William believes that the logicians' interpretation is 'wider and in a certain way superior' to that of the grammarians. William's terms derive from and clarify the grammatical ideas of the late eleventh century; but, by distinguishing so sharply between grammatical and logical modes of interpretation, William avoids the challenge offered to traditional logical concepts by an awareness of the workings of language.

In the Priscian commentaries of 1100–50 the same tendency can be seen. The eleventh-century commentary was revised in at least one version dating back to about 1100, but little of philosophical interest seems to have been added to it. Probably in the early 1120s, William of Conches composed a commentary on the *Institutiones*, which he revised some years later, when already advanced in age. William's commentary was used as a source by Peter Helias, in his *Summa super Priscianum*, composed before 1148.

William assigns a twofold function to names, both of individuals and types. Proper names signify both a particular substance (Socrates, for instance) and its individual quality (*Socratitas*, as Boethius had suggested in discussing the *De interpretatione*). Type-names signify universal things and some common quality. The way in which type-names signify universals is explained as being not by referring just to one individual, nor to all the individuals of the type, but by referring to any such individual, but to no one in particular: 'it signifies substance in such a way that it is not a particular substance'. To justify this position, William makes an interesting reference to the distinction between things, thoughts and words. Although there is no such thing as a substance which is not some particular substance, it is possible to think of a substance in this way; and the way in which we think and understand things is what we express in words.

William has touched on a very important point. Priscian had suggested principally that language referred directly to reality; the *De interpretatione* and Boethius' commentaries on it argued that language referred to thoughts. The conflict between these two views might be – indeed was, in the work of Abelard – the beginning of a deep analysis of the theory of meaning. But William seems not to notice that his recourse to thought as what is signified by language is at odds with the rest of his approach: for him, it seems to be an easy way out of a problem which threatened to obscure the clarity of his distinctions.

Peter Helias also observes (1:34–6) that speech is a representation of thought, not reality; and, like William, he does not allow this remark to modify his general approach. More clearly than any of his predecessors, Helias wishes to make the commentary of Priscian the province of the grammarian and to exclude logical and philosophical considerations so far as possible. To this end he makes use of a distinction, very similar to William of Champeaux's, between the ways of speaking of grammarians and logicians. To a grammarian, every name signifies both substance and quality; but, to the logician, a word like 'whiteness' signifies only a quality. Yet, says Helias (16:56–62), the grammarian and the logician do not disagree, but each speaks in the fashion proper to his discipline. Such a distinction spares a grammarian like Helias from exploring the philosophical consequences which his statements about grammar might suggest.

Fuller edition and study of twelfth-century grammatical texts might well alter this somewhat disappointing picture of the philosophical interests of grammarians. However, a small piece of evidence suggests that it might be substantially correct. A set of passages entitled *Tractatus glosarum Prisciani* records, first, what seem to be some very early twelfth-century discussions on subjects raised by the *Institutiones*, and then comments on the same area by masters of the late 1130s and 1140s. The earlier discussions seem to have had something of the philosophical vigour (and confusion) of the eleventh-century commentary; the masters of the mid-century – who include Albricus (Alberic, the successor of Abelard?), William of Conches and Thedricus (Thierry of Chartres?) – seem to have explained away the problems raised by Priscian's comments, rather than to have explored their philosophical implications.

Logic

There are four logical schools of the period 1100–50 about which something definite is known: that of Abelard, who taught logic from about 1104 onwards, and may have revised his logical textbook, the *Dialectica*, as late as the 1140s; of William of Champeaux, Abelard's teacher, at Notre Dame in Paris and, after 1108, at the Abbey of St Victor; of Adam of Balsham, who had a logical school near the Petit-Pont in the 1140s and later; and Alberic, Abelard's successor as a teacher on the Mt Ste Geneviève from about 1138 onwards. (The work of Robert of Melun, Alberic's colleague, seems to date from after 1150.)

The enthusiasm with which logic was studied from 1100 onwards owed little, in the first three decades of the century, to the discovery of new texts. The works of ancient logic generally studied – Porphyry's *Isagoge*, Aristotle's *Categories* and *De interpretatione*, Cicero's *Topics* along with Boethius' commentaries and monographs – were those known by the beginning of the eleventh century. Boethius' translation of the *Prior Analytics* is found in Thierry of Chartres's *Heptateuchon*, a collection of texts for school use compiled in about 1140. Abelard uses this version of the translation in his *Dialectica* and might have known it when he wrote his logical commentary *Ingredientibus* . . . (finished before about 1118). However, Abelard does not go beyond a rare quotation or allusion to this work: it is a text which neither he nor his contemporaries had absorbed into the mainstream of their logical thought. William of Champeaux and Alberic both worked on the basis of the texts of the 'Old' logic. Only Adam of Balsham, in the *Ars disserendi* which he wrote in the 1140s or later, shows a wider range of reading. He knows both the *De sophisticis elenchis*, introduced from about 1135, and the *Topics* of Aristotle, which first begins to be used a little later.

The interests of the four masters of these schools were predominantly technical. In the case of Abelard, this technical approach was complemented by a willingness to deal with philosophical problems whenever they arose. By contrast, Adam of Balsham's approach was explicitly formal: logic was for him the study of the principles of arguing – the investigation of a system in language, not of the relationship between language and reality or of reality itself. William of Champeaux seems to have been willing to stray into philosophical discussion on occasion: his views on the meaning of statements are preserved by Abelard (see above, p.128); he makes some comments on future contingents in a theological passage (see below, pp.140–1), and he had views on the nature of universals. The philosophical passages in texts from the school of Alberic appear, so far as they have been investigated at present, to derive in a rather unimaginative way, either from Abelard or Boethius; even the theory of universals probably current in this school (see below, pp.133–4) may well be a deformation of Abelard's.

The problem of universals is the one philosophical subject about which it is possible to reconstruct a many-sided argument among logicians of the earlier twelfth century, including some logicians who did not obviously belong to one of the four schools about which more is known. Most of the texts are anonymous; they borrow widely from one another, and it is rarely possible to date them or place them in order. But the historian is lucky in having two contemporary accounts which list the various opinions that were advanced. One is Abelard's, in his commentary *Ingredientibus* . . . (10:17–16:18) and his commentary *Nostrorum petitioni* . . . (513:13–522:32); the other John of Salisbury's in his *Metalogicon* (II.17; 91:11–96:2), written in the 1160s, but referring mainly to the ideas current when John was a student in the 1130s and 1140s. The former account has the benefit of that clarity which an acute mind can bring to the exposition of theories often confusedly expressed by their advocates; the latter is useful because, in some cases, it identifies the adherents of the views it mentions. Other contributors to the debate also list, and argue against, views about universals with which they disagree; but the comments of Abelard and John are, in their various ways, the fullest and most useful.

Most, though not all, of these twelfth-century thinkers are realists in their view of universals. They consider that, in some sense, universals are things; and their problem is to determine what sort of things. One type of realism is the theory of Platonic Ideas: that universals are separate from particulars, which are dependent on them for their being. It was not widespread, at least not in the context of logical discussions, in this period. John of Salisbury mentions Bernard of Chartres, at the beginning of the century, and Walter of Mortagne, in his own time, as its adherents. A text reporting logical teaching at the school of St Victor under William of Champeaux (incipit *Quid significet oratio* . . .) summarizes the Platonic doctrine of recollection (142), which would imply a Platonic theory of universals; but this was not William's own view.

William, at first – as Abelard reports (*Historia Calamitatum* 65:82–9) – had been an advocate of essential essence realism, according to which a species is a substance present essentially in all its members, which differ from one another by inferior forms (that is to say, accidents). This view, which is close to one expressed in Boethius' *Opuscula sacra*, did not stand up to scrutiny. Abelard attacked it violently and forced his master to adopt what was called an 'indifference' theory of universals.

The characteristic of indifference theories is, in effect, to identify particulars with the universal. Plato and Socrates are both men because man is in each of them, not essentially, but indifferently: that in respect of which Plato is a man is in no way different from that in respect of which Socrates is a man. An expression of this theory in its simplest form is found in one of William of Champeaux's theological sentences: 'we say that Peter and Paul are the same in that they are men . . . and that, for instance, each of them is rational, each of them is mortal. But, if we are to be correct, the humanity of each is not the same, but similar, since they are two [different] men' (192:116–20). Another early exponent of the indifference theory was Adelard of Bath in his *De eodem et diverso* (22:16 ff).

The thinkers who followed the indifference theory are divided by Abelard into two groups. One considered that universals consisted in the collection of all the individuals 'indifferently' of the same kind; the other that they consisted not only in the collection of individuals, but were to be found in each individual itself – that is to say, the species man would be not only the collection of all men, but also each man in that he is a man. John of Salisbury identifies Jocelyn, Bishop of Soissons, as an exponent of the first, collection theory. This theory is that defended in an anonymous treatise (incipit *Totum integrum . . .*), which deals with a number of logical subjects, including the nature of parts and wholes, and the relationship between the physical and logical analysis of an object. According to the writer (524–5), the species 'is not that essence of man which is in Socrates alone or that which is in any other individual, but the whole collection of such essences brought together from each single thing of this type'. Although 'essentially' this collection is many, it is, the writer says, considered to be one species, one universal thing, by the authorities, just as a people, though made up of many individuals, is said to be one.

The second type of indifference theory, in which universal and particular are more closely identified, was espoused, says John of Salisbury, by Walter of Mortagne, before he became a Platonist. Arguing from Boethius' dictum that everything which exists is singular in number, he held that universals were essentially one with particular things, and that Plato, for instance, is an individual, in that he is Plato; a species, in that he is a man; a genus, in that he is an animal; and a most general genus, in that he is a substance. A very similar line of argument is used to expound similar ideas in an anonymous treatise (incipit *Quoniam de generali . . .*), which, for this reason, is attributed by its editor to Walter. It is a thorough consideration of the problem of universals, summarizing and arguing against other current theories and supporting its own ideas against obvious objections.

Two other theories, although sharing points in common with the indifference theory, should be distinguished from it. Gilbert of Poitiers certainly makes use of the notion of indifference; but, as analysis shows (see below, pp.149 ff), the nature of his approach to the problem of universals is unique and intimately connected with his other ideas. In the school of Alberic, Abelard's successor on Mt Ste Geneviève, the approach to the problem of universals appears to have been characterized by the use of the term '*maneries*'. The meaning of this strange word, and the use to which it was put, is best illustrated in an anonymous treatise (incipit *Sunt quidam . . .*). Genera and species are, the writer says (68), 'manners' (*maneries*) of things; and (69) to predicate a genus of many things is simply to say that the things are of this or that manner. The writer agrees with the indifference theorists that one can say that the 'species man is in the single individuals', but this means no more than to say that 'every property of man comes together in each single man'. The word '*maneries*' seems to have been coined, and to be so used, in order to suggest that universals are not, in the proper sense, things; and indeed the writer allows that universals are both terms (*termini*) and things, although he insists that they are mainly things (66). Despite its links with indifference theories, this view of universals seems very much like a simplified version of Abelard's (see below, pp. 136–9), stripped of the psychological and linguistic aspects which make it so remarkable, and presented in a manner more in accord with the general debate.

A few thinkers in the early twelfth century stood aside from the realism of their contemporaries and sought a different type of explanation of the nature of universals. Both John of Salisbury and Abelard mention the theory that universals are not things, but thoughts. Abelard considers the theory to be applicable only to thoughts in the mind of God (see below, p. 139). John, who mentions Cicero and Boethius as sources of the theory, takes it as applying to the human mind; but he has little respect for its proponents.

At the end of the eleventh century, Roscelin had proposed that universals were merely words (see above, pp. 109–10). This opinion is very frequently mentioned, and rebutted, by the proponents of other theories; hardly ever is it advanced in its own right. One text, entitled *Sententia de universalibus secundum magistrum R.*, is an exception; it is also exceptional because it uses ideas developed in connection with grammar in a logical discussion. The author does not say simply, as Roscelin did, or is reputed to have done, that universals are words. Rather, he says that 'since things are considered in different ways according to the different meanings of the words used for them' (326), he will begin his discussion by looking at words. He refers to Priscian and says that a general word, like 'man', can be considered either appellatively or properly. Appellatively it refers to each individual who is a man and it signifies the fact that he has in him a certain universal nature – that he is a rational, mortal animal. Properly, the word 'man' means man, the universal, in its simplicity: it names this universal and 'makes it as it were a single subject' – as for instance in the sentence 'Man is a species'.

What is it that 'man', taken as a proper name, refers to? The writer explains that it is the potential material and figure (*figura*) of all individual men. It becomes in act a mortal animal (327), but only 'in figure', since it is the potential material of many different men whose actual material is, except in figure, different. The writer goes on (328) to add some psychological remarks, which seem to draw on Boethius' theory of abstraction in his second commentary to the *Isagoge* and his discussion of the mind in the commentaries to *De interpretatione* (see above, pp. 32–3), but use a fourfold division of human faculties. With his senses man perceives things as they are; with his imagination he can perceive things when they are absent. The reason, however, considers individuals as members of species: it understands what is signified by 'man' as an appellative word – that each individual man has in him a certain universal nature. Only the intellect considers the species in itself and, regarding Socrates, sees not the nature of man informing him, but the species man in its purity.

Although the writer does not clarify all of the ideas he raises, this is a remarkable little treatise, which puts forward a theory that bears more resemblance to Abelard's than any other of the time. Who was the writer, and did he work before or after Abelard? The idea, entertained by the work's editor, that the Master R. was Roscelin and the treatise therefore the work of a pupil, is attractive and not unreasonable: Roscelin may well have tried to modify his theory of universals as words in the sort of way indicated by this work. Abelard perhaps learned more from his early master than he liked to acknowledge.

Abelard's philosophy of logic

With the exception of some short glosses (incipit *Intentio Porphyrii* . . .) Abelard's thoughts on logic are contained in three works: a commentary (incipit *Ingredientibus* . . .) on the *Isagoge*, *Categories*, *De interpretatione* and Boethius' *De differentiis topicis*, written before 1118; a commentary on the *Isagoge* (incipit *Nostrorum petitioni* . . .), written in about 1124; and the *Dialectica*, an independent logical textbook which was probably begun, in some form, before 1118, but appears to have been revised, perhaps more than once, later in Abelard's life.

The features of Abelard's philosophy of logic which set him apart from the thinkers of his day are most clearly evident in his treatment of two very difficult subjects: universals, and the meaning of statements. For him, they are very closely connected. In each of his commentaries, he examines very fully the different theories, both ancient and contemporary, whereby universals are things: to all of them he finds convincing objections. Universals, he concludes (LI = *Ingredientibus* . . . 16:19–22; *Nostrorum petitioni*

. . . 522:10 ff) are not things, but words. However, they are not words in the sense of mere sounds, but rather words which have a meaning. The problem about universals is not, therefore, to determine what they are; but, having decided that they are words, to explain how and what these words signify. Like statements, the problem which universals pose is one of meaning.

Even where they professed otherwise (see above, p.129), contemporary commentators on Priscian worked on the assumption that there was a direct relationship between words and reality. The ancient logical tradition, as transmitted by the *De interpretatione* and Boethius' commentaries on it, taught differently. Words and sentences represented 'affections of the mind', in Aristotle's phrase. Abelard saw that these two approaches need not be mutually exclusive. It was by balancing the relationship between three elements – language, the workings of the mind, and reality – that Abelard produced a comprehensive theory of meaning. This relationship receives its most thorough exposition in the commentary *Ingredientibus* . . . . Much the same theory is given a more sophisticated, but much briefer treatment in the later commentary *Nostrorum petitioni* . . . . The *Dialectica* contains an important revision of Abelard's theory about the meaning of statements; but the section in which he discussed universals is missing from the work's only surviving manuscript.

In the commentary *Ingredientibus* . . ., Abelard proposes what was a widely accepted division of the mind into sense, imagination and intellect (LI 312:36 ff). But he discusses the imagination in unusual detail and defines it in a way especially suited to the requirements of his theory. Sense, he says, is merely perceiving without attention: one can sense even what one fails to notice (LI 317:27–9). Imagination is the fixing of a mind's attention on a thing (LI 317:35): listening to or looking at, as opposed to just seeing or hearing. One of the capacities of the imagination is to form mental pictures of what is no longer present to the senses (LI 313:33–314:6; 317:38–318:8); it can also conjure up pictures of objects that are unreal and were never present to the senses – imaginary castles, for instance (LI 20:28–33; 315:19–20). The intellect – which, unlike the other two parts of his mind, man does not share with the other animals – distinguishes the nature and properties of things by reason (317:36), placing them in a category, or in a genus and species (313:10–15).

Into this scheme Abelard fits certain ideas about psychology taken from Boethius' second commentary to the *De interpretatione*. Thoughts, the products of the intellect, derive from images, the product of the imagination: in classifying a thing, the intellect considers the same image of it from different aspects – the image of a man, for instance, as to its rationality, corporeality and spirituality (LI 25:1–26:3). But Abelard has a use for the notion of images which does not enter into Boethius' exposition. Images, he believes, may be not only of real and fictitious things, but of what are not things in the proper sense at all. Just as the mind can form an image of Socrates, a particular man, so it can form an image of man in general (LI 316:15–18). This image of man 'is a common and confused image of all men': 'a certain likeness which corresponds to all men so that it is common to all of them and peculiar to no one' (LI 21:28–34). There can be images, too, of abstract concepts, such as rationality or corporeality; and these images might be quite different from one person to another, and yet they are used to refer to the same concept (329:2–10).

Abelard believes that images also play an important part in the process by which statements are understood. When one considers the meaning of a statement such as 'Socrates is a man', one begins with the two images, of Socrates and man; by way of them, the intellect arrives at an understanding of the truth of the statement. And, should one wish to think of the statement again, one can call up a single image of it, in which the whole thought can be contemplated (LI 322:18–25).

Despite the importance which he lends to images, Abelard is insistent that they are neither what words – abstract or concrete – nor statements denote. The images are, he says, strictly speaking nothing: they are neither form nor substance (LI 314:25–31). It cannot be the purpose of statements or words to refer to them. Images, indeed, are used not for their own sake, but as signs for other things (LI 315:28–316:5). Why should Abelard be at such pains to define and discuss what he ends by describing as nothing? The seeming paradox becomes clear in the light of the other side of Abelard's theory, which explains – in the manner of the grammarians – what statements and universal-words actually do denote.

Abelard's clearest account of what statements refer to is found in the *Dialectica* (157:13–161:2). What is said – referred to – by a statement is not any thing: statements are not like (proper) names, which designate things simply. Abelard supports this view by adducing statements which can be demonstrated not to refer to things in a simple way, such as certain logically necessary and modal ones. For instance, the statement 'if it is a man, it is an animal' would, he says, be true, even if everything in the world were destroyed (*Dialectica* 160:17–21). And, before Socrates existed at all, the statement that it was possible for him to exist would have been true.

If statements do not denote things, what do they denote? According to Abelard they designate 'how things are related to one another, whether they go together or not'. They denote, not things, but 'a way of things being related' (*modus habendi*) (*Dialectica* 160:29–36). This analysis implies – as a passage shortly before in the *Dialectica* (157:31–160:13) in fact bears out – that Abelard has rejected the inherence theory of statements, commonly held among logicians and adopted instead an identity theory, closer to that considered by William of Champeaux (see above, p.128) to be characteristic of the grammarians. Abelard does not take the verb 'to be' used as the copula to signify the inherence of a quality in a subject, but rather to indicate that the two terms of the statement go together, that things are related in a particular way. At the time he wrote his commentary *Ingredientibus* . . . Abelard himself followed, with some misgivings, the inherence theory. By rejecting it in the *Dialectica*, he is able to bring his analysis of statements more closely in line with the general ideas about language and reality which he held even when he composed his earlier work.

Abelard's analysis of the reference of universal-words proceeds along similar lines to his theory about statements (LI 19:21–20:14). There is no such thing as man, either as an immaterial entity, or as a part of each man, which is denoted by the word 'man' used universally. But there is a reason, in the nature of things, why the word 'man' can be properly used of any man: namely, that he is a man. Men are alike 'in the condition of being a man' (*in statu hominis*). The condition of being a man is the 'common cause' of the use of the word 'man' – the reason why 'man' can be used to describe all men. But this 'condition of being something' is not, Abelard stresses, a thing: rather, it is the way things are.

When the two sides – psychological and linguistic – of Abelard's theory are brought together they form, not perhaps a complete and thoroughly satisfactory answer to his initial problems, but a satisfying and suggestive whole. What universal-words and statements denote are not things, but ways in which things are. However, in coming to an understanding of universal-words and statements, the intellect has the aid of the imagination, which can form images – themselves not things – of what is common to a species or of the relations between things mentioned in a statement. But it is the intellect, not the imagination, which has thoughts about what universal-words or statements actually denote – which, abstractly, understands what is the condition of being something or how things are related to one another. It is for this reason that only the intellect (LI 328:18–329:28) can judge the truth or falsehood of a statement.

The workings of Abelard's theory can be illustrated clearly by comparing his views on universals and the meaning of statements with those he inherited from the antique logical tradition. Alexander of Aphrodisias' theory of universals, put forward by Boethius in his second commentary to the *Isagoge* (see above, pp.31–2), held that universals were thoughts which had a basis in the nature of sensible things. For Abelard universals are words which refer not to any particular sensible thing or things, but to their condition of being. The imagination can form an image of the general characteristics of a species or genus, which, although itself not a thing, is a sign pointing to the condition of being which is the real reference of universal-words. The intellect alone, using the signs furnished by the imagination, can actually understand universal-words: but universals are not for Abelard, as they were for Alexander and Boethius, themselves thoughts. (Abelard does, in fact (LI 22:25–24:37), contemplate as a possibility the theory that the conditions of being of things are the same as the thoughts, derived by the intellect from the images of types of things; and that universal-words are based, therefore, not on a common cause – the condition of being – but on a common conception – the thought of this condition of being. Although he feels he cannot reject this theory out of hand, Abelard makes it clear that he does not favour it. God, he says, may have a clear conception in his mind of the conditions of being of things; but when man goes beyond what he senses, he has opinion rather than knowledge.)

According to the *De interpretatione*, statements referred to 'affections of the mind'; in his commentaries (see above, pp.32–3), Boethius interpreted these as thoughts. For Abelard, statements refer to reality. They do not, however, refer to things, but to a way of things being related. They can only be understood as being true or false by the intellect, but the imagination provides images which help the intellect to come to an understanding of statements and which allow the statement, once understood, to be recalled as a single unit.

Abelard examined other philosophical problems, often related to the theory of meaning, in the course of his logical treatises. His treatment of future contingents and divine prescience is particularly interesting, because it offers the rare opportunity to see Abelard taking an idea of his teacher's, William of Champeaux, and adapting it in his own much more sophisticated way.

Abelard discusses the question of future contingents in both the commentary *Ingredientibus* . . . (420:12 ff) and the *Dialectica* (213:29 ff). So far as the purely logical problem is concerned, he is very willing to follow Aristotle's own solution (see above, pp.22–3), that future contingent statements have no truth-value. Abelard finds this position unproblematic because of his theory of the meaning of statements. Statements refer to how things are, and it is perfectly possible that one should neither know, nor theoretically be able to know, how certain things are. Statements about future contingents are, by their nature, indeterminate – there is not even the theoretical possibility of deciding their truth that obtains in the case of 'There is an even number of stars in the sky'. They are not, however, unique among types of statements in being indeterminate. A statement such as 'A unicorn is a centaur or not' has no truth-value because there are no facts to which it can correctly or incorrectly refer; and there are statements about past or present things which cannot be determinate, because they deal with God and the secret natures of things beyond human comprehension (LI 422:41–423:39). In none of these cases does Abelard find anything troubling about not being able to assign a truth-value to a statement when the nature of the fact – the way of things being related to one another – which it denotes cannot be known.

God's knowledge of future contingent statements does, however, pose Abelard with a problem, since God must know whether they are true or false, and this would seem to destroy their contingency. It is Abelard's treatment of this aspect of the problem in his *Dialectica* (218:3–219:24) which yields an interesting comparison with one of William of Champeaux's theological sentences (195–6). Both thinkers wish to deal with the problem without resorting to Boethius' famous principle of God's timelessness (see above, p.41). The basis of their position is, for both, that God foresees future contingents, but *as* contingents, otherwise his foresight would not be correct. As William puts it: 'given that God has foreseen all that men will do through their free will, he has foreseen this in such a way that he has foreseen men going to do certain things but being able, by their wills, to do otherwise' (195:19–22). To this view there is a possible objection, which both thinkers notice. Their theory implies that, although God in fact foresees correctly all that has happened, it is possible for things to happen otherwise than God has foreseen (if it were not, then the things would not happen contingently). But, given that the indicative statement 'Something will happen otherwise than God has foreseen' implies the logical consequence that God is or was mistaken, does not the modal statement 'It is possible for something to happen otherwise than God has foreseen' (which their theory holds to be true) imply the modal logical consequence that it is possible for God to be mistaken – a position neither philosopher is willing to countenance? William answers the objection rather weakly (196:67–70). The indicative statement 'If something will happen otherwise than God had foreseen, God has or will be mistaken' is, he says, true but not necessary, because it can never be necessary that an impossibility (such as God's being able to err) follows from a possibility. Therefore, says William – but his logic is far from self-explanatory – it is possible that something should happen otherwise than God has foreseen, but impossible that God is or has been mistaken.

Abelard answers the objection in a more satisfying and subtler way: so subtly, indeed, that its sense has escaped the two modern editors of the *Dialectica*, who have emended a perfectly clear passage in the manuscript so as to make Abelard's argument here into nonsense. In the statement, 'If it is possible for something to happen otherwise than God has foreseen, it is possible for God to be mistaken', there are, he says, two possible interpretations of the antecedent. It can mean either (*a*) that something which God has foreseen has the possibility of happening otherwise; or (*b*) that there is the possibility that something will happen otherwise than God has foreseen. According to the latter interpretation (*b*), the antecedent is plainly false, Abelard believes: it is no more possible than that something should happen otherwise than it actually does happen. By the former interpretation (*a*), the antecedent is true, he says, but the consequent does not follow from it: since the possibility of happening otherwise in the antecedent refers not to God's foreseeing, but to what is foreseen, nothing follows from it about the possibility of God's being mistaken.

Abelard's argument may sound too ingenious to be convincing; but, in fact, it is a logical formulation of a position which he goes on to explain in less formal terms. No event can fail to correspond to God's providence; but, if something were going to happen otherwise than it in fact did, God's providence of it would have been different and would have corresponded to it accordingly. Our actions are not constrained by necessity because of God's prescience; rather, his knowledge includes the decisions of our free will.

Despite their predominantly technical interests, then, the logicians of the first half of the twelfth century engaged in philosophical discussion of sophistication and insight. The development of their views was influenced neither by theological objectives (even in the rare cases where a theological dogma, such as divine prescience, suggested a philosophical inquiry), nor by the wish to build or modify a metaphysical system. These characteristics were, in part, stimulated by the main source for these thinkers: the antique logical tradition as handed down by Boethius' commentaries. But, in one respect, their approach is very different from that of their late antique predecessors. For a Neoplatonist of the ancient world, the type of discussion generated by logical texts did not resolve questions such as the nature of universals, except in so far as logic was concerned. For a definitive answer, they would turn to their very different, systematic metaphysics, a higher philosophy dealing with a more real, intelligible universe. The twelfth-century logicians turned to no such higher philosophy. Christianity, indeed, provided a higher form of knowledge, which had replaced Platonic metaphysics in providing a picture of a supra-sensible universe. But it was knowledge of a different sort, which did not claim to be derived from reason and, in some cases, was beyond reasons's grasp. The autonomy of philosophical speculation, implicit in the logicians' works, would be stated openly by Gilbert of Poitiers, a thinker who, within the theological tradition, rivalled the philosophical achievements of the logicians.

13 *Theology*

The varieties of theology

The first fifty years of the twelfth century was a period of activity and change in theology, of the liveliest interest to the student of that discipline but most of it little relevant to the history of philosophy. The systematic theology of Anselm of Laon, William of Champeaux and their schools was concerned with the clarification of Christian doctrine on the basis of authoritative texts; it strayed into philosophy only when William failed to restrain the logician in him (see above, pp.132, 140–1; see also below for the contribution of this school to ethics). Hugh of St Victor, who carried on William's work at that abbey, was a dogmatic systematizer in his *De sacramentis* and his miscellaneous sentences and an educational encyclopedist in his *Didascalion*. In the first book of this work he applies a vague, Christianized Platonism to educational theory.

The mystical theology of Cistercian writers, such as Bernard of Clairvaux and William of St Thierry, is by its very nature unphilosophical (though by no means lacking in argument or order). Even when Bernard deals with a subject like free will, which normally occasions philosophical comment, his approach remains entirely that of the mystic and theologian. He is concerned not with the freedom of the will to be able to act, which he considers to be obvious, but with the problem of man's sinfulness, since he was created for ultimate beatitude. Consequently, he distinguishes three kinds of liberty (1005C): of nature (man's free will); of grace (man is reformed into innocence and made a new creature in Christ); and of life or glory (man is made sublime in glory, a creature perfect in spirit). Everything – whether it happens in spite of, against or in accordance with man's will – is the work of divine grace and so, as Bernard argues (1027D–8A), these distinctions are 'not indeed of free will, but of divine grace: creation; reformation; consummation'.

A theologian of very different character was Abelard; nevertheless, it is not principally in his theological work that his philosophical speculations should be sought. Besides several minor pieces and commentaries on St Paul's Letters to the Romans and the beginning of Genesis, he produced four pieces of theological writing: *Sic et non*, and the treatises known as *Theologia Summi Boni, Theologia christiana*, and *Theologia scholarium*. *Sic et non* consists of a collection of brief extracts from authoritative writings, from the Bible, Fathers and, occasionally, the pagan philosophers, arranged so that some support and some contradict a given position. Abelard's own contribution is restricted to a preface, in which he makes clear the principles behind the work. He does not call into question the authority of Scripture (101:292–3). To the Fathers he shows the greatest respect: often an apparent contradiction between their ideas can be resolved by an understanding of the different ways in which each used the same words (96:185–7). Where the disagreement cannot be resolved, the one who has made the strongest case must be chosen (96:190–1).

The three theological treatises, each one extant in several recensions, are rethinkings and elaborations of what remains basically the same work. The subject is the Trinity: only the *Theologia scholarium*, the latest of the three, announces – but does not realize – a much broader plan. The theological method which Abelard explicitly defends in these books was that implied in the preface to *Sic et non*: reason is useful in judging between different, conflicting human accounts of divine things, but cannot claim to reveal the ultimate truths about these mysteries themselves. The principle is extended in two ways. First, the importance of rational argument in attacking heresy is stressed: the arguments made by heretics with reason must be refuted by reason. Second, Abelard emphasizes the persuasive powers of reason: it does not yield a truer picture of the divine mysteries than faith, but it may be more widely convincing: very few men are spiritual, but almost all are capable of thought. Abelard entitles a section of the *Theologia Summi Boni* 'In praise of dialectic', but he is very clear in all three works about the limits of human reason in dealing with religious mysteries: neither he nor any mortal can offer to teach the truth about the Trinity, because they cannot know this: what he wishes to teach will be near to human reason and not contrary to Scripture, but merely a shadow of the truth (*Theologia Summi Boni* 36:15 ff).

One feature of Abelard's theological works illustrates the Christianizing of Platonism which had become dominant since the eleventh century, and is so noticeable in the writing of William of Conches. Each of the theological treatises contains a lengthy section giving the testimonies of both the Jews and the pagan philosophers about the Trinity, of which they are taken to have had some understanding, if not firm conviction. The treatment of the Platonic concept of the World-Soul, repeated in each of the treatises (*Theologia Summi Boni* 13:11 ff; *Theologia christiana* 100 ff; *Theologia scholarium* shorter version 450:1468 ff, longer version 1013A ff), provides an interesting reflection of Abelard's attitude to the ancient philosophical tradition. Plato, he insists, meant the World-Soul as a metaphor (*involucrum*) for the Holy Spirit; and he rejects, with vehemence, any suggestion that Plato might have wished it to be taken seriously. If there were already a World-Soul, why would individual souls have been created? And what could be more ridiculous than to consider the whole world as a rational animal? Had Plato meant the World-Soul literally, he would have been not the greatest philosopher, but the greatest of fools. The irony of Abelard's remark is that, whatever Plato's own position – a matter still debated by scholars – generations of his followers in antiquity were willing to do what Abelard considered the height of folly, and treat the World-Soul as a real, intelligible thing. The rigours of logical reasoning on the one hand, and the certainties of Christian faith on the other, had made Abelard, like many a modern philosopher, unable to take seriously the metaphysical concepts of Platonism.

The 'Opuscula sacra'

Among the texts studied in most detail by theologians of 1100–50 were Boethius' *Opuscula sacra*. Besides their theological discussion of trinitarian and christological doctrine, these works suggested a philosophical question produced by the juxtaposition of Platonic and Aristotelian analyses of the metaphysical constitution of things, with the Christian idea of God. The question was not simply that of the relationship between the Platonic Ideas and God: to this the Neoplatonic tradition itself provided the answer, widely adopted by Christian writers, of considering the Ideas as the thoughts of God. The *Opuscula sacra* raised a tougher problem: what is the relationship between God, the Ideas and the world of concrete wholes, objects made of matter but having, by virtue of their species, a given form?

The earliest of twelfth-century writers to have tackled this question is Bernard of Chartres. Bernard's works are lost and, from the description in John of Salisbury's *Metalogicon*, it is certain only that he wrote on the *Isagoge* and lectured on Priscian. Yet John of Salisbury's account of his opinions (*Metalogicon* 205:21–206:31) is devoted largely to the relation between God, matter and the Ideas (or, as he called it, the Idea); and the way he tackles the question suggests the influence of the *Opuscula sacra*, whether or not Bernard ever commented formally on them. The Idea is in the depths of the divine mind and requires no external cause. It is eternal, but not coeternal with the Trinity, being as it were the effect of the divine cause. Individual things are made up of matter and form and this form seems – but John of Salisbury's account is very unclear – to be the same as the Idea. Particular things *are*, Bernard says, not on account of the union between matter and form, but because of the form, which is the Idea and which is enduring (a reminiscence, it seems, of Boethius' maxim that 'all being comes from form' – see above, p.37). The creation of concrete wholes and the creation of Ideas are both said by Bernard to be works of the divine mind; but what their exact relation is to each other he does not clarify.

The relationship between God, the Ideas and matter is discussed in some detail in several commentaries to the *Opuscula sacra* of the mid-twelfth century. In Gilbert of Poitiers's work, it is examined within a tight argument, based on the author's views about the nature of philosophy and theology, which calls for detailed and separate examination. Three other commentaries deal with the question. Written in their surviving form probably just after Gilbert's (after about 1148), they have many passages and themes in common. This has led to their attribution by their editor to one man, Thierry of Chartres. It is very possible that some of the less philosophical material goes back to Thierry: for instance, the commentaries contain a 'Pythagorean' discussion of the Trinity in terms of unity and otherness, which is also found in the account of creation which is either a work of Thierry's or an account of his teaching (see above, pp.124–5). However, the character of each of the three commentaries is rather different, and the philosophical ideas each contains are not the same. Which of these ideas, if any, were Thierry's must remain a matter for conjecture.

One of the commentaries (incipit *Inchoantibus librum* . . .) covers the first of Boethius' treatises; and a fragment of commentary on the third treatise probably belongs to it. Its exegesis is close and ample, but not particularly learned in the references brought to bear on the text. By contrast, the second of these works (incipit

Quae sit auctoris . . .) is less close but more scholarly. It covers the first treatise and part of the fifth; whilst an abbreviation of it contains discussion of the first, third and fifth treatises. The author pauses often to sum up received knowledge, especially about logic (he has apparently also written a treatise on this subject). He shows an interest in negative theology and refers to pseudo-Dionysius and Hermes Trismegistus. The third commentary (incipit *Aggreditur propositum . . .*) is even more markedly scholarly and discursive; more authorities, including Priscian, are quoted; and the language is more convoluted.

In one very important way, the commentary *Inchoantibus librum . . .* simplifies Boethius' view of the structure of reality. Boethius had distinguished between God, the forms of things in their pure state, secondary forms (which are embodied in matter and described as images of the pure forms) and concrete wholes, made from matter and secondary forms. For the medieval writer, however, there is only one true form, God (83:65–8). Only by contact with matter is this form determined into such-and-such a type of thing – humanity, treeness or whatever (83:75–6). Forms can have no specific existence apart from individuals: if, says the commentator, no individual man were to exist, then the form humanity would not perish; but it would lose its specific identity and return to the simplicity of the divine form (84:81–4).

The writer of the commentary *Quae sit auctoris . . .* also argues that God is the one true form (167:38–9) and that matter is a necessary condition for the existence of all other forms (169:5–7). But he considers that forms, although created 'about matter' (*circa materiam*), are nevertheless distinct from it and exist in the divine mind (169:90–4). Like Boethius he distinguished between these pure forms and those which derive from them, like images, and are embodied in matter (176:40–3). The commentator now has to explain the relationship between pure forms and God, which he does traditionally, by saying that the forms are ideas in the mind of God. But how can God remain one if he contains this diversity? At one point (176:45–50), the writer states, without explanation, that the many exemplars of things are all one exemplar in the divine mind. In his commentary on treatise III (according to the abbreviation – 409:51 ff) he tries to explain this notion a little. God is said to be one or simple. Plurality requires unity in order to be, whereas unity does not require plurality. God is simplicity winding into itself all things; plurality is the unwinding of this simplicity. The writer is not inclined to take his explanation beyond such metaphors.

The commentary *Aggreditur propositum* . . . is more competent and sophisticated in its philosophy than the others. Far more definitely than in the first two, a distinction is made between act and potentiality (*possibilitas*). The presence of this Aristotelian idea has led to the suggestion of indirect contact with Aristotle's *Metaphysics*, perhaps through the work of the Arabic astronomer Abu Ma'-shar; but the concept is also discussed in Boethius' commentaries on the *De interpretatione* and had been used a century and a half earlier by Gerbert (see above, p.83). The theory put forward in this commentary (275:11 ff) combines aspects of the arguments of *Inchoantibus librum* . . . and *Quae sit auctoris* . . . . Forms are ideas in the mind of God, but they become many, rather than one, only when embodied in matter, which is described, following Augustine, as potentiality. By generating forms from this potentiality, God produces a 'certain perfection in act'; because he gives this perfection its being he is its form.

Gilbert of Poitiers

The most detailed, complex and sophisticated twelfth-century commentary on the *Opuscula sacra* is by Gilbert of Poitiers. Gilbert's commentary is also the most original in its arguments. Originality in a commentary may seem, at first sight, paradoxical; especially since Gilbert represents himself as the faithful interpreter of Boethius, and his exegesis is characterized by its thoroughness – not a word of his text is left unexplained. But, according to Gilbert (53:18 – 54:29), the *Opuscula sacra* deliberately conceal their doctrine by a difficult and condensed style of exposition. His elaborate reasonings – often running for pages where Boethius's fill just a few lines – are designed to bring out clearly the true meaning behind his author's words. The modern reader – rightly – is not likely to be convinced that Gilbert's commentary provides a guide to understanding what Boethius really intended. Nevertheless, he should take Gilbert's self-professed role of exegete seriously. The commentary on the *Opuscula sacra* is the only definitely authentic work of Gilbert's which contains his arguments on philosophical questions. Yet it remains a commentary – a close explanation – of texts which are concerned for the most part with problems not of philosophy but theology. Accordingly, Gilbert's discussions are aimed, not at resolving philosophical problems for their own sake, but at bearing out the christological and trinitarian doctrines advanced by Boethius. An account of Gilbert's philosophy, such as that which follows, will mislead, unless it is taken in this context: it presents just an aspect of Gilbert's thought, which can only be fully understood in the light of his aims as an exegete and theologian.

In the course of his commentary, Gilbert considers many of the philosophical topics which interested his contemporaries: universals and particulars, singularity and individuality, the categories, matter and form and the different meanings of the verb 'to be'. His discussion of all these areas involves Gilbert's characteristic distinction between what he calls '*quod est*'s and '*quo est*'s.

Everything except God is what it is (*quod est*), Gilbert considers, by virtue of something which makes it so (*quo est*). For instance, John is what he is (John) by John-ness; a man is what he is (a man) by humanity; a white thing is white by whiteness; a rational thing rational by rationality. John, the man, the white thing and the rational thing are all *quod est*s; ★John-ness, ★humanity, ★whiteness and ★rationality are *quo est*s [an asterisk will be used to designate *quo est*s]. Gilbert keeps clearly to this distinction throughout his commentary, although he uses a bewilderingly varied terminology to refer to it (for instance, he uses the term 'substance' (*substantia*) on some occasions to mean *quo est* and on some to mean *quod est*). Some *quo est*s are simple, like ★whiteness; some are complex, like ★John-ness – the combination of everything which goes to make John what he has been, is and will be.

From this brief description, it is not difficult to grasp what Gilbert means by *quod est*s. They are things, according to their various possible descriptions with respect to substance (for example, a man) or accidents (for example, a white thing). *Quo est*s need rather more explanation. According to Gilbert, they are singular (144:58–60, 145:95–100) and really existing, but only in conjunction with their *quod est*s. The ★humanity which makes me a man (my *quo est*) is not the same as the ★humanity which makes *you* a man (your *quo est*); indeed, it is because our *quo est*s are each singular that we, their *quod est*s, are also singular (144:58–62; 145:95–100). These singular *quo est*s are not mere concepts: they exist in reality just as *quod est*s exist. Epistemologically and ontologically, *quo est*s and *quod est*s are completely interdependent. *Quod est*s can only be conceived through their cause; *quo est*s through their power to make: 'a white thing through ★whiteness; ★whiteness through its making white' (245:77–81). *Quo est*s cannot even even exist in reality apart from their corresponding *quod est*s, while *quod est*s need their *quo est*s to be what they are: for example, '★bodiliness is nothing in reality (*in actu*) unless it is in a body. And what we call a body is not one unless there is ★bodiliness in it' (279:10–12).

Gilbert bases his approach to the problem of universals on his theory of *quo est*s. A number of his contemporaries held 'indifference' theories of universals: all men, they said (for instance), belong to the species man because each man is *not different* from any other man in being a man (see above, pp. 132–3). Gilbert agrees; but, for him, what makes each man a man is his ★humanity. Each man's ★humanity is singular: it makes just that man – for instance, just John – a man. But it has exactly the same effect on John as Peter's ★humanity has on Peter, and each other man's ★humanity on each other man. Gilbert describes such *quo est*s, which each have exactly the same effect, as being 'exactly similar' (*conformes*); and he calls a collection of exactly similar *quo est*s (and also the collection of their *quod est*s) one 'dividual' (*diuiduum*) (144:64–5; 270:75–7). Gilbert, then, has a clear explanation of why singulars belong to their various genera and species: they do so because of their *quo est*s, which make them exactly alike certain other singulars. But Gilbert is vague about exactly what universals are. At one point (269:39–50) he suggests that a *quo est* which makes its *quod est* exactly similar to other *quod est*s is a universal – an odd statement, since Gilbert also holds that all *quo est*s are singular. At another point (312:100–13) he explicitly equates universals with dividuals, the collections of exactly similar *quo est*s or *quod est*s.

Gilbert does not provide a full and explicit account of universals (in the manner of contemporaries such as Abelard), because the text on which he is commenting does not provoke one. Conversely, he gives a subtle and detailed discussion of singularity and individuality (terms which most twelfth-century thinkers blurred), because the *Opuscula sacra* make extensive use of these concepts. For Gilbert, singularity and individuality are distinct. Everything which exists – *quo est*s and *quod est*s – is singular (270:73). All individuals, therefore, are singular; but not every singular is an individual (144:55–7; 270:71–4). Only those *quo est*s (and their corresponding *quod est*s) which do not belong to a dividual are individuals. But which are they? A dividual is a collection of *quo est*s which have exactly similar effects (or of their corresponding *quod est*s): of, for instance, the ★humanities which make men men (or of the men who are made men by these ★humanities). A *quo est* will therefore be individual if its effects are NOT exactly similar to those of any other, and its corresponding *quod est* will also be individual. The *quo est*s which fulfil this condition are complex *quo est*s, such as ★John-ness and ★Peter-ness (144:63–8; 270:74–80). Whereas John's ★humanity makes *him* a man in exactly the same way as Peter's ★humanity makes *him* a man, his ★John-ness does not make him exactly similar to anything else. And so both John and ★John-ness are individuals.

It might seem from this account that Gilbert would classify the sun (and its *quo est*, ★sun-ness) as individuals: there is, has been and will be only one sun, and nothing else is exactly the same as it. But Gilbert's requirements for individuality turn out to be stricter (273:50–74). In reality (*in actu*) there neither is, has been nor will be anything exactly similar to the sun; but potentially (*natura* – 'by nature') there might be many suns. Only those *quo est*s which make something to which, even potentially, nothing else is exactly similar are to be classed, along with their *quod est*s, as individuals. Here Gilbert is basing himself on the difference between proper names and names for sorts of things (including those sorts which happen only to have one member); indeed, he even refers (273:50–3) to the terminology of the grammarians (*nomina propria/nomina appellatiua*). The word 'sun' is a common (appellative) noun. But a proper name – for instance, 'the Sun' – might be given to that particular object which can be seen in the sky and rises and sets on the earth daily. Gilbert could say, similarly, that there is a *quo est*, ★the Sun-ness, which is itself individual and makes its *quod est*, the Sun, individual. What, then would be the difference between ★the Sun-ness and ★sun-ness? ★The Sun-ness would include all those accidental characteristics which have made the Sun what it is: for instance, that it was so many million miles from the earth at such and such a time. This answer throws an interesting light on Gilbert's theory. In the *De trinitate*, Boethius describes variety of accidents as the basis for numerical difference (see above, pp. 37–8). Gilbert's theory of individuals, at first sight so far removed from Boethius, also seems implicitly to rely on variety of accidents.

When Gilbert discusses universals and individuality in terms of *quod est* and *quo est*, he is engaging in what, following Boethius's threefold division of the branches of knowledge (see above, p. 37), he calls physics or 'natural science' (*scientia naturalis* – 80:51 ff.). The second of Boethius's divisions is mathematics. Gilbert's view of mathematics has little to do with numbers or with the 'mathematicals' of Neoplatonic thought which Boethius probably had in mind. According to Gilbert, the mathematician considers *quo est*s 'other than they are, that is abstractly' (84:70–1). The mathematician's point of view, therefore, is different from that of the natural scientist, who is concerned wth *quo est*s as they are naturally, in concretion: that is to say, combined to form complex *quo est*s (for instance, ★whiteness, ★humanity, ★rationality, ★knowledge and many more, all concreted in the complex *quo est* which makes John what he is). Mathematical analysis artificially separates these *quo est*s: its task is to place *quo est*s into the nine of Aristotle's categories other than substance (cf. above, pp. 20–1). ★Whiteness, for instance, belongs to the category of quality. ★Humanity belongs to two different categories – quality and having (*habitus*): to be human necessarily involves rationality, which is a quality, and the *having* of a soul (117:84–118:91).

The third of Boethius's branches of knowledge is theology. For the most part, the type of theology which occupies Gilbert concerns the relations between persons of the Trinity and between Christ's divine and human natures. Such theology can make use of reasoning from natural science, but not simply or directly. The arguments of natural science must be 'transumed proportionately' for theological purposes (e.g. 143:42–7): they are to be applied analogously and with qualification. Much of Gilbert's commentary is devoted to this difficult task of adaptation. But when Gilbert glosses the division of knowledge in *De trinitate*, the requirements of his authoritative text lead him to put forward a rather different notion of theology. Theology, he says, concerns not only God, but an Idea (*idea*) and formless matter (*yle*) (85:97–100). This type of theology, it becomes clear (100:13–28; 195:100–7), discusses the derivation of bodies. Following (but distorting) Calcidius, Gilbert suggests that formless matter is formed by an immaterial Idea into four pure elements (*sincerae subsantiae*) – fire, water, earth and air; and that from them derives the fiery, watery, earthy and airy matter of sensible things. This account of the physical formation of things is a complement, not an addition or an alternative, to the theory of *quo est*s and *quod est*s. It explains from what the bodies of corporeal things are derived, whereas the theory of *quod est*s and *quo est*s analyses how things, corporeal and incorporeal, are the sort of things they are. Many commentators of Gilbert – beginning with John of Salisbury (*Metalogicon* II 17) – have overlooked this important distinction between Gilbert's physical theory and his ontological one. They have interpreted Gilbert as arguing that the *quo est*s are images, innate in matter, of immaterial Ideas, mistakenly seeing him as a thinker who, in the manner of Boethius (see above, pp. 37–8), made use of both Platonic Ideas and Aristotelian embodied forms to explain the constitution of things.

Gilbert's discussion of the physical concerns which so fascinated thinkers like William of Conches (see above, pp. 122–3) is remarkable for its brevity. Of far more interest to Gilbert than the general question of bodies and their derivation was a question about a particular sort of body – the human body and its relation to the soul.

The relationship between body and soul is an example of a philosophical problem which was much discussed in antiquity and again from the thirteen century onwards, but which was mostly ignored by early medieval thinkers. They were usually content to say that the soul was entirely present everywhere in the body, echoing a patristic formula used to describe God's omnipresence in the universe. For instance, in his short treatise *De anima* (probably from the 1090s), Gilbert Crispin writes: 'One and the same soul exists entire in the various parts and pieces of the human body. There is not more of it in a large part [of the body] or less of it in a smaller part, because everywhere [in the body] it remains one in number' (161:6–8). Half a century later, Gilbert of Poitiers knew vaguely from Calcidius of Aristotle's view (so challenging to a Christian thinker) that the soul is related to the body as form is to matter. But there is little sign that he understood Aristotle's position, and he rejects it completely: the soul is not, he says, a form, 'but rather a substance – that is a thing which has in it forms and accidents of various sorts' (271:17–272:18). None the less, Gilbert is keen to show the intimate manner in which two different substances, body and soul, can be linked together as parts of the same whole.

He is enabled to do so by a view about parts and wholes which, as a general position, seems remarkably weak. Gilbert argues (90:42–50) that the *quo est* of a whole includes all the *quo est*s of all its parts (except for ones which are negative – such as ★incorporeality – and ones which concern logical categories – such as ★being-a-part: 272:35–42). Applied to the relationship between, for instance, a man (the whole) and one of his hands (the part), Gilbert's view has impossible consequences, since it implies that the whole man, as well as his hand, has five fingers and is eight inches long. But when Gilbert's view is restricted to the relationship between soul and body (as it is when he gives examples for it), it becomes powerful and convincing. An important aspect of the unity of a man's body and his soul is that the characteristics of each belong to the whole person. For instance, my body is white and my soul is rational. But whiteness and rationality are also qualities of the compound of body and soul which constitutes the whole person I am; and I am white because my body is white and rational because my soul is rational. Gilbert can explain the ontological basis of this unity. The *quo est* which makes my soul what it is is part of the complex *quo est* which makes me what I am. And so, for example, the ★rationality by which my soul is rational is numerically the same as the ★rationality by which I am rational; the same ★whiteness which makes my body white makes me white (cf. 94:42–64).

The union between human soul and body is one which, according to Christian faith, will at some time be sundered. Christian thinkers face the task of reconciling the wholeness of mortal human beings with the immortality of their souls. Gilbert approaches this problem by explaining that *quo est*s which produce their *quod est*'s substance, quality and quantity are those which give it its 'nature', whereas those which produce merely the other accidents of their *quod est* only give it its 'status'. Among the *quo est*s which give a whole man his nature are ★bodiliness and ★spirituality, and ★embodiment and ★ensouledness. But there is an important difference between these two pairs. Whereas ★bodiliness gives a man's body its nature and ★spirituality gives his soul its nature, his soul is given only its status by ★embodiment and his body only its status by ★ensouledness (319:56–321:97). And, although 'mortality' is part of the definition of a man ('a rational, mortal animal'), ★mortality does not give the whole man his nature, but just his status (321:98–323:63).

In his discussion of body and soul, Gilbert treats in detail a topic which attracted little attention from his sophisticated contemporaries. By contrast, Gilbert's commentary on the third of the *Opuscula sacra* deals, although from a different point of view, with a question much debated by the best logicians of the twelfth century. Boethius's treatise is a Neoplatonic analysis of the difference between the being and goodness of God and the being and goodness of his creatures (see above, pp. 38–9). For Gilbert, however, the central problem which it raises is a logical and ontological one about the meaning of the verb 'to be'. Twelfth-century logicians were familiar with the distinction between the existential function of 'to be' ('is' = exists) and its predicative function ('is' as the sign binding subject to predicate) – a theme which their predecessors had already explored (see above, pp. 108–9). How then, they asked themselves, should 'is' be interpreted in sentences like 'John is a man'? Does it just bind subject and predicate, or does it also indicate existence? The first alternative has the implication – which many twelfth-century scholars wished to avoid – that the verb 'to be' means something quite different from one sort of sentence to another. The second alternative runs into difficulties with regard to sentences concerning things which do not (or cannot) at present exist: it seems to suggest, for instance, that 'Unicorns are white' implies the existence of unicorns.

Gilbert approaches the problem (193:51–194:77) from a different position. He envisages, not two sorts of meaning for 'to be', but four: (1) purely existential; (2) indicating that by virtue of which something is what it is; (3) indicating being-something; (4) purely predicative. When the natural scientist says 'John is a man', he uses 'is' in sense (2), since ★humanity is the *quo est* which makes John what he is, a man. Gilbert adds that some natural scientists would hold that 'is' in this sentence also has sense (3); whereas others consider that 'is' has sense (3) – and that sense only – just in statements about quality and quantity ('John is white', 'John is six-foot tall'). The purely predicative sense (4) of 'to be' is found in statements concerning the seven Aristotelian categories other than substance, quality and quantity ('John is Henry's son', 'John is in the room'). But when theologians use 'to be', their statements must be analysed differently. It is their job to talk about God; and of God alone can 'is' be used in its purely existential sense (1) (because God alone has being by virtue of himself). Theologians, then, can use 'to be' in sense (1), but only when referring to the deity. And if they discuss the species and genera of created things, their statements must be taken merely as indicating that the things are something (sense 3), not that they are by being a certain sort of thing (sense 2). However, a theologian can use 'to be' of created things in another way, non-literally: he can say 'the man is', where 'is' takes an existential meaning by transference from God, the man's creator.

Whereas many of his contemporaries were worried by the idea that 'to be' could have more than one meaning, Gilbert is willing to allow that the word has various, quite different functions, depending both on the statement which contains it, and the discipline (natural science or theology) to which that statement belongs. At the same time, by his restriction to God of the literal use of the purely existential sense of 'to be', Gilbert avoids any suggestion that statements about non-existent things imply the existence of their objects. But his treatment of 'to be' raises as many problems as it solves: in particular, how can the purely existential sense of being (1) be distinguished from being-something (3)? Only in the context of Gilbert's wider theological and exegetical purposes is it possible to find an adequate answer. Like much in Gilbert's commentary, his analysis of 'to be' is subtle and sophisticated, but also incomplete and ultimately baffling when viewed in the isolation of his 'philosophy'.

14 *Abelard and the beginnings of medieval ethics*

In the main, the philosophy of 1100–50 was restricted to the same, narrow though important, range of themes which had stimulated philosophical reflection in the preceding medieval centuries: the philosophy of logic, a few metaphysical questions suggested by the contact between logic and theology (freedom and necessity; being as existence and being-something), along with the somewhat vague metaphysical issues raised by the heritage of antique philosophy. Most of what is newest in earlier twelfth-century thought, such as Abelard's theory of meaning and Gilbert of Poitiers's theory of mathematical speculation, was developed within these areas of interest. But there is one substantial exception. In two of his works, the *Collationes* and *Scito teipsum*, Abelard begins to develop a truly philosophical ethics. Medieval thinkers before him had, indeed, discussed good and evil, sin and punishment, virtue and vice: but they had been either moralizers, urging certain sorts of behaviour rather than analysing the nature of morality; theologians, basing themselves on the authority of Scripture; or metaphysicians, interested in goodness in relation to the origin and ultimate perfection of the world, rather than in reference to moral conduct. By applying to ideas current within these traditions the analytical habit of mind he had gained from commenting logical texts, Abelard succeeds in formulating the beginnings of what is recognizable as an ethical theory: an explanation of what moral concepts are, and of their relation to human choice and deliberation. It is this – as comparison reveals – which makes his ethics philosophical, whilst that of his contemporaries remains speculative theology.

The *Collationes*, composed in about 1136, consists of (and is sometimes entitled) a dialogue between a Jew, a (pagan) philosopher and a Christian. It is very different, however, from the apologetic dialogues of similar format, such as those composed by Gilbert Crispin (see above, p. 104). In the first section, where the philosopher talks to the Jew, the question at issue is whether the law of the Old Testament, the Old Law, is preferable to natural law, man's instinctive and rational ability to act well. No definite conclusion is reached or judgment given; but the philosopher, who quotes the Old Testament with as much facility as the Jew, seems to have gained the upper hand in the argument. The second part of the (unfinished) work contains a discussion between the philosopher and the Christian. Their debate becomes concentrated on the question of the highest good and the nature of goodness; both philosopher and Christian argue rationally, rather than by reference to authoritative texts; and the Christian becomes not the representative of faith as opposed to reason, but the more perceptive and logically acute of two men engaged in philosophical dispute.

It is towards the end of the dialogue (160:3136 ff) that the most interesting ethical discussion takes place. Abelard analyses the ways in which the word 'good' is used, distinguishing between its predication of things or people, of the meaning (*dicta*) of statements (that is, states of affairs, events), and of actions. By illustrating the ways in which 'good' is used non-morally, he is able, by a process of elimination, to reach a conclusion about the nature of moral good.

'Good', Abelard recognizes, is sometimes used of things, animals and people to mean good at doing something. A good craftsman is one who is skilled at his craft; a good horse is strong and swift. For Abelard, this is a non-moral type of use: even something bad can be called 'good' in this manner: for instance, a good thief is one who steals well.

'Good' as used of the meaning of statements – states of affairs – is also, Abelard suggests, non-moral. Indeed, his very example of 'good' used of a state of affairs is one in which 'good' most obviously cannot be taken morally; 'it is good that there is evil'. This might seem a perverse or even self-contradictory statement; but in the context of the metaphysical theory of goodness adopted by Abelard, and expounded in the *Collationes*, it illustrates succinctly why states of affairs cannot be described as good or bad in the moral sense at all. One aspect of patristic teaching which Abelard accepted without question was God's providential ordering of the universe (cf. 168:3349 ff). If every event, each state of affairs, is part of a divinely ordained plan, and God, as Abelard believed, is perfectly good and all powerful, then every event must be good: 'whatever is done by whomsoever, because they come from the best disposition of divine providence, they are predestined and thus happen rationally and well' (166:3312–167:3314). If there is evil in the universe, then it must be there because of the goodness of God's ultimate providence: it is good that there is evil, although evil is in no sense good (162:3211–163:3215).

Abelard's argument would seem to lead to the position that every state of affairs is good, and so the word 'good' is entirely redundant, when used of events. He escapes from this conclusion by suggesting that, when we say that an event is good, it is 'as if we say that it is necessary to fulfil some excellent disposition of God, which is entirely hidden from us' (170:3404–6). To predicate goodness of events is therefore to make a guess about the course of divine providence; and presumably – although Abelard does not draw the consequence explicitly – any event which has taken place must be good, because it will have been part of God's providential design. Abelard has saved 'good' from being entirely otiose as a description of events; but he has made goodness of events something separate from moral goodness. In many theories of ethics, to be morally good is to bring about a good (or, at any rate, less bad) state of affairs. But by Abelard's theory, every state of affairs is good if it actually come about. If goodness of events were the measure of moral goodness, it might enable Abelard to make a guess about the moral status of some future action, but anything which actually had been done would, of necessity, have been morally good.

Is moral goodness, then, applicable only to actions in themselves, regardless of their consequences? Abelard quickly shows the untenability of this position (160:3158–161:3162). An act considered in itself, as if it were a thing, does not hinder or obstruct any good thing, but it cannot be considered of use in itself. Abelard seems, in the course of his argument, to shift inexplicably from talking about a trivial, chance act, such as an unintended movement of the finger, to talking about every sort of act. In fact, he has very good reason for this shift: in itself – without regard to its consequences or the mental state of its agent – every action is like a trivial, unintended one (which is, however considered, without measurable consequence and without relation to the mind of the man who committed it).

Abelard has left little alternative: having eliminated the efficacy with which things perform their function, states of affairs (and thus the consequences of actions), as the objects or criteria of moral goodness, he is free to urge that it is the intention with which an act is carried out that is the measure of moral goodness or evil (163:3229 ff): 'the good man', says the Christian in the dialogue, 'does not seem to differ from the bad man in that what he does is good, but rather, that he does it well' (163:3229–30).

Abelard probably began *Scito teipsum* ('Know thyself') shortly after he stopped work on the *Collationes*; and it takes up his discussion of morality at almost exactly the point where the earlier work had left it. Granted that a man acts well when he acts from a good intention, what precisely, it asks, is a good intention? *Scito teipsum*, however, differs from the *Collationes* in an important respect. Its ethics are specifically Christian. The figure of the philosopher has vanished from the scene, and with him Abelard's wish to keep to the common ground shared by pagan and Christian. *Scito teipsum* (which, in the book that survives, considers its subject only from the point of view of wrongful action) is about sin, rather than evil; scriptural and patristic authority is frequently adduced; and the definition of sin is unashamedly theological: to sin is 'to show contempt for the creator, that is, not at all to do what we believe we should do on his account, or not to cease doing what we believe we should stop doing on his account' (6:3–6).

Abelard's use of religious language and dogma does not reduce the philosophical bearing of this work. On the contrary, by dispensing him from the task of saying what kind of intention is good or bad – which would have demanded a piece of moralizing, not a treatise about morality – it leaves him free to tackle a genuinely philosophical problem about the relationship between will, choice and moral action.

It might seem, says Abelard, that it is the will to do an evil deed which makes a man guilty. But this cannot be so because, he contends, there are many cases where a man sins – he shows contempt for God – by performing an action which he does not wish to do. For instance (6:24–8:23) a man who, having taken every step to escape a pursuer who wishes to kill him, eventually murders him as the only means of saving his own life, does not *wish* to kill his adversary, although he consents to do so. Or (16:16–18) one might want to sleep with a woman one knows to be married and yet not *wish* to commit adultery, in the sense that one would have far preferred her to have been single. In a very strict sense – that they were not necessary, and that they were chosen – Abelard allows that actions such as these were willed; but he insists that, in an important sense of the word, the guilty man did not *wish* to perform the action which manifested contempt for

God. Evil will, therefore, except in the strictest sense, is not a necessary part of the definition of evil intention.

Nor is evil will, argues Abelard, a sufficient definition of evil intention. The man who has an evil will and successfully resists acting in accord with it cannot be accused of sinning: on the contrary, to place the will of God before one's own is surely deserving of merit (10:28 ff).

By a process of elimination, similar in manner to that found in the *Collationes*, Abelard has, if not demonstrated, then at least given evidence for the truth of the contention which, in fact, he places near to the beginning of his work. To have an evil intention is not to have an evil will: it is to consent to that which we should not do (4:28–9). It is when we consent to do what we should not that we show contempt for God. We do not show contempt when we hold an evil will, to which we have not as yet consented; and our contempt is not lessened (14:19–24) if we do not actually succeed in doing that to which we have consented. Even though a sinner might in fact gain extra pleasure by actually performing the wrongful deed, this pleasure does not add to the sin, because there is nothing sinful in carnal pleasure in itself (18:1–22:5).

Abelard goes on to make it quite clear that his discussion of sin is quite distinct from a discussion of justice and punishment as it should be exercised by humans. It is right that men should be rewarded or punished on earth according to their works rather than their intentions, partly because it is for God, not men, to judge intentions (40:6–12), and partly because in human punishment there is the consideration of deterrence. People should be discouraged from performing acts which cause harm to others (42:21 ff); and even the woman who, whilst trying to keep her baby warm, accidentally smothers it, should be punished severely, in order to make other women avoid such accidents (38:13–22). Men judge by acts; but sin – which it is for God alone to judge – lies purely in the intention, the consent to an evil will.

Abelard did not think in isolation; and a study of the theological sentences of two of his teachers, Anselm of Laon and William of Champeaux, and their school reveals many parallels with Abelard's ethical ideas. The idea that intention was more important than the act itself in assessing sinfulness was widespread (and had good patristic precedent). Anselm himself (61:6–7) says that 'whatever is not done from a good intention is an evil and a sin for him by whom it is done'. Anselm also (76:1–16) studied the notion of contempt for God, although he did not make it into a formal definition of sinning. A division of the act of sinning into stages, along with the recognition that to experience a temptation to which one might not accede is not in itself sinful, is found in another passage by Anselm (73:1–74:56), and William of Champeaux is even closer to Abelard, in that he regards the giving of consent to evil passions as the determinant of sin (222:12–14). Indeed, the only individual notion in Abelard's analysis of the psychology of sinning which does not find a parallel in the school of Laon, except where its members seem themselves to be under the influence of Abelard, is the idea that actions *never* play a part in determining a man's sinfulness. Rather, the *Enarrationes in Matthaeum* – a work perhaps by Anselm himself, perhaps by a pupil – mention specifically (*MPL* 162:1294) that a good intention cannot make a bad action good.

Does this mean that in his ethical work Abelard merely systematized, and perhaps drew out the extreme consequences of a body of doctrine which he had learned from one or both of the two teachers he seems so much to have despised? Certainly Abelard seems to have been indebted for individual concepts and arguments to Anselm and William; but these individual borrowings or parallels obscure a great difference in overall approach and purpose. The ethical passages in the *Collationes* show Abelard examining goodness using the techniques he had developed in his logic, and asking himself in what different ways the word 'good' may be used. In *Scito teipsum*, Abelard continues the investigation. Having decided that 'good' in the moral sense has its application determined only by a man's intention, he investigates, in equally precise terms, the logical structure of intending. Anselm, William and their pupils were interested, rather, in giving an accurate, psychological analysis of how one sins, and apportioning blame to the different stages of the action. Where they emphasize that a state of mind, rather than the action itself, brings guilt, this seems to be because – as good disciples of Augustine – their concern was for the goodness or evil of a man's soul. They are not trying to propose a utilitarian morality of consequences; but neither do they show any philosophical awareness of the differences between the use of 'good' of events, and the use of 'good' of intentions.

Even where William of Champeaux (221:1–18) seems to argue along lines parallel to Abelard's, the similarity turns out to be an illusion. Beginning from the patristic commonplace, that evil is not a substance and therefore not created by God, William locates evil in the free will of man: not in the free will in itself, but whenever it chooses to do evil. But then he has to allow that, when the free will becomes evil by choosing wrongly, this choice is nevertheless good, because God permits it. This is the paradox from which Abelard drew out the definition of moral good as being determined by intention; but for William it is no paradox at all, merely an assertion that in no sense does God himself create evil. Abelard's is the approach and purpose of a philosopher, William's of a speculative theologian; and Abelard's rediscovery of ethical philosophy an illustration, in miniature, of that larger rediscovery of philosophical manners of investigation, which had occupied almost five centuries and to which Abelard's own work provides a crowning achievement.

Abbreviations

AHDLMA	*Archives de l'histoire doctrinale et littéraire du moyen âge*
AL	*Aristoteles Latinus* (Bruges/Paris: Desclée de Brouwer)
BGPMA	*Beiträge zur Geschichte der Philosophie des Mittelalters: Texte und Untersuchungen* (Münster: Aschendorff)
CC(cm)	*Corpus Christianorum (continuatio medieualis)* (Turnhout: Brepols)
CIMAGLC	*Cahiers de l'Institut du moyen-âge grec et latin,* Université de Copenhague
CSEL	*Corpus Scriptorum Ecclesiasticorum Latinorum* (Vienna and other towns: Tempsky and other publishers)
MGH	*Monumenta Germaniae Historica* (various German towns and publishers)
MPL	*Patrologiae cursus completus* accurante J.-P. Migne (Paris: Migne, 1844–64)
MRS	*Mediaeval and Renaissance Studies*
SM	*Studi medievali* 3a serie
SSL	*Spicilegium sacrum lovaniense: études et documents* (Louvain: 'spicilegium sacrum lovaniense')

Bibliography

The bibliography is divided into two sections. The list of Primary Works records the editions of all texts to which reference is made in the course of the book, and one or two other texts, which are mentioned generally or in passing, although not quoted. Where, for any reason, more than one edition is mentioned, an asterisk denotes that to which page references are made. Translations into English are also listed whenever they exist. Editions of Greek philosophical texts and of patristic works are not given: good texts of the former will generally be found in the *Oxford Classical Texts* series or in the classical texts published by Teubner; good texts of the latter are available in many cases in the series *CSEL* and *CC*. J.-P. Migne's *Patrologia latina* (*MPL*) contains a very wide collection of patristic writing, but its texts are often less than reliable. The later volumes of *MPL* contain many of the primary texts of early medieval philosophy: these editions are mentioned below only where they have not been replaced by more modern ones.

The list of Secondary Works is arranged according to the chapters and sections of the book. It is not intended as a complete record of works used in writing this study, but rather as a list of the most important secondary material on each area of early medieval philosophy. Further bibliographical information can be obtained from the works listed.

In cross-references to the list of secondary works, the first figure represents the chapter, and the second figure the section: thus 'above 2, 1' means 'see above, chapter 2, section one'.

PRIMARY WORKS

(1) Firmly attributed works

Abbo of Fleury	*Syllogismorum categoricorum et hypotheticarum enodatio*, A. Van de Vyver (ed.) (Bruges: De Tempel, 1966); *Quaestiones grammaticales*, *MPL* 139, 521–34.

Abelard

Logical works Commentary *Intentio Porphyrii* . . . in *Pietro Abelardo: Scritti di logica*, M. dal Pra (ed.) (Florence: Nuova Italia, 1969, 2nd edn); Commentary *Ingredientibus* . . ., B. Geyer (ed.), in *Peter Abaelards philosophische Schriften BGPMA* 21, 1–4 (1919–33): the authentic text of the final sections of the *De interpretatione* commentary is edited by L. Minio-Paluello in *Twelfth Century Logic: Texts and Studies* II *Abaelardiana inedita* (Rome: Edizioni di storia e letteratura, 1958); and the glosses to *De differentiis topicis* are printed in dal Pra, *ed. cit.*; Commentary *Nostrorum petitioni* . . ., in Geyer, *ed. cit.*; *Dialectica*, L. M. de Rijk (ed.) (Assen: Van Gorcum, 1970).

Theological works   *Theologia Summi Boni*, H. Ostlender (ed.) *BGPMA* 35, 2–3 (1939); *Theologia christiana*, E. Buytaert (ed.), in *Petri Abaelardi Opera theologica CC(cm)* 12 (1969); *Theologia scholarium*, shorter redactions in Buytaert, *ed. cit.*, longer redaction in *MPL* 178; *Sic et non*, B. B. Boyer and R. McKeon (eds) (Chicago and London: University of Chicago Press, 1976); other theological works in *MPL* 178 and *CC (cm)* 11.

Ethical works   *Collationes*, R. Thomas (ed.) (as *Dialogus inter Philosophum, Iudaeum et Christianum*) (Stuttgart and Bad Cannstatt; Fromann Holzboog, 1970); *Scito teipsum*, D. E. Luscombe (ed.) (as *Peter Abelard's Ethics*) (Oxford University Press, 1971).

Autobiography   *Historia calamitatum*, J. Monfrin (ed.) (Paris: Vrin, 1962).

Translations   Discussion of universals from Commentary *Ingredientibus* . . . in R. McKeon, *Selections from Medieval Philosophers* (New York: Scribner's, 1929); *Theologia christiana*, extracts trans. in J. R. McCallum, *Abelard's Christian Theology* (Oxford: Blackwell, 1948); *Collationes* trans. (as *Dialogue between a Jew, a Christian and a Philosopher*) by P. J. Pay   (Toronto: Pontifical Institute of Mediaeval Studies, 1979); *Scito teipsum* in Luscombe, *ed. cit.*; *Historia calamitatum* (and also letters) in *The Letters of Abelard and Heloise*, trans. B. Radice (Harmondsworth: Penguin, 1974).

Adalbold of Utrecht

Commentary on Boethius, in R. B. C. Huygens (ed.), 'Mittelalterliche Kommentare zum *O qui perpetua* . . .', *Sacris Erudiri* 6 (1954), pp. 373–427.

Adam of Balsham — *Ars disserendi*, L. Minio-Paluello (ed.), *Twelfth Century Logic: Texts and Studies* 1 (Rome: Edizioni di storia e letteratura, 1956).

Adelard of Bath — *De eodem et diverso*, H. Willner (ed.) *BGPMA* 4, 1 (1903); *Quaestiones naturales*, M. Müller (ed.), *BGPMA* 31, 2 (1934).

Agobard of Lyons — Letter to Fredegisus, *MGH Epistulae* v, pp. 210–21.

Alcuin — *Works*, *MPL* 100–1.

Anselm of Canterbury — *Works*, F. S. Schmitt (ed.), Vols 1 and 11 (Edinburgh: Nelson, 1946) contain the treatises; some philosophical fragments are edited in F. S. Schmitt and R. W. Southern, *Memorials of St Anselm* (Oxford University Press, 1969). **Translations** *Monologion, Proslogion*, Gaunilo's critique and Anselm's reply, trans. J. Hopkins and G. Richardson (London: SCM, 1974); *Proslogion*, Gaunilo's critique and Anselm's reply, trans. with facing Latin text and philosophical commentary M. J. Charlesworth (Oxford University Press, 1965); *Cur Deus homo*, trans. anonymously (London: Griffith, Farrar, Okeden and Welsh, 1889); *De veritate, De libero arbitrio* and *De casu diaboli*, trans. J. Hopkins and H. Richardson as *Truth, Freedom and Evil: Three Philosophical Dialogues* (New York: Harper Torchbooks, 1967); *De grammatico*, trans. in D. P. Henry, *The De grammatico of St Anselm: the Theory of Paronymy* (Notre Dame University Press, 1964), along with the Latin text and very full logical commentary; philosophical fragments trans. in J. M. Hopkins, *A Companion to St Anselm* (below, ch. 9, 2); a translation of *Cur Deus Homo* into French by R. Roques (Paris: Editions du Cerf, 1963) contains the Latin text and very full annotation.

Anselm of Laon — Theological sentences in O. Lottin, *Psychologie et morale* (below, ch. 10).

Apuleius — Logical and philosophical works (including the *Asclepius*), P. Thomas (ed.) (Stuttgart: Teubner, 1971 – reprint of 1908 edn).

Aristotle — Translations into Latin: see Boethius and *Categoriae Decem*

Berengar of Tours — *De sacra coena*,* A. F. and T. H. Vischer (eds) (Berlin: Haude & Spener, 1834). There is a more recent edition by W. H. Beekenkamp (1941).

Bernard of Clairvaux *De gratia et libero arbitrio, MPL* 182, 1001–30.

Bernard Silvestris *Cosmographia*, P. Dronke (ed.) (Leiden: Brill, 1978).

Boethius **Treatises on the arts** *De arithmetica* and *De musica*, D. Friedlein (ed.) (Leipzig: Teubner, 1867).

Logical works Translations from Aristotle in *AL*: I *Categories, Isagoge* (1961–6); II *De interpretatione* (1965); III *Prior Analytics* (1962); V *Topics* (1969) – (all) L. Minio-Paluello (ed.); VI *De sophisticis elenchis* (1975), B. G. Dodd (ed); monographs in *MPL* 64: a better edition of *De syllogismis hypotheticis* by L. Obertello (Brescia: Paideia, 1969); commentaries on *Isagoge*, S. Brandt (ed.) (Vienna: Tempsky, and Leipzig: Freytag, 1906) (*CSEL* 38); commentary on *Categories, MPL* 64, 159–294; commentaries on *De interpretatione*, C. Meiser, (ed.) (Leipzig: Teubner, 1877–80); commentary on Cicero's *Topics*, in Cicero, *Opera omnia*, V, I J. C. Orelli and J. G. Baiter (eds) (Zürich: Orelli, 1833). *Opuscula sacra*, H. F. Stewart, E. K. Rand and S. J. Tester (eds) (London: Heinemann, and Cambridge, Mass.: Harvard University Press 1973 – rev. edn) – also includes the *Consolation*; *Consolation of Philosophy*, L. Bieler (ed.), *CC* 94 (1957).

Translations *De topicis differentiis*, trans. E. Stump (Ithaca and London: Cornell University Press, 1978); *Opuscula sacra* and *Consolation*, trans. in Stewart, Rand and Tester, *ed. cit.*; the *Consolation* is also found in many other English translations.

Bovo of Corvey Commentary on Boethius in Huygens, *ed. cit.* (above, Adalbold of Utrecht)

Calcidius Translation of *Timaeus* and commentary to it edited by J. H. Waszink (London: Warburg Institute, and Leiden: Brill, 1975 – 2nd edn).

Cassiodorus *Institutiones* R. A. B. Mynors (ed.) (Oxford University Press, 1937).

Clarembald of Arras See Thierry of Chartres.

Damian, Peter *De divina omnipotentia* P. Brezzi (ed.) (Florence: Valecchi, 1943), with Italian translation.

Eriugena See John Scottus.

Fredegisus *De substantia nihili* in *MGH Epistulae* IV, pp. 552–5.

Garland	*Dialectica*, L. M. de Rijk (ed.) (Assen: Van Gorcum, 1959).
Gaunilo of Marmoutier	Reply to Anselm's *Proslogion*: see Anselm of Canterbury
Gerbert of Aurillac	*De rationali et ratione uti*, in A. Olleris, *Oeuvres de Gerbert* (Clermont-Ferrand: Thibaud, and Paris: Dumoulin, 1867), pp. 297–310; Letters, F. Weigle (ed.), *MGH Die Briefe der deutschen Kaiserzeit* II. **Translation** Letters, trans. H. P. Lattin (New York: Columbia University Press, 1961).
Gilbert Crispin	*Dispute of a Christian with a Heathen*, C. C. J. Webb (ed.), *MRS* 3 (1954), pp. 55–77; *Dispute of a Christian with a Jew*, B. Blumenkranz (ed.) (Utrecht and Antwerp: Spectrum, 1956).
Gilbert of Poitiers	Commentary on Boethius, N. M. Häring (ed.) (Toronto: Pontifical Institute of Mediaeval Studies, 1966).
Gottschalk	Surviving prose works in *Oeuvres théologiques et grammaticales de Godescalc d'Orbais*, C. Lambot (ed.), *SSL* 20 (1945).
Honorius Augustodunensis	Works, *MPL* 172; *Elucidarium*, in Y. Lefèvre (ed.), *L'Elucidarium et les lucidaires* (Paris: Broccard, 1954); *Clavis physicae*, P. Lucentini (ed.) (Rome: Edizioni di storia e letteratura, 1974).
Isidore of Seville	*Etymologiae*, W. M. Lindsay (ed.) (Oxford University Press, 1911).
John Scottus	*De praedestinatione*, G. Madec (ed.), *CC(cm)* 50 (1978); *★MPL* 122; *Periphyseon* I–III, I. P. Sheldon-Williams (ed.) (Dublin Institute for Advanced Studies, 1968–81); I–V H. J. Floss (ed.) in *★MPL* 122; homily on the prologue to *John*, E. Jeauneau (ed.) (Paris: Editions du Cerf, 1969); commentary on *John*, E. Jeauneau (ed.) (Paris: Editions du Cerf, 1972); commentary on pseudo-Dionysius' *Celestial Hierarchy*, J. Barbet (ed.) *CC(cm)* 31 (1975); translations of Dionysius in *MPL* 122; translation of Gregory of Nyssa, M. Cappuyns (ed.), *Recherches de théologie ancienne et médiévale* 32 (1965), pp. 205–62; translation of Maximus the Confessor's *Ad thalassium* in edn. of the Greek text, *CC series graeca* 7. **Translations** *Periphyseon* I–III in Sheldon-Williams, *ed. cit.*; *Periphyseon* (abridged), trans. M. L. Uhlfeder (Indianapolis: Bobbs-Merrill,

1976). French translations and very full annotation are provided in Jeauneau's editions of the Homily and Commentary on the Gospel of St John.

John of Salisbury   *Metalogicon* C. C. J. Webb (ed.) (Oxford University Press, 1929).
Translation *Metalogicon* trans. D. D. McGarry (Berkeley and Los Angeles: University of California Press, 1955).

Lanfranc   *De corpore et sanguine domini*, MPL 150, 407–42.

Macrobius   Commentary on *Somnium Scipionis*, J. Willis (ed.) (Leipzig: Teubner, 1970).
Translation Commentary, trans. W. H. Stahl (New York and London: Columbia University Press, 1952).

Manegold of Lautenbach   *Liber contra Wolfelmum*, W. Hartmann (ed.) (Weimar: Böhlaus Nachfolger, 1972).

Martianus Capella   *De nuptiis Philologiae et Mercurii*, A. Dick (ed.) (Stuttgart: Teubner, 1969 – rev. edn).
Translation *De nuptiis*, trans. in W. H. Stahl, R. Johnson and E. L. Burge, *Martianus Capella and the Seven Liberal Arts* (New York and London: Columbia University Press, 1977).

Notker Labeo   *De syllogismis*, in *Die Schriften Notkers und seiner Schule*, P. Piper (ed.) (Freiburg im Breisgau and Tübingen: Mohr, 1881).

Peter Helias   *Summa super Priscianum*, section 'De constructione', J. E. Tolon (ed.), *CIMAGLC* 27–8 (1978); further extracts are given in De Rijk, *Logica modernorum* II–1 (below, ch. 12).

Plato   See Calcidius.

Ralph, *pupil of Anselm*   Works, unpublished, in *Oxford Bodleian Laud. lat. 363*; extracts in R. W. Southern, 'St Anselm and his English pupils' (below, ch. 9, 3).

Ratramnus of Corbie   *De anima ad Odonem*, D. C. Lambot (ed.) (Namur: Godenne, and Lille: Giard, 1952).

Remigius of Auxerre   Commentary on Boethius' *Consolation of Philosophy*, unpublished: details of manuscripts in Courcelle, *La consolation* (below, ch. 4, 4); extracts – including the whole of the comment to Book 3, metrum 9 – in *Saeculi noni auctoris in Boetii consolationem philosophiae commentarius*, E. T. Silk (ed.) (Rome: American Academy in Rome, 1935); Commentary on Martianus Capella, C. Lutz (ed.) (Leiden: Brill, 1962–5).

Roscelin   Letter to Abelard and fragments collected in Reiners, *Der Nominalismus* (below, ch. 9, 4).

Thierry of Chartres	Work on creation, reported or copied by Clarembald of Arras: *De sex dierum operibus* in *Commentaries on Boethius by Thierry of Chartres and his School*, N. M. Häring (ed.) (Toronto: Pontifical Institute of Mediaeval Studies, 1971).
William of Champeaux	Theological sentences in O. Lottin, *Psychologie et morale* (below, ch. 10).
William of Conches	*Philosophia mundi*, ★*MPL* 172, 41–102: a better edition, with German translation is now available, G. Maurach (ed.) (Pretoria: University of South Africa, 1980); *Dragmaticon*, printed as *Dialogus de substantiis physicis* by W. Gratarolus (Argentoratus, 1567) (a photomechanical reproduction of this edn. has been published by Minerva of Frankfurt); Commentary on Boethius – extracts in C. Jourdain 'Des commentaires inédits . . . sur la Consolation de Philosophie de Boèce', in *Notices et extraits des manuscrits de la bibliothèque impériale* 20, 2 (Paris: Imprimerie impériale, 1865), pp. 40–82; Commentary on Macrobius – unpublished: details of manuscripts in E. Jeauneau, 'Gloses de Guillaume de Conches sur Macrobe: note sur les manuscrits', *AHDLMA*, 27 (1960), pp. 17–23; Commentaries on Priscian – unpublished: extracts in de Rijk, *Logica modernorum* II-1 (below, ch. 12); details of manuscripts in E. Jeauneau, 'Deux rédactions des gloses de Guillaume de Conches sur Priscien', *Recherches de théologie ancienne et médiévale* 27 (1960), pp. 212–47 (this and the article on the Macrobius glosses are both reprinted in Jeauneau's *Lectio philosophorum* (below, ch. 10); commentary on *Timaeus*, E. Jeauneau (ed.) (Paris: Vrin, 1965).

(2) Anonymous works

(i) Treatises with titles

Categoriae Decem	*AL* I, 1–5, L. Minio-Paluello (ed.) (1961).
De dialectica (and other passages from St Gall, 9th cent.)	In Piper, *ed. cit.* (above, Notker Labeo).
De mundi constitutione (12th cent.)	*MPL* 90, 881–910.
Libri Carolini (8th cent.)	H. Bastgen (ed.) *MGH* Legum III, Concilia Supplementband.

Sententia de universalibus secundum Magistrum R. (12th cent.; Roscelin?)

In B. Hauréau, *Notices et extraits de quelques manuscrits latins de la Bibliothèque Nationale* (Paris: Klincksiek, 1892).

Tractatus glosarum Prisciani (12th cent.)

Extracts in K. M. Fredborg, 'Tractatus glosarum Prisciani in MS Vat. Lat. 1486', *CIMAGLC*, 21 (1977), pp. 21–44.

(ii) Untitled treatises

Omnia tribus constant . . . (circle of Alcuin: Candidus?)

In Marenbon, *From the Circle . . .* (below, ch. 5, 2).

Quid significet oratio . . . (school of St Victor)

Extracts in de Rijk, *Logica modernorum* II–1 (below, ch. 12).

Quoniam de generali . . . (Walter of Mortagne)?

In Hauréau, *ed. cit.* (above, *Sententia . . . secundum Magistrum R.*).

Sunt quidam . . . (school of Alberic)

In M. Grabmann, 'Ein *Tractatus de universalibus* und andere logische inedita aus dem 12. Jahrhundert im *Cod. lat.* 2486 der Nationalbibliothek in Wien', *Mediaeval Studies*, 9 (1947), pp. 56–70.

Totum integrum . . . (12th cent.; probably a fragment of a commentary)

V. Cousin, *Ouvrages inédits d'Abélard* (Paris: Imprimerie royale, 1836), pp. 507–50).

Usia graece . . . (circle of Alcuin)

In Marenbon, *From the Circle* (below, ch. 5, 2).

(iii) Glosses and commentaries

To:–	Incipit	
BOETHIUS *Consolation of Philosophy*	*Carmina cantus delectabiles . . .* (9th cent.)	Unpublished. In Vatican lat. 3363.
	Expositio rationem . . . (10th cent.?)	In H. Silvestre, 'Le commentarie inédit de Jean Scot Erigène' (below, ch. 8, 2).
	Inuocatio haec philosophiae . . . (10th cent.)	In Huygens, *ed. cit.* (above, Bovo of Corvey).
	Iste Boetius . . . (9th cent.; St Gall)	Unpublished. Extracts and details of manuscripts in Courcelle, *La consolation* (below, ch. 4, 4).
BOETHIUS *Opuscula sacra*	*Aggreditur propositum . . .* (12th cent.)	In *Commentaries on Boethius*, Häring, ed. (above, Thierry of

		Chartres) (called the 'Glosa')
	Inchoantibus librum . . . (12th cent.)	In ibid. (called the 'Commentum').
	Quae sit auctoris . . . (12th cent.)	In ibid. (called the 'Lectiones')
	Quinti dicebantur . . . (9th/10th cent.)	In E. K. Rand, *Johannes Scottus* (Munich, 1906 – reprinted photomechanically Frankfurt: Minerva, 1966).
Categoriae Decem	Ninth and tenth-century glosses	Extracts and details of manuscripts in Marenbon, *From the Circle* (below, ch. 5, 2).
MARTIANUS CAPELLA, *De nuptiis*	*Martianus in isto . . .* (9th cent.; partly the work of John Scottus) (incipit in Paris: Bibliothèque Nationale 12960, *Huius fabulae . . .*)	Book I in E. Jeauneau, *Quatre thèmes érigéniens* (Montreal: Institut d'études médiévales, and Paris: Vrin, 1978) (from Oxford: Bodleian Auct. T. II. 19); complete edn. from Paris: Bibliothèque Nationale 12960, by C. E. Lutz, Johannes Scotus *Annotationes in Martianum* (Cambridge, Mass.; Medieval Academy of America, 1939).
	Titulantur hi duo . . . (9th/10th cent.; incipit varies – this is from Leiden: BPL 87)	Books II and IV, C. E. Lutz (ed.) (Dunchad *Glossae in Martianum*) (Lancaster, Pa.; American Philological Association, 1944).
PLATO *Timaeus*	Eleventh-century glosses	Extracts and details of manuscripts in Gibson, 'The study of the "Timaeus"' (below, ch. 8, 2).
PORPHYRY *Isagoge*	Tenth-century glosses (Icpa)	Cl. Baeumker and B. von Walterhausen, eds as *Frühmittelalterlichen Glossen des angeblichen*

		Jepa zur Isagoge des Porphyrius, BGPMA 24, 1 (1924).
PRISCIAN	Eleventh-century	*(1488 edn
Institutiones	commentary	Arrivabenus); *extracts (on verb 'to be') in Hunt, 'Studies on Priscian' (below, ch. 9, 4). The commentary is printed in a number of early editions of Priscian; for details of these and of manuscripts, see Gibson, 'The early scholastic glosule' (below, ch. 9, 4).

SECONDARY WORKS

No attempt is made here to give a full bibliography for the antique sources and background to early medieval philosophy (the subject of Chapters 1–3). A few general books are listed, but the reader is referred especially to *The Cambridge History of Later Greek and Early Medieval Philosophy*, A. H. Armstrong, ed. (Cambridge University Press, 1970) for a general introduction and further bibliography.

Chapter 1   Platonism in the ancient world

(1) Plato
F. M. Cornford, *Plato's Cosmology* (London: Kegan Paul, and New York: Harcourt Brace, 1937) – a translation of the *Timaeus* with full commentary.

(2) From Platonism to Neoplatonism
P. Merlan, *From Platonism to Neoplatonism* (The Hague: Nijhoff, 1968 – 3rd edn).
Plotinus   J. M. Rist, *Plotinus: The Road to Reality* (Cambridge University Press, 1967).
Latin Platonism   P. Courcelle, *Late Latin Writers and Their Greek Sources* (trans.) (Cambridge, Mass.: Harvard University Press, 1969).

Chapter 2   Neoplatonism and the Church Fathers

(1) Augustine's treatment of pagan philosophy
R. Arnou, article, 'Platonisme des Pères', in *Dictionnaire de théologie catholique* XII, cols 2258–392 – a wide-ranging account of patristic Platonism.

(2)   Greek Christian Platonists
F. Siegmund, *Die Überlieferung der Griechischen Christlichen Literatur* (München-Pasing: Filsen, 1949) – on transmission to Latin West.

(3)   Iamblichus, Proclus and the pseudo-Dionysius
S. Gersh, *From Iamblichus to Eriugena* (Leiden: Brill, 1978); R. Roques, *L'univers dionysien* (Aubier: Montaigne, 1954).

Chapter 3   The antique logical tradition

General histories of logic
W. and M. Kneale, *The Development of Logic* (Oxford University Press, 1962) – a concise, technical survey from the beginnings to the present day; C. Prantl, *Die Geschichte der Logik im Abendlande* I and II (2nd edn) (Leipzig: Hirzel, 1855, and 1885) – these volumes cover the period from Aristotle to about 1200 in much greater detail.

(1)   Aristotle
J. L. Ackrill, *Aristotle's 'Categories' and 'De interpretatione'* (Oxford University Press, 1963) – a translation with full philosophical commentary.

(2)   Logic in late antiquity
A. C. Lloyd, 'Neoplatonic and Aristotelian logic', *Phronesis* 1, pp. 55–72 and 146–60.

Chapter 4   Boethius

General books on Boethius
H. Chadwick, *Boethius: the Consolations of Music, Logic, Theology, and Philosophy* (Oxford University Press, 1981) – a comprehensive and detailed study of life and writings; M. Gibson (ed.), *Boethius: His Life, Thought and Influence* (Oxford: Blackwell, 1981) – learned discussions by various scholars on many aspects of Boethius.

(2)   The logical works
J. Shiel, 'Boethius's commentaries on Aristotle', *MRS* 4 (1958), pp. 217–44 – argues that the commentaries are translations of marginalia: compare with Chadwick's account; H. J. Brosch, *Der Seinsbegriff bei Boethius* (Innsbruck: Rauch, 1931). Sections on Boethius' logic are found in Tweedale, *Abailard . . .* (below 12, 3), and De Rijk, *Logica . . .* (below 12).

(3)   The *Opuscula sacra*
V. Schurr, *Die Trinitätslehre des Boethius im Lichte der 'Skythischen Kontroversen'* (Paderborn: Schöningh, 1935).

(4)   The *Consolation of Philosophy*
J. Gruber, *Kommentar zu Boethius De Consolatione Philosophiae* (Berlin: De Gruyter, 1978) – a line-by-line commentary; F. Klingner, *De Boethii consolatione Philosophiae* (Berlin: Weidmann, 1921) – literary and philosophical sources; P. Courcelle, *La consolation de philosophie dans la tradition littéraire* (Paris: Etudes augustiniennes, 1967) – studies on philosophical sources and influence.

Chapter 5   The earliest medieval philosophers

(1)   From Cassiodorus to Alcuin
General surveys P. Courcelle, *Histoire littéraire des grandes invasions germaniques* (Paris: Etudes augustiniennes, 1964 – 3rd edn); M. L. W. Laistner, *Thought and Letters in Western Europe; A.D. 500 to 900* (London: Methuen, 1957).
Cassiodorus J. J. O'Donnell, *Cassiodorus* (Berkeley and London: University of California Press, 1979).
Isidore J. Fontaine, *Isidore de Séville et la culture classique dans L'Espagne Wisigothique* (Paris: Etudes augustiniennes, 1959).
Irish learning L. Bieler, *Ireland, Harbinger of the Middle Ages* (trans.) (Oxford University Press, 1963) – over-enthusiastic; M. MacNamara (ed.), *Biblical Studies: The Medieval Irish Contribution* (Dublin: Dominican Press, 1976) – includes trans. of important Bischoff article.
Bede C. Jenkins, 'Bede as exegete and theologian', in A. Hamilton Thompson (ed.), *Bede: His Life, Times and Writings* (Oxford University Press, 1935).
Alcuin P. Hunter Blair, 'From Bede to Alcuin', in G. Bonner (ed.), *Famulus Christi* (London: SPCK, 1976) – on his education; A. Van de Vyver, 'Les étapes du développement philosophique du haut moyen-âge', *Revue belge de philologie et d'histoire* 8 (1929), pp. 425–52 – on his logic; M. T. d'Alverny, 'La Sagesse et ses sept filles', *Mélanges . . . Felix Grat* 1 (Paris: Pecqueur-Grat, 1946), pp. 245–78 – on the preface to *De grammatica*; P. Meyvaert, 'The authorship of the "Libri Carolini": observations prompted by a recent book', *Revue bénédictine* 89 (1979), pp. 29–57 – summarizes and contributes to the debate about the authorship of the *Libri Carolini*.

(2)   The circle of Alcuin
J. A. Marenbon, *From the Circle of Alcuin to the School of Auxerre* (Cambridge University Press, 1981); J. A. Endres, *Forschungen zur Geschichte der frühmittelalterlichen Philosophie*, BGPMA 17 (1915) – outdated but still useful; C. Ineichen-Eder, 'Theologisches und philosophisches Lehrmaterial aus dem Alcuin-Kreise', *Deutsches Archiv für Erforschung des Mittelalters* 34 (1978), pp. 192–201 – on the material in MS Munich: Clm 18961.

Chapter 6   Philosophy in the age of John Scottus Eriugena

(1)   Ratramnus of Corbie and Macarius the Irishman

Martin of Laon   J. J. Contreni, *The Cathedral School of Laon from 850 to 930: Its Manuscripts and Masters* (München: Arbeo-Gesellschaft, 1978).

Sedulius Scottus   S. Hellmann, *Sedulius Scottus (Quellen und Untersuchungen zur lateinischen Philologie des Mittelalters* hrsg. L. Traube I, 1) (1906 – reprinted Frankfurt: Minerva, 1966).

Ratramnus   J.-P. Bouhot, *Ratramne de Corbie: histoire littéraire et controverses doctrinales* (Paris: Etudes augustiniennes, 1966) – a general study; P. Delehaye, *Une controverse sur l'âme universelle au IXe siècle* (Louvain: Nauwelaerts, 1950) – on the controversy with Macarius.

Gottschalk   J. Jolivet, *Godescalc d'Orbais et la Trinité* (Paris: Vrin, 1958) – on his use of grammar in theology.

(2), (3), (4)   John Scottus Eriugena

Bibliography   M. Brennan, 'A bibliography of publications in the field of Eriugenian studies, 1800–1975', *SM* 18, 1 (1977), pp. 401–47.

General studies   M. Cappuyns, *Jean Scot Erigène: sa vie, son oeuvre, sa pensée* (Louvain and Paris: Desclée de Brouwer, 1933) – still the best biographical and scholarly study; also, *Jean Scot Erigène et l'histoire de la philosophie* (Paris: CNRS, 1977) (*Colloques internationaux du centre de la recherche scientifique* 561) – short articles, some important, by many writers on Eriugena's background, thought and influence.

Translations from Greek   E. Jeauneau, 'Jean Scot Erigène et le grec', *Archivium latinitatis medii aevi* 41 (1979), pp. 5–60.

Sources   J. Dräseke, *Johannes Scottus Erigena und dessen Gewährsmänner in seinem Werke De divisione naturae libri V* (Leipzig: Dieterich, 1902); *Eriugena: Studien zu seinen Quellen* (Heidelberg: Winter, 1980) (*Abhandlungen der Heidelberger Akademie der Wissenschaften*, phil.-hist. Klasse, 1980, 3) – proceedings of a conference: detailed studies of individual sources; G. d'Onofrio, 'Giovanni Scoto e Boezio: tracce degli "Opuscula sacra" e della "Consolatio" nell'opera eriugeniana', *SM* 21, 2 (1980), pp. 707–52 – on the importance of Boethius to Eriugena.

Philosophical studies   H. Bett, *Johannes Scotus Erigena: A Study in Medieval Philosophy* (Cambridge University Press, 1925) – outdated but still useful; J. J. O'Meara and L. Bieler (eds), *The Mind of Eriugena* (Dublin: Irish University Press, 1973) – proceedings of a conference; also includes papers on sources and influences; T. Gregory, *Giovanni Scoto Eriugena: tre studi* (Florence: Sansoni, 1963) – the *Periphyseon* in the context of Neoplatonism: on this, see also Gersh, *From Iamblichus* (above 2, 3); R. Roques, *Libres sentiers vers l'érigénisme* (Rome: Ateneo, 1975) – the *Periphyseon* in the context of pseudo-Dionysius and the patristic tradition.

Chapter 7   The aftermath of Eriugena: philosophy at the end of the ninth and beginning of the tenth century

(1)   The influence of Eriugena
Marenbon, *From the Circle* (above 5, 2) – on his contemporaries and immediate followers; P. Lucentini, *Platonismo medievale: contributi per la storia dell'Eriugenismo* (Florence: Nuova Italia, 1979); N. M. Häring, 'John Scottus in twelfth-century angelology', in *The Mind of Eriugena* (above 6, 2–4) – limits of his influence in the twelfth century.

(2)   The traditions of glosses to school texts
Martianus glosses   G. Schrimpf, 'Zur Frage der Authentizität unserer Texte von Johannes Scottus' "Annotationes in Martianum"', in *The Mind of Eriugena* (above, 6, 2–4); and C. Leonardi, 'Glosse eriugeniane a Marziano Capella in un codice leidense', in *Jean Scot Erigène et l'histoire* (above, 6, 2–4) – both on the relationship between various different glossed manuscripts of *De nuptiis*; C. Leonardi, 'I codici di Marziano Capella', *Aevum* 33 (1959), pp. 443–89 and 34 (1960), pp. 1–99, 411–524 – on the study and commentary of *De nuptiis*, based on a census of the manuscripts.
Glosses to the *Consolation of Philosophy*   Courcelle, *La consolation* (above, 4, 4) – fundamental; F. Troncarelli, 'Per una ricerca sui commenti altomedievali al *De Consolatione* di Boezio', in *Miscellanea in memoria di Giorgio Cencetti* (Turin: Bottega d'Erasmo, 1973) – valuable criticism of Courcelle's method and conclusions.
Glosses to Boethius's *Opuscula sacra*   M. Cappuyns, 'Le plus ancien commentaire des "Opuscula sacra" et son origine', *Recherches de théologie ancienne et médiévale* 3 (1931), pp. 237–72 – on manuscripts and authorship; G. Schrimpf, *Die Axiomenschrift des Boethius (De Hebdomadibus) als philosophisches Lehrbuch des Mittelalters* (Leiden: Brill, 1966) – on philosophical influence of Treatise III throughout the Middle Ages.
Glosses to the *Categoriae Decem*   Marenbon, *From the Circle* (above 5, 2).
Logic at St Gall   L. M. de Rijk, 'On the curriculum of the arts of the trivium at St Gall from *c.* 850–*c.* 1000', *Vivarium* 1 (1963), pp. 35–86.

(3)   Remigius of Auxerre
Courcelle, *La consolation* (above 4, 4) – discusses Remigius' whole range of work as a commentator.

Chapter 8   Logic and scholarship in the tenth and earlier eleventh century

(1)   Tenth-century logic
General surveys   A. Van de Vyver, 'Les étapes' (above 5, 1); and 'Vroeg-Middeleewsche wijsgeerige Verhandelingen', *Tijdschrift voor Philosophie* 4 (1942), pp. 156–99 – both fundamental; O. Lewry, 'Boethian

logic in the medieval west', in Gibson (ed.), *Boethius* (above 4) – a useful summary.

Use of logical sources J. Isaac, *Le peri hermeneias en occident de Boèce à Saint Thomas* (Paris: Vrin, 1953) – on *De interpretatione*; C. Jeudy, 'Israel le grammairien et la tradition manuscrite du commentaire de Rémi d'Auxerre à l'"'Ars Minor" de Donat', *SM* 18, 2 (1977), pp. 185–205 – on date and authorship of the *Isagoge* glosses; L. Minio-Paluello, 'Note sull'-Aristotele latino medievale: XV- Dalle "Categoriae Decem" . . . al testo vulgato aristotelico boeziano', *Rivista di filosofia neo-scolastica* 54 (1962), pp. 137–47, reprinted in his *Opuscula: the Latin Aristotle* (Amsterdam: Hakkert, 1972) – on the *Categories*.

Notker De Rijk, 'On the curriculum' (above 7, 2).

Abbo P. Cousin, *Abbon de Fleury-sur-Loire* (Paris: Lethielleux, 1954) – biography; A. Van de Vyver, 'Les oeuvres inédites d'Abbon de Fleury', *Revue bénédictine* 47 (1935), pp. 125–69 – scientific and logical work.

Gerbert A contemporary account of Gerbert's teaching and his dispute on the division of philosophy is given by Richer in his *Historia* (G. Waitz (ed.), *MGH*, Scriptorum rerum germanicarum, Hannover: Hahn, 1877), III, 43 ff; F. Picavet, *Gerbert: un pape philosophe* (Paris: Leroux, 1897); U. Lindgren, *Gerbert von Aurillac und das Quadrivium* (Wiesbaden: Steiner, 1976) – scientific and mathematical education and interests.

(2) Antique philosophy and the Christian scholar
General studies E. Garin, *Studi sul platonismo medievale* (Florence: Le Monnier, 1958) – eleventh to sixteenth centuries; T. Gregory, *Platonismo medievale: studi e ricerche* (Roma: Istituto storico italiano per il medio evo, 1958) – eleventh and twelfth centuries.

Glosses to the *Timaeus* M. Gibson, 'The study of the "Timaeus" in the eleventh and twelfth centuries', *Pensamiento* 25 (1969), pp. 183–94; R. Klibansky, *The Continuity of the Platonic Tradition during the Middle Ages* (London: Warburg Institute, 1939) – a general survey of the whole topic, rather outdated.

Glosses to Boethius' *Consolation* Courcelle, *La consolation* (above 4, 4) – fundamental general study; J. Beaumont, 'The Latin tradition of the *De consolatione philosophiae*', in Gibson (ed.) *Boethius* (above 4) – a summary of Courcelle and more recent work; D. K. Bolton, 'The study of the *Consolation of Philosophy* in Anglo-Saxon England', *AHDLMA* 44 (1977), pp. 33–78 – revisions of Remigius; H. Silvestre, 'Le commentaire inédit de Jean Scot Erigène au mètre IX du livre III du "De consolatione philosophiae" de Boèce', *Revue d'histoire ecclésiastique* 47 (1952), pp. 44–122 – study of *Expositio rationem* . . . commentary, with unconvincing attempt to attribute it to Eriugena.

Manegold of Lautenbach W. Hartmann, 'Manegold von Lautenbach und die Anfänge der Frühscholastik', *Deutsches Archiv* 26 (1970), pp. 47–149.

Chapter 9   Logic and theology in the age of Anselm

(1)   Dialectic and its place in theology
General study   A. J. Macdonald, *Authority and Reason in the Early Middle Ages* (Oxford University Press, and London: Milford, 1933) – useful survey, needs correction by reference to more specialized monographs.
Lanfranc   M. Gibson, *Lanfranc of Bec* (Oxford University Press, 1978) – biography; M. Gibson, 'Lanfranc's notes on patristic texts', *Journal of Theological Studies* 22 (1971), pp. 435–50.
Berengar   A. J. Macdonald, *Berengar and the Reform of Sacramental Doctrine* (London: Longman, 1930).
The controversy on the eucharist   J. de Montclos, *Lanfranc et Berengar: la controverse eucharistique du XIe siècle*, SSL (1971); R. W. Southern, 'Lanfranc of Bec and Berengar of Tours', in R. W. Hunt, W. A. Pantin and R. W. Southern (eds), *Studies in Medieval History Presented to Frederick Maurice Powicke* (Oxford University Press, 1948) – the importance of dialectic in the dispute.
Peter Damian J. Gonsette, *Pierre Damien et la culture profane* (Louvain and Paris: Béatrice-Nauwelaerts, 1956).

(2)   Anselm
General study   J. M. Hopkins, *A Companion to the Study of St Anselm* (Minneapolis: Minnesota University Press, 1972).
Biography   R. W. Southern, *Anselm and his Biographer* (Cambridge University Press, 1966) – an intellectual as well as political study; F. S. Schmitt, 'Zur Chronologie der Werke des hl. Anselm von Canterbury', *Revue bénédictine* 44 (1932), pp. 322–50 – chronology of writings.
The 'ontological argument'   K. Barth, *Anselm: fides quaerens intellectum* (trans.) (London: SCM, 1960) – Anselm's proof as theological: highly influential; E. Gilson, 'Sens et nature de l'argument de Saint Anselme', *AHDLMA* 9 (1934), pp. 5–51; D. P. Henry, – 'The *Proslogion* proofs', *Philosophical Quarterly* 5 (1955), pp. 147–51 – Boethian influence; C. Hartshorne, *Anselm's Discovery: A Re-examination of the Ontological Proof for God's Existence* (La Salle: Open Court, 1965) – the argument from the point of view of modern philosophy or religion; R. R. La Croix, *Proslogion II and III: A Third Interpretation of Anselm's Argument* (Leiden: Brill, 1972) – unity of the *Proslogion*: has a very full bibliography of philosophical studies of the ontological argument.
Logic and language   D. P. Henry, *The Logic of St Anselm* (Oxford University Press, 1967); and also *Medieval Logic and Metaphysics* (London: Hutchinson, 1972) – highly technical, fundamental studies.

(3)   Anselm's pupils and influence
General   R. W. Southern, 'St Anselm and his English pupils', *MRS* 1 (1941–3), pp. 3–34; A. Daniels, *Quellenbeiträge und Untersuchungen zur Geschichte der Gottesbeweise im dreizehnten Jahrhundert*, BGPMA 8 (1909) – influence of ontological argument.

Honorius Augustodunensis J. Endres, *Honorius Augustodunensis: Beitrag zur Geschichte des geistigen Lebens im 12. Jahrhundert* (Kempten and Munich: Kösel'schen, 1906); M.-T. d'Alverny, 'Le cosmos symbolique du XIIe siècle', *AHDLMA* 20 (1953), pp. 31–81 – on the *Clavis physicae*.

(4) Logic and grammar at the end of the eleventh century
Priscian commentary R. W. Hunt, 'Studies on Priscian in the eleventh and twelfth centuries', *MRS* 1 (1941–3), pp. 194–131 (part 1) – survey of the tradition up to Peter Helias; M. Gibson, 'The early scholastic "glosule" to Priscian, "Institutiones grammaticae": the text and its influence', *SM* 20, 1 (1979), pp. 235–54.
Roscelin J. Reiners, *Der Nominalismus in der Frühscholastik, BGPMA* 8 (1910); F. Picavet, *Roscelin: philosophe et théologien d'après la légende et d'après l'histoire* (Paris: Alcan, 1911).

Chapter 10 Masters and schools

General studies C. H. Haskins, *The Renaissance of the Twelfth Century* (Cambridge, Mass.: Harvard University Press, 1927) – outdated but unreplaced; M. Grabmann, *Die Geschichte der scholastischen Methode* I and II (1909 and 1911 – reprinted Basel and Stuttgart: Schwabe, 1961) – on the schools in general, although concentrating on theology; E. Lesne, *Histoire de la propriété ecclésiastique en France* V: *Les écoles de la fin du VIIIe siècle à la fin du XIIe* (Lille: Facultés catholiques, 1940); R. L. Poole, *Illustrations of the History of Medieval Thought and Learning* (London: SPCK, 1920 – 2nd edn) – still useful; G. Paré, A. Brunet and P. Tremblay, *La renaissance du XIIe siècle: les écoles et l'enseignement* (Paris: Vrin, and Ottawa: Institut d'études médiévales, 1933); and P. Delehaye, 'L'organisation scolaire au XIIe siècle', *Traditio* 5 (1947), pp. 211–68 – both on how teaching was conducted.
Anselm and the school of Laon O. Lottin, *Psychologie et morale aux XIIe et XIIIe siècles* V: *Problèmes d'histoire littéraire* (Gembloux: Duculot, 1959).
William of Champeaux and the school of St Victor J. Châtillon, 'De Guillaume de Champeaux à Thomas Gallus . . . Chronique d'histoire littéraire de l'école de Saint-Victor', *Revue du moyen âge latin* 8 (1952), pp. 139–62, 245–72.
Gilbert of Poitiers H. C. van Elswijk, *Gilbert Porreta. Sa vie, son oeuvre, sa pensée, SSL* 33 (1966).
Abelard J. G. Sikes, *Peter Abailard* (Cambridge University Press, 1932) – rather outdated; R. Klibansky, 'Peter Abailard and Bernard of Clairvaux: a letter by Abailard', *MRS* 5 (1961), pp. 1–27; *Abélard en son temps*, J. Jolivet (ed.) (Paris: Les belles lettres, 1981) – papers on historical and intellectual backgrounds.
Thierry F. Vernet, 'Une épitaphe inédite de Thierry de Chartres', in *Recueil de travaux offert à M. Clovis Brunel* II (Paris: Société de l'école des chartes, 1955).

Adelard and the scientists   D. C. Lindberg (ed.), *Science in the Middle Ages* (Chicago and London; Chicago University Press, 1978) – very general introduction; C. H. Haskins, *Studies in the History of Medieval Science* (Cambridge, Mass.: Harvard University Press 1927 – 2nd edn).

The school of Chartres   A. Clerval, *Les écoles de Chartres au moyen-âge* (Paris: Picard, 1895) – fundamental study of Chartres: unreplaced for detail; R. W. Southern, 'Humanism and the school of Chartres', in *Medieval Humanism and other Studies* (Oxford: Blackwell, 1970) – questions the importance of Chartres; N. Häring, 'Chartres and Paris revisited', in J. R. O'Donnell (ed.) *Essays in Honour of Anton Charles Pegis* (Toronto: Pontifical Institute, 1974) – attacks Southern; R. W. Southern, *Platonism, Scholastic Method and the School of Chartres* (University of Reading, 1979) – defence and extension of earlier position; E. Jeauneau, *Lectio Philosophorum* (Amsterdam: Hakkert, 1974) – a collection of articles: many important details on Chartres.

Contemporary accounts   Abelard's *Historia calamitatum* and John of Salisbury's *Metalogicon* (II, 10) – particularly important; R. B. C. Huygens, 'Guillaume de Tyr étudiant: un chapitre (xix, 12) de son "Histoire" retrouvé', *Latomus* 21 (1962), pp. 811–29 – an account of studies between about 1145 and 1165.

Chapter 11   The antique philosophical tradition: scholarship, science and poetry

General   W. Wetherbee, *Platonism and Poetry in the Twelfth Century* (Princeton University Press, 1972); P. Dronke, *Fabula: Explorations into the Uses of Myth in Medieval Platonism* (Leiden and Cologne: Brill, 1974)

(1)   William of Conches
T. Gregory, *Anima mundi: la filosofia di Gugliemo di Conches e la scuola di Chartres* (Florence: Sansoni, 1955) – philosophical study; E. Jeauneau, 'L'usage de la notion d'integumentum à travers les gloses de Guillaume de Conches', *AHDLMA* 24 (1957), pp. 35–100 – on metaphorical interpretations; E. Jeauneau, 'Macrobe, source du platonisme chartrain', *SM* 1, 1 (1960), pp. 2–24 – on glosses to Macrobius.

(2)   Minor cosmological works
De mundi constitutione   Garin, *Platonismo* (above 8, 2).
Work attributed to Thierry   Southern, *Platonismo* (above 10) – discussion of authorship.
Further glosses and commentaries to antique philosophical texts   Jeauneau, *Lectio* (above 10) – discussion of various anonymous commentaries on Boethius, Martianus Capella and the *Timaeus*; Courcelle, *La consolation* (above 4, 4) – on commentaries to the *Consolation*.

(3)   Bernard Silvestris
B. Stock, *Myth and Science in the Twelfth Century* (Princeton University Press, 1972) – detailed study of the *Cosmographia*.

Chapter 12   Grammar and logic

General   L. M. de Rijk, *Logica Modernorum* II, 1 (Assen: Van Gorcum, 1967) – important studies of the theory of meaning, both in grammatical and logical works.

(1)   Grammar
J. Pinborg, *Logik und Semantik im Mittelalter: ein Überblick* (Stuttgart: Frommann, and Bad Canstatt: Holzboog, 1972) – very clear summary; K. M. Fredborg, 'The dependence of Petrus Helias' Summa super Priscianum on William of Conches' Glose super Priscianum', *CIMAGLC* 11 (1973), pp. 1–57.

(2)   Logic
Availability of texts   M. Grabmann, 'Bearbeitungen und Auslegungen der Aristotelischen Logik aus der Zeit von Peter Abelard bis Petrus Hispanus', *Abhandlungen der Preussischen Akademie der Wissenschaften*, phil. hist. Klasse 5 (1937); Minio-Paluello, *Opuscula* (above 8, 1) – collection of very important articles on Latin translations of Aristotle; L. M. de Rijk, *Logica Modernorum* 1 (Assen: Van Gorcum, 1962) – especially on *De sophisticis elenchis*.
Alberic and his school   L. M. de Rijk, 'Some new evidence on twelfth-century logic: Alberic and the school of Mont Ste Geneviève (Montani)', *Vivarium* 4, pp. 1–57.
Adam of Balsham   L. Minio-Paluello, 'The "Ars disserendi" of Adam of Balsham "Parvipontanus"', *MRS* 3 (1954), pp. 116–69).
Theories of universals   Prantl *Geschichte* II (above 3) – still the fullest account.

(3)   Abelard's philosophy of logic
J. Jolivet, *Arts du langage et théologie chez Abélard* (Paris: Vrin, 1969) – penetrating and detailed study of Abelard's theory of meaning and his use of it; M. M. Tweedale, *Abailard on Universals* (Amsterdam: North Holland, 1976) – detailed analysis of texts by a modern philosopher.

Chapter 13   Theology

(1)   The varieties of theology
General   A. M. Landgraf, *Introduction à l'histoire de la littérature théologique de la scolastique naissante* (trans.) (Montreal: Institut d'études médiévales, and Paris: Vrin, 1973) – lists editions, manuscripts and secondary work; J. de Ghellinck, *Le mouvement théologique du XIIe siècle* (Bruges: 'De Tempel', Bruxelles: l'Universelle, and Paris: Desclée de Brouwer, 1948) – survey; M.-D. Chenu, *La théologie au douzième siècle* (Paris: Vrin, 1957) – collection of articles studying the ideas and their sources.
Bernard of Clairvaux   E. Gilson, *La théologie mystique de Saint Bernard* (Paris: Vrin, 1934).

Hugh of St Victor   R. Baron, *Science et sagesse chez Hugues de Saint-Victor* (Paris: Léthielleux, 1957).

Abelard as a theologian   J. Cottiaux, 'La conception de la théologie chez Abélard', *Revue d'histoire ecclésiastique* 28 (1932), pp. 247–95, 533–51, 788–828; D. E. Luscombe, *The School of Peter Abelard* (Cambridge University Press, 1970) – on his theological influence: full bibliography on theological works.

(2)   The *Opuscula sacra*
Bernard   E. Gilson, 'Le platonisme de Bernard de Chartres', *Revue néoscolastique de philosophie* 25 (1923), pp. 5–19.

Commentaries   Southern, *Platonism* (above 10) – on authorship of the treatises; R. Lemay, *Abu Ma'Shar and Latin Aristotelianism in the Twelfth Century* (Beirut: American University at Beirut, 1962) – on possible Aristotelian influence.

(3)   Gilbert of Poitiers
Elswijk, *Gilbert Porreta* (above 10) – biography and study of thought; N. M. Häring, 'The case of Gilbert de la Porré, Bishop of Poitiers (1142–54)', *MS* 13 (1951), pp. 1–40 – clear exposition of some aspects of his thought; M. E. Williams, *The Teaching of Gilbert Porreta on the Trinity as found in the Commentaries on Boethius* (Rome: Gregorian University, 1951); M. A. Schmidt, *Gottheit und Trinität nach dem Kommentar des Gilbert Porreta zu Boethius De trinitate* (Basel: Verlag für Recht und Gesellschaft, 1956) – dense philosophical discussion.

Chapter 14   Abelard and the beginnings of medieval ethics

P. Delhaye, '"Grammatica" et "Ethica" au XIIᵉ siècle', *Recherches de théologie ancienne et médiévale* 25 (1958), pp. 59–110 – the classical moralizing tradition; R. Thomas, *Der philosophisch-theologische Erkenntnisweg Peter Abaelards im Dialogus inter Philosophum, Judaeum et Christianum* (Bonn: Röhrscheid, 1966) – analysis of the *Collationes*; R. Blomme, *La doctrine du péché dans les écoles théologiques de la première moitié du XIIᵉ siècle* (Louvain: Publ. universitaires de Louvain, and Gembloux: Duculot, 1958) – fundamental study of ethics in the school of Laon and in Abelard.

Further reading

The Cambridge History of Later Medieval Philosophy, A. Kenny, N. Kretzmann and J. Pinborg (eds) (Cambridge University Press, 1982), has a little material on the period 1050–1200, but is mainly devoted to the period 1200–1500. It contains summaries of the main areas of philosophical inquiry in the later Middle Ages and extensive bibliography.

Additional Notes and Bibliography

These notes refer to and briefly discuss some of the most important work on medieval philosophy which was overlooked in *Early Medieval Philosophy* or which has appeared since the first edition was published. Cross-references to the sections of these additional notes and bibliography are preceded by an asterisk.

Additional abbreviations

CHLMP	N. Kretzmann, A. Kenny, J. Pinborg (eds), *The Cambridge History of Later Medieval Philosophy*, (Cambridge University Press, 1982)
Individuation	J.J.E. Gracia, *Introduction to the Problem of Individuation in the Early Middle Ages*, (Munich, Vienna: Philosophia Verlag, 1984)

PRIMARY WORKS

(1) Firmly attributed works

Abbo of Fleury	*Quaestiones Grammaticales* ed. A. Guerreau-Jalabert (Paris: les Belles Lettres, 1982).
Abelard	**Theological works** Commentary on *Romans*, E. M. Buytaert (ed.), *CC (cm)* 11 (1969); *Soliloquium*, C. Burnett (ed.), *SM* 25, 2 (1984), pp. 857–94 (with English transl.).
	Translation *Theologia Summi Boni* trsl. into French (*Du Bien Suprême*) by J. Jolivet (Montreal/Paris: Bellarmin/Vrin, 1978).
Gilbert Crispin	Works. A. Sapir Abulafia and G. Evans (eds) (Oxford U.P., 1986).

(2)   Anonymous works

(i)   Treatise with title

De mundi	C. Burnett (ed.) (London: Warburg Institute,
Constitutione	1985) (with English transl.)

(iii)   Glosses and commentaries

To:–	Incipit	
BOETHIUS		
Consolation of	*Carmina cantus*	In Troncarelli,
Philosophy	*delectabiles . . .* (but)	*Tradizioni*
	cf. ⋆7.2)	(below ⋆5.1)
PLATO		
Timaeus	*Socrates de republica*	Unpublished. Extracts
	(early 12th cent.)	and details of
		manuscripts in Dutton,
		'The *Glosae*' (below
		⋆13.2)

SECONDARY WORKS, AND ADDITIONAL NOTES

General Works

M. Haren, *Medieval Thought. The Western Intellectual Tradition from Antiquity to the 13th Century* (Houndmills: Macmillan, 1985) – a well-researched account of sources, influences and milieux. *Individuation* – one of the most rigorous studies of an aspect of thought in the period: especially valuable on Boethius, John Scottus and Gilbert of Poitiers.

'Chapter 3.2   Logic in late antiquity
General S. Ebbesen, 'Ancient Scholastic Logic as the Source of Medieval Scholastic Logic' = *CHLMP* Chapter 4 – especially good on the relations between logical and grammatical theory.

Chapter 4   Boethius
General L. Obertello (ed.), *Congresso internazionale di studi boeziani: Atti* (Rome: Herder, 1981) – specialized articles on different aspects of Boethius's work.

Chapter 4.2   Boethius. The logical works
Topics N.J. Green-Pedersen, *The Tradition of the Topics in the Middle Ages: the Commentaries on Aristotle's and Boethius' Topics* (Munich: Philosophia Verlag, 1984) – detailed attention to the *De topicis differentiis* and its influence.
Glosses to the *Prior Analytics* (cf. p. 28) J. Shiel ['A Recent Discovery: Boethius' Notes on the Prior Analytics', *Vivarium* 20 (1982),

pp. 128–41] argues convincingly that the glosses to the *Prior Analytics* printed in *AL* III are Boethius's.

Chapter 4.3   Boethius. The *Opuscula sacra*
Theological background   B.E. Daley, 'Boethius' Theological Tracts and Early Byzantine Scholasticism', *Mediaeval Studies* 46 (1984), pp. 158–91.
Numerical difference in *De trinitate* (cf. pp. 37–8)   A much clearer and more detailed discussion is given in *Individuation*, pp. 97–107.

Chapter 4.4   Boethius. The *Consolation of Philosophy*
God is outside time (cf. p. 41)   This position of Boethius's has been the subject of much recent discussion by philosophers. Is the concept of a timeless God coherent? Is it compatible with divine omniscience? And is it theologically inevitable? R. Sorabji [*Time, Creation and the Continuum* (London: Duckworth, 1983), pp. 253–67, cf. pp. 115–16] provides a clear discussion, with full references, which also illuminates Boethius's links with the Greek Neoplatonists and with Augustine.

Chapter 5.1   From Cassiodorus to Alcuin
Cassiodorus and Boethius (cf. p. 45)   F. Troncarelli [*Tradizioni Perduti. La 'Consolatio Philosophiae' nell'Alto Medioevo* (Padua: Antenore, 1981)] has argued that a learned edition of the *Consolation of Philosophy*, complete with rhetorical glosses and a life of the author, was produced in the circle of Cassiodorus.

Chapter 5.2   The circle of Alcuin
Alcuin and the *Usia graece* . . . passages (cf. p. 48)   D.A. Bullough ['Alcuin and the Kingdom of Heaven: Liturgy, Theology and the Carolingian Age' in U.-R. Blumenthal (ed.), *Carolingian Essays* (Washington, D.C.: Catholic University of America, [1983]), pp. 1–69, esp. pp. 22–31] finds considerable – though not necessarily conclusive – evidence against Alcuin's authorship of Passage VII. In his view, it is more probably a late fifth or early sixth-century work, rediscovered by Carolingian scholars.

Chapter 6   Philosophy in the age of John Scottus Eriugena
General   G.H. Allard (ed.), *Jean Scot Ecrivain* (Montreal/Paris: Bellarmin/Vrin, 1986) – articles which deal especially with Eriugena's language and his use of the arts of language.

Chapter 6.4   John Scottus Eriugena. The *Periphyseon*
General   G. Schrimpf, *Das Werk des Johannes Scottus Eriugena im Rahmen des Wissenschaftsverständnisses seiner Zeit. Eine Hinführung zu Periphyseon*, BGPMA 23 (1982), views the *Periphyseon* in the context of ninth-century aims and schemes of study. W. Beierwaltes has made important contributions to understanding the *Periphyseon* in the context of

Neoplatonic thought: 'Eriugena. Aspekte seiner Philosophie' in *Die Iren und Europa im früheren Mittelalter*, ed. H. Löwe (Stuttgart: Klett-Cotta, 1982), pp. 799–818; 'Marginalien zu Eriugenas "Platonismus" ' in H.-D. Blume and F. Mann (eds), *Platonismus und Christentum* (Münster: Aschendorff, 1983), pp. 64–74; 'Language and Object. Reflexions on Eriugena's Valuation of the Function and Capacities of Language' in *Jean Scot Ecrivain* (above ★6), pp. 209–228.
Biography   M. Brennan, 'Materials for the Biography of Johannes Scottus Eriugena', *SM* 27, 1 (1986), pp. 413–60.

Chapter 7.1   The Influence of Eriugena
Eriugena's close followers (cf. p. 71)   Another piece of evidence for Eriugena's great influence on his own generation has recently been discovered: a set of brief comments (incipit *Imago Dei. . .*) on the verses in *Genesis* about the creation of man [edited and discussed by E. Jeauneau, 'Un "dossier" carolingien sur la création de l'homme (Genèse I, 26–III, 24)', *Revue des Etudes Augustiniennes*, 28 (1982), pp. 112–32]. The comments are found in a manuscript of the second half of the ninth century, and they are dedicated to a king (who may well be Charles the Bald). They combine ideas and language very close to the *Periphyseon* with passages based on Augustine.

Chapter 7.2   The Tradition of Glosses to School-Texts
Glosses to the *Consolation* (cf. pp. 74–5)   Troncarelli [*Tradizioni perduti* (above ★5.1)] has now edited and discussed the *Carmina cantus delectabiles. . .* glosses (in Vatican lat. 3363; their incipit, according to his edition, should be *Victor habebit innumeros. . .*). He considers that they derive from glosses prepared by King Alfred's helper, Asser, and used in Alfred's Old English translation of the *Consolation*. Troncarelli points out that the passage in which the World Soul is equated with the sun is in fact a quotation from Bede's *De temporum ratione*.

Chapter 8.1   Tenth-century Logic
'Icpa', glossator of the *Isagoge* (cf. p. 81)   Thanks to the work of Colette Jeudy ['Israel le grammairien' (above 8.1)], it is now possible to identify this figure as Israel, an Irishman who died in about the middle of the tenth century and who had among his pupils St Bruno. Edouard Jeauneau ['Pour le dossier d'Israel Scot', *AHDLMA*, 52 (1985), pp. 7–72] has edited and discussed a set of passages associated with Israel. Among them can be found an examination of the Trinity (definitely by Israel himself) which draws heavily on Boethius's *De trinitate*, and two other passages also related to Boethius's *Opuscula Sacra*; a discussion of the soul which echoes the concerns and language of the Carolingian *Usia graece. . .* passages (see above, pp. 48–50); and various pieces connected with the *Categoriae Decem* and the tradition of glosses to this work (see above, pp. 76–7). In some of the material there are definite signs of Eriugenian influence.

Chapter 9.2 Anselm
Anselm as a logician (cf. pp. 101–3) D.P. Henry gives a brief account of his views on Anselm as a logician in 'Predicables and Categories' = *CHLMP* Chapter 5, pp. 128–42.

Chapter 9.4 Logic and Grammar at the End of the Eleventh Century
Garland's *Dialectica* (cf. p. 109) E. Stump, 'Dialectic in the Eleventh and Twelfth Centuries: Garlandus Compotista', *History and Philosophy of Logic* 1 (1980), pp. 1–18, shows that the account of topical arguments in Garlandus's *Dialectica*, although based on Boethius, differs from its source by emphasizing the evaluation rather than the discovery of arguments. On the theory of topics in the eleventh and twelfth centuries, see also Green-Pedersen, *The Tradition of the Topics. . .* (above, ★4.2).

Chapter 10 Masters and Schools
General An important collection of essays on intellectual life in the twelfth century is provided in R.L. Benson and G. Constable (eds), *Renaissance and Renewal in the Twelfth Century* (Oxford U.P., 1982). Shortly to be published is P. Dronke (ed.) *The Cambridge History of Twelfth-Century Philosophy*, which will contain detailed studies of thinkers such as Abelard, Thierry of Chartres, William of Conches, Bernard Silvestris and Gilbert of Poitiers, along with more general surveys (including examination of the ancient sources and arabic influences). Valuable discussion about twelfth-century methods of studying texts is found in N.M. Häring 'Commentary and Hermeneutics' in *Renaissance and Renewal* (above), pp. 173–200 and in E. Jeauneau, 'Jean de Salisbury et la lecture des philosophes', *Revue des Etudes Augustiniennes* 29 (1983), pp. 145–74 = M. Wilks (ed.), *The World of John of Salisbury* (Oxford: Blackwell, 1984), pp. 77–108.

General works on individual twelfth-century thinkers Abelard: J. Barrow, C. Burnett, D. Luscombe, 'A Checklist of the Manuscripts containing the Writings of Peter Abelard and Heloise and other Works closely associated with Abelard and his School', *Revue d'histoire des textes* 14/15 (1984/5), pp. 183–302. C. Mews, 'On Dating the Works of Peter Abelard', *AHDLMA* 52 (1985), pp. 73–134 – an important revision of accepted views.

The School of Chartres (pp. 116–7) R.W. Southern produces more evidence for the pre-eminence of Paris over Chartres as a scholastic centre in 'The Schools of Paris and the School of Chartres', in *Renaissance and Renewal* (above), pp. 113–37. And C.S.F. Burnett ['The Contents and Affiliation of the Scientific Manuscripts written at, or brought to, Chartres in the Time of John of Salisbury' in *The World of John of Salisbury* (above), pp. 127–60] shows that Chartres was not very receptive to the new scientific translations of the twelfth century.

Chapter 11.2   Minor cosmological works

De mundi constitutione   In the preface to his new edition (above, ★Primary works), Burnett suggests that this piece is a collection of material, rather than the work of a single author.

Chapter 12.3   Abelard's Philosophy of Logic

Chronology (cf. p. 135)   Mews ['On Dating' (above)] suggests the following datings: *Intentio Porphyrii*. . . 1102–8; *Dialectica* and *Ingredientibus*. . . 1117–21; *Nostrorum petitioni*. . . 1120–4.

Inherence and identity theories of predication (cf. p. 138)   Two recent studies [K. Jacobi, 'Peter Abelard's Investigations into the Meaning and Function of the Speech Sign "Est" ' in S. Knuuttila and J. Hintikka (eds), *The Logic of Being. Historical Studies* (Dordrecht/Boston/Lancaster/Tokyo: Reidel, 1986), pp.145–80; and N. Kretzmann, 'The Culmination of the Old Logic in Peter Abelard' in *Renaissance and Renewal* (above), pp. 488–511] show that Abelard's thoughts about predication were much more subtle and complicated than the account here suggests. In particular, Abelard was keen to explore the unusual theory that propositions have an underlying form of two rather than three parts, so that *Socrates est currens* ('Socrates is running') should properly be analysed as *Socrates currit* ('Socrates runs').

Chapter 13.1   The varieties of theology

General   M.M. Davy *Initiation médiévale. La philosophie au douzième siècle* (Paris: Michel, 1980) – valuable for its treatment of relations between ancient philosophy and monastic thought.

Chapter 13.2   The *Opuscula Sacra*

Bernard of Chartres   In a recent article ['The Uncovering of the *Glosae super Platonem* of Bernard of Chartres', *Mediaeval Studies* 46 (1984), pp. 192—221], P.E. Dutton has drawn attention to the influence of a set of early twelfth-century glosses to the *Timaeus* (incipit *Socrates de re publica* . . .) and pointed out that they (like Bernard of Chartres) follow Boethius's distinction between immaterial Ideas and the images of these Ideas in matter. Dutton argues that it was Bernard himself who composed the glosses. Although, from his account of the glosses' contents, this suggestion is not implausible, Dutton's external evidence is far from conclusive.

Chapter 13.3   Gilbert of Poitiers

L.O. Nielsen, *Theology and Philosophy in the Twelfth Century* (Leiden: Brill, 1982) – the first half of this (misleadingly widely-titled) book contains a very detailed study of Gilbert's thought. J.A. Marenbon, 'Gilbert of Poitiers' in Dronke (ed), *Cambridge History of Twelfth-Century Philosophy*, pp. 328–52 – suggests that Gilbert's thought cannot be understood unless his exegetical and theological aims are taken into account. (Although the re-written section on Gilbert for this edition of

Early Medieval Philosophy reflects – and in some cases clarifies – my analyses in this longer discussion, it approaches the subject from a rather different angle).

Chapter 14   Abelard and the beginnings of medieval ethics
Dating of Abelard's ethical works (cf. pp. 157 and 160)   Mews ['On Dating. . .' (above)] suggests c. 1125–6 for the *Collationes* and 1138–9 for *Scito teipsum*.

Index

Aachen, 46
Abbo of Fleury, 81–3
Abelard, Peter, 71, 80, 109–10, 150,
   152; life of, 114–15, 117–18; as
   philosophical logician, 128–39;
   rediscovery of ethical philosophy
   by, 157–67; as theologian, 144–5;
   Collationes, 157–62; *Dialectica*, 110,
   130, 135–8, 140–1; *Historia
   calamitatum*, 132; *Ingredientibus* . . . ,
   128, 131, 135–40; *Intentio
   Porphyrii* . . . , 135; *Nostrorum
   petitioni* . . . , 131, 135–6; *Scito
   teipsum*, 157, 160–2; *Sic et non*, 144;
   *Theologia Summi Boni/Christiana/
   scholarium*, 144–5
Abu Ma'shar, 148
Achard of St Victor, 116
Adalbold of Utrecht, 86–8
Adam of Balsham (Parvipontanus),
   116, 130–1
Adelard of Bath, 114, 117, 124–5, 132
adoptionist heresy, 47, 52
Agobard of Lyons, 51
Alberic, follower of Abelard, 115,
   130–1, 133–4
Alcuin, 46–53, 60, 80
Aldhelm, 46
Alexander of Aphrodisias, 31, 33, 139
allegory: in biblical exegesis, 17, 64; in
   Martianus Capella, 11; in the
   twelfth century, 125–7; *see also*
   metaphor
Ambrose, 16, 60, 64
Ammonius Saccas, 17
Andrew of St Victor, 116
Angelôme of Luxeuil, 60
Anselm, Archbishop of Canterbury,

94–105, 113–14. *Cur Deus Homo*,
   95–7, 103–5; *De concordia*, 95–7,
   103–5; *De grammatico*, 102–3, 106,
   108; *De libero arbitrio*, 97; *De veritate*,
   97; *Epistola de incarnatione Domini*,
   110; *Monologion*, 95–7, 101–2;
   Proslogion, 94–5, 98–101
Anselm of Laon, 114–15, 143, 161–2
Apuleius: *Asclepius* probably
   misattributed to, 11–12; *De dogmate
   Platonis*, 7; *Peri hermeneias*, 23, 47, 49,
   82
Aquinas, Thomas, 94
Arabs, 95, 113, 117
Aristotle, 3, 7–8, 59; relationship with
   Plato, 6–7, 21, 24, 31, 35, 126;
   Categories, 20–1, 24–5, 28, 30, 32,
   47, 53, 66–7, 80–2, 106, 113, 130,
   135; *De anima*, 32, 153; *De
   interpretatione*, 20–4, 28, 30, 32–3, 47,
   53, 81–3, 94, 101, 106, 113, 129–30,
   135–6, 139; *De sophisticis elenchis*, 23,
   28, 35, 82, 130; *Metaphysics*, 21, 148;
   Posterior analytics, 23, 28, 35, 82;
   Prior analytics, 23, 28–9, 35, 82, 130;
   Topics, 23, 28, 35, 82, 130; *for
   commentaries see under* Abelard
   (*Ingredientibus* . . .); Boethius;
   Porphyry
Arno, Bishop of Salzburg, 48
Asclepius, 11–12
Augustine, 49–50, 52, 58, 60–1, 63–4,
   67, 69–70, 94, 162; as an authority
   for early medieval logicians, 25–6,
   47, 91; and Neoplatonism, 10,
   14–16, 19, 25, 39, 42, 54, 57, 75, 98;
   City of God, 14, 84; *Confessions*, 14,
   25; *De dialectica*, 25–6; *De diversis*